0|92

||||| ||||| ||||| ||||| ||||| |||||
D0114013

WITHDRAWN

Sending My Heart Back
Across the Years

Sending My Heart Back Across the Years

TRADITION AND INNOVATION IN NATIVE AMERICAN AUTOBIOGRAPHY

Hertha Dawn Wong

New York   Oxford
OXFORD UNIVERSITY PRESS
1992

Oxford University Press

Oxford   New York   Toronto
Delhi   Bombay   Calcutta   Madras   Karachi
Petaling Jaya   Singapore   Hong Kong   Tokyo
Nairobi   Dar es Salaam   Cape Town
Melbourne   Auckland

and associated companies in
Berlin   Ibadan

Copyright © 1992 by Oxford University Press, Inc.

Published by Oxford University Press, Inc.,
200 Madison Avenue, New York, New York 10016

Oxford is a registered trademark of Oxford University Press

Library of Congress Cataloging-in-Publication Data
Wong, Hertha Dawn
Sending my heart back across the years :
tradition and innovation in native
American autobiography / Hertha Dawn Wong.
p.   cm.   Includes bibliographical references and index.
ISBN 0-19-506912-9
1. Indians of North America—Biography—History
and criticism. 2. Autobiography.   I. Title.
E89.5.W66   1992   818.009′4920009297—dc20
91–36639

The following sections of chapters have been published previously in other forms:
an early, much different, version of parts of Chapters 1 and 2 was published as
"Pre-Literate Native American Autobiography: Forms of Personal Narrative," *MELUS*
14.1 (1987) 17–32; a different version of one section of Chapter 6 appeared as "N. Scott
Momaday's *The Way to Rainy Mountain:* Contemporary Native American
Autobiography," *American Indian Culture and Research Journal* 12.3 (1988) 15–31;
and a portion of Chapter 3 was published, in slightly different form, as "Pictographs as
Autobiography: Plains Indian Sketchbooks of the Late Nineteenth and Early Twentieth
Centuries," *American Literary History* 1.2 (1989) 295–316.

2 4 6 8 9 7 5 3 1

Printed in the United States of America
on acid-free paper

Preface

When I began writing this book in 1984, I had little idea that I was part Native American, one of the unidentified mixed-bloods whose forebears wandered away from their fractured communities, leaving little cultural trace in their adopted world. In 1986, when my mother told me that her grandparents had been Indian (her grandmother was from the Plains, and her grandfather from what was then called Indian Territory), I found a new insight into the meaning of irony. I had believed that I was a non-Indian writing as an outsider about Native American autobiographical traditions. Did my newly discovered part-Indian heritage now make me an "insider," someone who might speak with the authority of belonging? "Of course not," was my first response. Because my ancestry is German, Scotch-Irish, and French as well as Native American, because I do not believe that blood quantum alone determines Indian identity, and because we do not have a community to which to return, I felt that I could write only as dimly related to, but outside of, the indigenous communities of the United States. But over the years, I have met other displaced mixed-blood people, all of us wrestling with the various labels, the rankings of legitimacy and illegitimacy, imposed on us by others and accepted or resisted by ourselves. Such absolute and dualistic categories (either/or, Indian/non-Indian, insider/outsider), constructed and imposed by those in power (and often adopted or internalized by native people), do not and cannot comprehend the complexities of multiple ethnicity. As many people have pointed out, so much of twentieth-century Native American experience, particularly in California, where so many urban and mixed-blood Indians do not fit the categories constructed for them, *is* the experience of this multiple marginality.

When I am asked the inevitable question, "Are you Indian?" what, then, do I say? "Yes, kind of"? Native people of mixed descent, particularly those who have been displaced from their communities, often have a *choice* to make about self-identification, a problematic luxury unavailable to full-bloods or those who, undeniably, "look Indian." For years I have been wrestling with how to answer this question with honesty and integrity. Like many urban mixed-blood Indians, I am not a member of a native community, but much of what my mother taught me reflects traditional values long associated with Native American cultures (although she did not label her teachings "Indian").

Finally, it seems, questions of identity are intensely personal; they can be resolved only with a sound conscience, a good spirit, and the help of family or community. They cannot be answered once and for all, but must be reconsidered perpetually. Part of our challenge is to reconstruct disrupted family histories, to examine the silences, erasures, and editings left by those who have gone before us. To deny my part-Indian family is to erase them and to perpetuate the historical invalidation of native people. To pretend that I have some kind of ethnic authority to speak on behalf of others would be dishonest and irresponsible. Insisting on either position is unfulfilling; locating a boundary zone from which to speak is difficult. According to my mother's findings, my great-grandmother was from a Plains tribe; and according to records at the Oklahoma Historical Society, my great-grandfather may have been Creek or Chickasaw or Choctaw or perhaps Cherokee, but several generations later their great-granddaughter is an undocumented mixed-blood person. So I write from the borders (a very crowded space these days) as one who observes and listens with openness and sensitivity, but who, of course, presents only a particular angle of vision.

Stories of our lives, told (or withheld) by our families and retold or edited by us, shape our identity. Self-narration is part of the process of self-construction and self-representation. When our stories change, when silences are spoken or narrative vacancies become inhabited, we are transformed. Over the years, the unfolding narrative of my family history and the narrative of this book on autobiography have taken on striking parallels. Both are concerned with one of the fundamental activities of autobiography: reconstructing a past from the present moment and laboring to understand how our ancestors' long-ago stories shape and reshape our self-narrations today.

As in all such endeavors, there are many people to thank. In the earliest stages of the project, when many academic advisers warned that if I wrote about Native American autobiography I would face terminal unemployment, Robert F. Sayre and Wayne Franklin were enthusiastic supporters. They have continued to be invaluable mentors. Thanks is due also to those scholars who made it possible to write about Native American autobiography in an English Department. Lynne Woods O'Brien's slim volume on Plains Indian autobiography initiated my interest in nonliterate autobiographical forms, while H. David Brumble's suggestive introduction to his bibliography of Native American autobiographies inspired me to continue. Since then, the work of Gretchen Bataille, H. David Brumble, Arnold Krupat, Kathleen Mullen Sands, A. LaVonne Brown Ruoff, and others has contributed to the growing discourse on Native American autobiography.

James Olney has been generous with his time and expertise. His 1988 NEH Summer Seminar on Autobiography offered a fruitful atmosphere in which to revise part of the manuscript. In 1989, the National Endowment for the Humanities awarded me a summer stipend that allowed me to devote myself to further revisions. I am particularly grateful to those at the California State University, Chico, who offered me substantial released time from teaching so that I could continue my work. Thanks also to the University of California, Berkeley, for assistance with the considerable expenses of obtaining photographs and permissions.

Many staff members of various museums, institutions, and libraries have provided invaluable assistance. Richard Buchen and Craig Klyver, both from the Braun Research Library at the Southwest Museum in Los Angeles, assisted in my search for and preparation of photographs for the sketchbooks of Zo-Tom, Howling Wolf, and the Cheyenne diarist. John Aubrey, curator of the Edward E. Ayer Collection at the Newberry Library in Chicago, was generous of spirit and time, inadvertently leading me to the Cheyenne autographs in Wuxpais' sketchbook. Joseph Porter, curator of the Western Historical Collection at the Joslyn Art Museum in Omaha, provided timely assistance as well. I am indebted to John Ewers, retired ethnographer at the Smithsonian Institution, and others who provided clues in locating the Zo-Tom and Howling Wolf sketchbooks. In addition, I am grateful to Hilda Neihardt Petri for permission to use Standing Bear's drawings which, belong to the John G. Neihardt Trust, as well as to the staff of the Western Historical Manuscripts Collection of the University of Missouri, Columbia, for their assistance in preparing them. A heartfelt thank you to Karen Daniels

Petersen, who has been consistently generous with her vast knowledge of Plains Indian pictographic sketchbooks.

Special thanks to the many people who read the innumerable versions of this manuscript, particularly Susan Jaret McKinstry, Steven Crum, Tom Fox, and Cheryl Allison Leisterer, and to Andrea Lerner, who, with a gentle nudge and lively intellect, helped me to reenvision my preface. I am grateful to Jonathan Brennan for his precise indexing and editorial skills, to Rebecca Dobkins for her remarkable organizational assistance, and to two special people at Oxford University Press: Irene Pavitt for her editorial expertise and Elizabeth Maguire for her support. Thank you also to my Native American students and friends in Minnesota, South Dakota, and California who continue to teach me about community, and to my family, particularly Dianne and Chaarles Sweet and Ruth, George, and Judith Wong, who have been sources of inspiration. My most special thanks, though, goes to Richard Wong, who diligently read every draft of this book in its many incarnations since 1984 and who has offered me unfailing and exceptional support for almost twenty years.

Berkeley, Calif.   H. D. W.
November 1991

Contents

Sending My Heart Back
Across the Years

I am sending my heart back across the years.

Cheyenne description of autobiographical memory

Introduction

In the past three decades, autobiography has earned its place as a distinct genre in the study of literature. Even more recent is the study of Native American autobiography in English departments. Most literary scholars insist that autobiography is "a distinctive product of Western post-Roman civilization," "a late phenomenon in Western culture" that "expresses a concern peculiar to Western" individuals.[1] However, long before Anglo ethnographers arrived in North America, indigenous peoples were telling, creating, and enacting their personal narratives through stories, pictographs, and performances. To date, most of the scholarship in this area has been done by historians, anthropologists, and linguists who examine Native American life histories (narratives collected primarily in the late nineteenth and early twentieth centuries) as ethnographic documents. Only a few articles—by William Bloodworth, H. David Brumble, Lynne Woods O'Brien, Arnold Krupat, Kathleen Mullen Sands, William F. Smith, Jr., and R. D. Theisz—discuss the literary aspects of Native American autobiography. At this time, only five books of literary scholarship have been devoted to this subject.

One of the first full-length considerations of Native American autobiography is Gretchen Bataille and Kathleen Mullen Sands's *American Indian Women: Telling Their Lives* (1984). In this monograph, the authors intended to correct a history of devaluation of Indian women by examining, in their literary and ethnographic contexts, five transitional personal narratives by Native American women. In *For Those Who Come After: A Study of Native American Autobiography* (1985), Arnold Krupat applies contemporary literary theory to the study of Native American autobiographies from the late nineteenth to the early twentieth century with the aim of encouraging "some small degree of rapprochement between the two separate camps of theorists and Native Americanists."[2]

3

In a chapter of his most recent book (*The Voice in the Margin: Native American Literature and the Canon* [1989]), Krupat extends his theoretical considerations to discuss the dialogism of Native American autobiography.[3] While Bataille and Sands present a descriptive introduction to Native American autobiography, Krupat provides a solid critical and theoretical foundation for its study. Both discussions, however, negate the possibility of pre-European contact[4] tribal traditions of personal narrative. Bataille and Sands state that autobiography was "not an indigenous form,"[5] while Krupat insists that "Indian autobiographies are not a traditional form among Native peoples but the consequence of contact with white invader-settlers, and the product of a limited collaboration with them" (*For Those Who Come After* xi).[6] If we apply Western definitions to the study of the self-narrations of indigenous people, these scholars are absolutely correct. Native American autobiographical narratives are not based on Euro-American notions of self, life, and writing. As we consider the autobiographical activities of non-Western cultures, however, it is crucial to reexamine our approaches. As Karl Kroeber notes in an essay on traditional Native American literatures: "It is our scholarship, not Indian literature, which is 'primitive' or undeveloped."[7] Similarly, we might say: it is Eurocentric theory, not Native American autobiography, that is lacking.

Unlike Bataille, Sands, and Krupat, Lynne Woods O'Brien suggests the existence of pre-contact native "oral, dramatic, and artistic expressions" of one's life. In her early, short, and often neglected book, *Plains Indian Autobiographies* (1973), O'Brien introduces the possibility of nonliterate autobiography and calls for further consideration of this form.[8] Although she does not develop her discussion, her work provides a starting point for a consideration of nonwritten autobiographical traditions. Fifteen years later, in *American Indian Autobiography* (1988), H. David Brumble developed this discussion. He presents a historical consideration of Native American autobiography, comparing "preliterate" native autobiographies with the classical oral traditions of the Greeks and Romans and charting the development of native autobiography in general.[9] My book both continues and extends the work of O'Brien and Brumble. My focus, intended to be suggestive rather than encyclopedic, is a detailed consideration of a select number of distinctly native traditions of self-narration and their later interaction with Euro-American forms of autobiography.

Such an endeavor leads to numerous questions. How do Native

American assumptions about self, life, and writing (the roots of auto-bio-graphy) differ from Western assumptions? Are there areas of agreement? More important, how can we acknowledge the geographical, cultural, and linguistic differences of the many diverse tribes and yet generalize about Native American autobiographical forms? Since pre-Columbian indigenous peoples had no written language, is it possible to ascribe autobiographical activity to them? Can autobiography be oral or artistic rather than written? If so, what are the differences between a three-dimensional storytelling performance or a two-dimensional pictographic painting and the mono-dimensional linearity of written narrative? How does the often noted emphasis on event in Native American personal narrative (e.g., personal stories about specific battles, visions, and coming-of-age transitions) relate to the diurnal rhythms of Western forms such as diaries and journals?

More specific questions arise for late-nineteenth- and early-twentieth-century life histories. When Native Americans began to communicate their personal narratives to Euro-Americans, their traditional narrative forms encountered new challenges. Recent literary theory suggests that language is on the border between self and Other; thus to use language is to engage in a power struggle between these two opposing forces. Such a struggle is intensified when one communicates a sense of self through another individual from another culture in a different language. How, then, does a Native American express a genuine sense of self when that self is mediated by the language of a member of the dominant culture? How does one construct and maintain an identity in a hostile world? Is the act of expressing one's self in the language and forms of the ''enemy'' an attempt at communication, an indication of negotiation, or an act of capitulation?

Addressing these questions and using contemporary autobiography theory as well as literary and anthropological approaches, this study traces the changes in Native American autobiography from pre-contact oral and pictographic personal narratives through late-nineteenth- and twentieth-century life histories to contemporary autobiographies. My purpose is to expand the Eurocentric definitions of autobiography to include nonwritten forms of personal narrative and non-Western concepts of self and to highlight the interaction of traditional tribal modes of self-narration with Western forms of autobiography. This study, then, considers Native American autobiography from the context of auto-biography theory, delineates distinctly Native American oral and pictographic traditions of personal narrative and their interaction with Euro-American autobiographical modes, and examines the relationship between nineteenth-century Native American oral modes of personal narrative and Euro-American "female" forms of autobiography.

This book is organized into six chapters. The first chapter presents the theoretical framework, examining Native American traditions of personal narrative in the context of autobiography theory. In order to consider Native American autobiographical forms, it is necessary to expand Western definitions of autobiography to include nonliterate modes of self-narration. A discussion of Native American autobiography creates more than the usual controversy among scholars of autobiography who have reached little agreement about how to define the term precisely. Literary, cultural, and historical scholars, however, refer repeatedly to the three roots of the word *autobiography* (self-life-writing). The word itself reveals European assumptions about the importance of the *individual* life and the necessity of *writing*. The emphasis on the autonomous individual and writing is not particularly relevant to pre-Columbian Native American autobiography. It is tempting to coin a more appropriate term, such as *communo-bio-oratory* (community-life-speaking) or *auto-ethnography*[10] (self-culture-writing). The first allows for a communal identity and orality; the second for a sense of self determined by one's cultural discourse. At this point, one might ask: Why, then, insist that pre-contact indigenous people engaged in autobiographical expression? My interest is in expanding current definitions of autobiography, which all too often have not recognized non-Western self-conceptions and their consequent expressions and representations. There are, I believe, forms of autobiographical narrative other than accounts of the lives of autonomous individuals written by themselves. If one assumes that self-narration is the fundamental act of autobiography, one must recognize a variety of forms besides literary autobiography. Considering such forms as oral and pictographic personal narratives as autobiography, for example, acknowledges differences in modes of self-narration due to culture, gender, and historical period.

In addition to recognizing aboriginal forms of personal expression, a study of Native American autobiography should be aware of the long-term development of tribal concepts of self. Not all tribes had the same sense of identity, however. There is no generic Indian sense of self. Each tribe (or sometimes even each band or clan) had a distinctive language (or dialect), religion, and philosophy. Although it is possible to make some useful generalizations about Native Americans as a whole, it is important to acknowledge and respect individual tribal differences. Therefore, throughout the following discussion, relevant ethnographic and historical information is included.

In contrast to distinct native notions of self, life, and language, certain characteristics of oral composition seem to transcend cultural boundaries. What I originally thought were Native American storytelling styles turned out to be similar to such diverse oral traditions as those of ancient city-state Greeks (discussed in detail by Brumble)[11] and contemporary rural Irish. Also, many of the most often quoted generalizations about Native American identity and its literary expression are remarkably parallel to current feminist discussions of women's autobiography. Both female and Native American autobiographical narratives focus on a communal or relational identity and tend to be cyclical rather than linear.

After the theoretical section in Chapter 1, the book is organized by the three basic historical periods of Native American literature: (1) the pre-Columbian period, which includes oral and pictographic forms of personal narrative (Chapter 2); (2) the late-nineteenth- and early-twentieth-century transitional period, which includes what have been referred to as "as-told-to"[12] life histories (which were solicited, translated, and edited by Euro-American editors), a few autobiographies written by Indians, and numerous pictographic autobiographies (Chapters 3–5); and (3) the contemporary period, which includes oral self-narrations and written autobiographies that combine Native American and Euro-American forms and themes (Chapter 6). Although these categories emphasize the historical shift from orality to literacy as well as the transition from pre-contact tribal life to post-contact reservation or urban life, they are not intended as an evolutionary model of "progress." The word *transitional,* for instance, means simply "changing," not "developing" or "progressing."

More specifically, Chapter 2 surveys pre-contact nonwritten modes of personal narrative such as naming practices, coup tales (Plains Indian tales of heroic achievement in battle), and pictographic hide and tipi paintings. Problems arise, of course, in obtaining and interpreting materials. Most of the personal stories and much of the autobiographical artwork that survive were solicited by Euro-Americans who translated and edited the works of "native informants." In addition, many of the narratives were collected during the late nineteenth and early twentieth centuries. With these autobiographical traces, we can only speculate about pre-contact narrative traditions. Nonetheless, these nonwritten autobiographical modes suggest the basis of *native* traditions of autobiography. For this historical period, published oral autobiographical narratives are examined. Among those considered are Plains Indian oral coup tales (such as stories collected by men like James Schultz who lived among the Blackfeet) and late-nineteenth- and early-twentieth-century personal narratives rendered in pictographic painting on hides and tipis (such as Mah-to-toh-pa's painted buffalo-hide robe, described by George Catlin, and Kiowa and Kiowa–Apache pictographic tipis painted by native men and described by nineteenth-century ethnologist James Mooney and contemporary ethnographer John Ewers).

Chapters 3 through 5 deal with transitional autobiographies–pictographic and oral life histories that were solicited, translated, and edited, for the most part, by Euro-American ethnographers, historians, and others. A useful division is a historical one: those autobiographers who spoke, created, or performed their life stories before 1890 and those who did so after 1890. (The year 1890, the date of the first Wounded Knee massacre and the "closing of the frontier," is a useful year to demarcate those with more experience of prereservation life and those with primary experience of reservation life.) Native American autobiographers of this period modified existing tribal narrative forms to meet the demands of new audiences, occasions, and purposes. Discussion of transitional autobiographers in Chapter 3 includes an examination of an anonymous Cheyenne pictographic diarist who constructed his own book (pre-1890) and a comparison of Zo-Tom and Howling Wolf (pre-1890) with White Bull (post-1890), all of whom drew their pictographic personal histories, adding written explanations and modifying conventional Plains Indian pictographic principles to assist their white readers.

Chapter 4 focuses on four native autobiographers, three who spoke and one who wrote life histories. With the advent of reservation life, aboriginal autobiographers, such as the Crows Plenty-Coups and Pretty-Shield and the Winnebago brother and sister Sam Blowsnake and Mountain Wolf Woman, collaborated with Anglo editors, modifying native autobiographical forms. With the exception of that of Blowsnake, who wrote his personal narrative for Paul Radin in the Winnebago syllabary, these works illustrate some of the modes of production and editorial techniques of oral collaborative life histories solicited by Euro-American ethnographers and Indian enthusiasts.

Chapter 5 is devoted to two well-known early-twentieth-century autobiographers who remember prereservation life. Nicholas Black Elk and Charles Alexander Eastman represent two historical streams of Native American autobiography, the first arising from oral native traditions, and the second from borrowed Euro-American forms such as the Christian conversion narrative. Black Elk, collaborating with John G. Neihardt, *spoke* his life history, while Eastman, collaborating with his wife and editor, Elaine Goodale Eastman, *wrote* his autobiography. Special consideration is given to the problems of bicultural and collaborative autobiographies—the difficulties of one self being mediated by another individual from another culture in another language. Also noted are how pre-contact autobiographical modes were modified to fit new forms, to address new audiences, and to serve new purposes.

The final chapter deals with how Native American oral (and to a lesser extent pictographic) traditions of personal narrative have been reconfigured today in such contemporary works as N. Scott Momaday's *The Way to Rainy Mountain* and *The Names* and Leslie Marmon Silko's *Storyteller*. Momaday, Silko, and other Native American authors combine past and present genres, themes, and stories, consciously striving to synthesize native forms of personal narrative and contemporary Euro-American modes of autobiography, the spoken voice and the written word. Such contemporary autobiographers reclaim and revivify indigenous forms of personal narrative; at the same time, they enrich and extend Western traditions of autobiography.

Before the arrival of the ethnographer, with notebook in hand, native people had many means of telling their lives. Stories, pictographic narratives (and other artwork), and performances were all such means. When interaction with Europeans began, Native Americans, while finding their self-conceptions challenged, still used traditional native forms to narrate their life experiences. It was not until the nineteenth century, when native peoples were herded onto reservations, that Euro-American ethnographers, missionaries, and other professional people began collecting Indian life histories in earnest. In general, Euro-Americans asked their native informants about issues that interested them (the Custer battle, for instance) rather than allowing indigenous people to select their own concerns. The late-nineteenth- and early-twentieth-century collaborative autobiography, then, is especially complex because it reflects a dual perspective—the editor's and the raconteur's (two individuals from two different cultures working together to attempt to construct a coherent singular identity).[13] Even though the final shape and content of life histories were determined by the editors, Native American narrators often told their life stories in their own indigenous narrative forms. Similar tribal modes of personal narrative may be found in some contemporary autobiographies written by Native Americans, only now this is by conscious design. Today, Native American autobiographers are attempting to resurrect and redefine tribal oral pasts in Western written forms, creatively adapting the two traditions and imaginatively extending the possibilities of autobiography.

1 / Native American Self-Narration and Autobiography Theory

Of the few literary scholars involved in the study of Native American autobiography, most have avoided pre-contact Native American autobiographical modes, choosing instead to discuss the late-nineteenth- and early-twentieth-century oral life histories that were solicited, translated, recorded, and edited by Euro-American amanuenses. William Bloodworth distinguishes "anthropological" (often referred to as "as-told-to")[1] autobiography from what he regards as "authentic" Native American autobiography, which "springs from the desires of Native Americans to tell the stories of their individual lives" rather than from the wishes of a Euro-American anthropologist. In contradistinction to Bloodworth, Kathleen Mullen Sands writes that "the most distinctive characteristic" of American Indian autobiography is the "collaboration of the narrator and recorder editor." Likewise, H. David Brumble refers to Native American autobiographies as "bicultural documents" that are interesting because of the questions raised by the collaboration between the subject and the collector, and because they record the transition from a preliterate to a literate people in 150 short years. Arnold Krupat, who offers the most comprehensive and theoretical discussion of Native American life histories, states that "the principle constituting the Indian autobiography as a genre [is] the principle of *original bicultural composite composition.*" Indian autobiography, he concludes, is "a ground on which two cultures meet," "the textual equivalent of the frontier."[2]

Sands and Krupat agree on the importance of the "bicultural composite composition" of Native American autobiography. This is a valid definition for a particular historical period (for much of the nineteenth and twentieth centuries),[3] but it overlooks pre-contact Native American personal narratives. Because Western definitions of autobiography have been applied to the study of indigenous personal narratives, some scholars have concluded that Indian autobiography did not exist prior to European contact. But Native American autobiographical expressions are not based on Euro-American notions of self, life, or writing. Before the arrival of Europeans, indigenous people had numerous oral and pictographic forms in which to share their personal narratives. Certainly, these narratives were told in different forms, with different emphases, for different audiences and purposes, but they *were* told. William Smith recognizes this when he defines Indian autobiography as "verbal expressions, whether oral or written," of American Indian lives. His focus is on these "verbal expressions" as a mixture of personal narrative and cultural essay. Lynne Woods O'Brien, among the first to mention the possibility of nonliterate autobiography, refers to Plains Indian autobiographies as "oral, dramatic, and artistic expressions by native individuals about their own lives."[4] Thus she includes such forms as songs, storytelling, dances, visions, and artwork. H. David Brumble, one of the most convincing advocates for pre-contact native autobiography, delineates "six fairly distinct kinds of pre-literate autobiographical narratives": coup tales, informal autobiographical tales, self-examinations, self-vindications, educational narratives, and stories of quests for visions and power (22).

Certainly, these autobiographical modes do not conform to dominant Euro-American notions of autobiography, which emphasize autonomous individuality and insist that autobiography is the story of one's life written by oneself. Instead, pre-contact indigenous autobiographical forms emphasize a communal rather than an individual self; they often narrate a series of anecdotal moments rather than a unified, chronological life story; and they may be spoken, performed, painted, or otherwise crafted, rather than written. Three-dimensional storytelling performances and two-dimensional pictographic stories challenge interpretive approaches based on the mono-dimensional linearity of written narrative. Such a self-narration, what Elizabeth Bruss has called "an autobiographical act"[5]—an illocutionary act that creates and narrates personal identity—can be oral or artistic as well as written. One of the major problems with considering spoken, performed, and painted (or otherwise artistically created) self-narrations as autobiography (other than the fact that to do so strains the root meanings of the word) is that such pre-contact indigenous autobiographical expressions, unmediated by a Euro-

American consciousness, are difficult to find. What is accessible is, once again, a "bicultural collaboration," since a Euro-American ethnographer had to translate and record in writing the early "oral, dramatic, and artistic forms" of Native American personal narrative. A consideration of pre-contact autobiographical narratives, then, is necessarily speculative. Another difficulty has to do with the assumptions about self, life, and writing that underlie Western autobiography but that were not shared by indigenous peoples.

Native American Concepts of Self, Life, and Language

To consider pre-Columbian Native American autobiographical forms, we must first reconsider the roots of the word *autobiography* (self-life-writing). Defining a Native American identity is an especially treacherous endeavor, since such diverse native cultures and nations cannot be collapsed into one undifferentiated category. When Columbus supposedly "discovered" America, thinking he had reached the Indies, he misnamed the native peoples "Indians." These "Indians" were never a homogeneous group. According to Michael Dorris, "the pre 1492 Western Hemisphere was among the most linguistically and culturally plural areas the world has ever known"; throughout North and South America, native peoples were composed of more than three hundred distinct culture groups, from differing geographical regions, who spoke anywhere from one thousand to two thousand languages (with many more dialects).[6] Not only were there different tribal notions about what constitutes a self, there were individual differences as well. Contrary to some romanticized notions of communal identity, even within a specific tribe, individuality abounded. For all the tribal and individual distinctions, however, it is possible to make a few generalizations about the concepts of self, life, and language shared by many of the pre-Columbian indigenous peoples of what is now the United States.

First, a Native American concept of self differs from a Western (or Euro-American) idea of self in that it is more inclusive. Generally, native people tend to see themselves first as family, clan, and tribal *members,* and second as discrete individuals. There is less of a sense of what Karl J. Weintraub calls "individuality"—"a personality conception, the form of self that an individual may seek," which distinguishes him or her from the cultural community.[7] Instead of emphasis on an individual self who *stands apart* from the community, the focus is on a communal self who *participates within* the tribe. Using an analogy from modern physics, Howard Gardner discusses "particle" versus "field" societies—those that emphasize the importance of each individual and those that accentuate the centrality of the nation as a whole. According to Gardner's model, Euro-American society is fascinated with the isolated, autonomous person evident in the "Western notion of the solitary hero," while Native American societies are concerned with the environment, which is seen as "the determining force in an individual's life."[8] That is, the former emphasizes individuality; the latter, communality. Gardner describes the distinction between "field" and "particle" societies this way: "For Jean-Paul Sartre, an apostle of the French literary tradition, 'Hell is other people.' For individuals in a field society, 'One's self *is* other people'— and when one's fellows have been shorn away, there is hardly an irreducible core of 'self' left" (272). Native American tribes or nations, then, were primarily "field" societies, more concerned with the group than the individual. The result is what Susan Friedman calls a relational identity (35), what Krupat refers to as a "dialogic" self (*Voice* 133).

Besides the inclination to locate identity in family, clan, and tribal affiliation, there is the tendency to see identity in a spiritual context, to place one's self in relation to the cosmos. Many indigenous people share the belief that *"all things in the universe are dependent on one another"* (emphasis Beck and Walters).[9] This awareness of interdependence results in a deep respect for everything in the natural world as well as a profound personal responsibility for helping to maintain balance. Rather than standing above natural forces, pre-contact Native Americans stand with them; rather than conquering the elements, they interact harmoniously with them. Thus individual identity, although it is recognized and honored, is subordinate to tribal identity, which is subsumed in a sense of cosmic interconnection.

Often, the sense of a relational self is connected intimately to a specific landscape. According to Paula Gunn Allen, of Laguna descent, "the fundamental idea embedded in Native American life and culture in the Southwest" is "[w]e are the land. . . . [T]he Earth is the mind of the people as we are the mind of the earth."[10] Allen insists that this is no mere metaphor; it is "not a matter of being 'close to nature,'" but that "[t]he earth is, in a very real sense, the same as ourself (ourselves)" (191). Allen is referring to Native Americans today, but her comments can be applied to earlier indigenous attitudes from which her ideas derive.

This notion of feeling an intimate connection to the earth is not limited to southwestern Indians. Native Americans from various regions see their deceased relatives who have returned to the earth as nourishing their physical and spiritual existence. According to Sioux and Ojibway legends, red pipestone was thought to be ''the flesh and blood of their ancestors which was used to make ceremonial pipes.''[11] The symbolism of the pipe attests to the reciprocity between Plains Indian identity and the land. White Buffalo Woman, who first brought the pipe to the people, teaches them:

> . . . the Earth is your Grandmother and Mother, and She is sacred.
> . . . The bowl of this pipe is of red stone; it is the Earth. Carved in the stone and facing the center is this buffalo calf who represents all the four-leggeds who live upon your Mother. The stem of the pipe is of wood, and this represents all that grows upon the Earth. And these twelve feathers which hang here where the stem fits the bowl are from *Wanbli Galeshka*, the Spotted Eagle, and they represent the eagle and all the wingeds of the air. All these peoples, and all the things of the universe, are joined to you who smoke the pipe—all send their voices to *Wakan-Tanka*, the Great Spirit.[12]

Smoking a ceremonial pipe whose material substance is obtained from the earth and its creatures (pipestone, sumac, buffalo hide, and feathers) on important occasions, then, links the people not only to their tribal past (and their ancestors), but to one another in the present and to Wakan-Tanka, the Great Spirit, in the present and future.

Traditional Native American self-conceptions thus are defined by community and landscape. In many cases, this identity is also dynamic; that is, it is in process, not fixed. Native American autobiographical expressions tend to tell a portion of a person's life—a dramatic or a transitional experience such as a Plains Indian coup story, in which a warrior recounts his brave deeds in battle, or a Papago puberty purification ceremony, in which a young woman announces the onset of menstruation and thus her ''coming of age.''[13] Another, quite different, example of a Native American sense of a changing self might be the Navajo emphasis on going, in contrast to the Western stress on being.

According to Margot Astrov, ''Navaho is a language of the verb, in contrast to English which relies chiefly on the use of the noun.'' Thus Astrov describes ''the concept of motion'' as ''the perennial current on which Navaho culture is carried along,'' and she discusses the importance of this ''concept of motion'' in the language, creation myth, chants, curing ceremonies, and daily lives of the Navajo.[14] Furthering Astrov's discussion, Gary Witherspoon has worked out at least 356,200 variations of the verb "to go" in Navajo:[15]

> . . . the principal verb in the Navajo language is the verb "to go" and not the verb "to be," which is the principal verb in so many other languages but is of relatively minor importance in Navajo. This seems to indicate a cosmos composed of processes and events, as opposed to a cosmos composed of facts and things. (49)

The Navajo emphasis on dynamic processes would certainly include a sense of self that embodies the "concept of motion," a self that is continually shifting, changing, going.[16] In many tribes, evidence of a sense of a "self-in-process" is seen in the many names an individual takes or receives during his or her lifetime. As individuals mature, they take new names to reflect their important accomplishments and changing identities.

Such generalizations are, of course, highly suspect for many reasons. It is difficult to recover a genuine sense of any culture in history, especially a culture different from one's own. The very notion of "genuineness" or "authenticity" is problematic, arising as it does from a nineteenth-century Romantic impulse to locate and recover "pure" origins: the transcendental fount of creative inspiration, the presumed innocence of childhood, or the pure (i.e., unsullied by "civilization") artifacts of "primitive" cultures. Such notions ignore the cultural exchange between and among pre-contact indigenous people who were not waiting for the arrival of Europeans to "develop." Similarly, when these generalities about Native American cultures are applied uncritically to all tribes, the result may be a contemporary form of savagism[17]—intellectualizing a cluster of romantic notions about "the long ago Indians."

Although the concept of self may be somewhat different for a Native American than for a Euro-American, the purpose of expressing one's self is not so different. It seems, at first, that a Westerner *writes* an autobiography to set himself or herself *apart from* (better than, different from, richer than, more successful than) other members of his or her society, whereas a pre-contact Native American *speaks* a personal narrative to become more fully *accepted into* (a fuller participant in) his or her community. If a Native American sense of self is associated with tribal identity, to realize fully a sense of Indian identity is to realize one's link to the tribe. But all autobiography, European or Native American, involves a degree of socializing an individual into the community. The autobiographer has a culturally defined audience in mind, and that culture-audience, in part, shapes the autobiographer's self-narrative. In fact, according to postmodern theorists, autobiographers can construct narrative self-representations only by using the available cultural discourses. Religious conversion narratives, the basis for much Western autobiography and some Native American autobiography as well, served as a type of ritual that conferred a social sanction on the converted teller's new status: I was different from (less than, a greater sinner than, etc.) you, but now I am one of you (equal in the eyes of God, a forgiven sinner, etc.). In his secular autobiography, Benjamin Franklin identified himself with the newly liberated America so that his individual development and America's national growth were related. Often autobiographers reveal themselves as both different from and related to their social contexts. Thus whether we call it "tribal identity" or "national consciousness" or "social context," autobiographers, Euro-American and Native American alike, are shaped by their environmental and cultural milieus.

Life, the second root of autobiography, seems to be unassailably straightforward, but what makes a life important or meaningful is profoundly culture specific. The autobiographical expressions of pre-contact Native Americans tend to be event oriented. In the same way an occasional poem is recited for a particular event, these self-narrations arise at certain meaningful moments, recording an important happening—a marriage or a vision, for instance.

Since these personal narratives are event oriented, from a Western perspective they appear to be fragmented. Unlike Roy Pascal's early insistence that the "proper theme" of autobiography ("the autobiography of the whole man") requires that such a work be written by an older person, usually a man, who can review an entire life (148, 178), pre-contact native people tended to narrate their lives as they were living them. Rather than shaping a past life in the present, they shaped a present (and sometimes a future) life in the present moment. Once again, this process is more like that of a diarist capturing the immediacy of the recent moment in a dairy entry than that of a memoirist pondering and reformulating the long-ago past into a unified and chronological narrative.

Although the events of one particular life are focused on, the entire community may be included in the individual's recounting of the events. For example, after a battle a Sioux warrior returned to the tribe to tell his story of his part of the action. Certainly, the telling was important for his individual glory (a compelling motive behind the bravery of most

Plains Indian warriors), but it was also important for the honor of the tribe, which often helped the warrior articulate his brave actions. After his story was told and affirmed by fellow combatants, the women might have contributed spontaneous songs about the warrior's bravery, thus exalting him and therefore the whole tribe.

Different though it may seem at first glance, this tribal participation in telling the events of an individual's life is a type of collaborative autobiography. This is not the bicultural collaboration that Sands, Brumble, and Krupat discuss, but an intracultural collaboration. The community, which is the primary source of identity for the individual, contributes to the individual's personal narrative not merely passively, by its social codes and cultural discourses, but actively by joining in the storytelling, singing, and dancing, thereby accepting, affirming, and exalting the individual/tribal identity.

In fact, all autobiography, in whatever culture or historical period, is collaborative. The idea of an audience implies shaping one's experiences to suit or, perhaps, to confound the expectations of one's readers or listeners, who, of course, are also shaped by a cultural framework or a set of cultural discourses. Even if one chooses to think of one's *self* as the audience, there is a type of collaboration between one's private self and one's public self (if they can ever be distinguished from each other). In fact, from a Bakhtinian perspective, a self is not autonomous and unified, but relational and multiple.[18] Anthropologists have long recognized the close relationship of one's self and one's culture; the term ''life history,'' referring to both one's individual history and one's cultural milieu, attests to this. Theorists of autobiographical studies share this understanding as well. In his introduction to *The American Autobiography,* Albert E. Stone calls autobiography ''individual stories and cultural narratives'' simultaneously.[19]

The third root of autobiography, writing, poses the most troublesome problem when considering early Native American autobiographical narratives because aboriginal Americans had no written language. If we replace the word *writing* with the word *language,* however, the scope of autobio*graphy* extends to include ''speech'' and ''signs.'' The spoken self-narratives of pre-contact Native Americans include songs, chants, and stories. The signed self-expressions include pictographs (signs that represent persons, events, and/or concepts) and sign language.

Shifting the focus from writing to language, which includes signs and speech, allows us to consider pre-contact Native American forms of personal narrative in terms of autobiography. Language for Native Americans, however, especially for pre-Columbian Native Americans, is considered sacred. To speak is not a casual affair, but a holy action. Words not only describe the world, but actively create and shape that world. The Navajo creation myth, for instance, emphasizes the sacred and powerful nature of language. The world is created by the thoughts of the gods made manifest in "speech, song, and prayer" (Witherspoon 15–16). Out of his medicine bundle, First Man creates Są'ah Naagháii (First Boy, the personification of Thought) and Bik'eh Hózhǫ́ (First Girl, the personification of Speech), who together create Estsánatlehi (Changing Woman, the Earth). As the "holy people" thought and spoke the world into existence, so do the first *Diné* (the Navajo term for themselves, which means simply "the people") think and speak the earth into being.

Są'ah Naagháii and Bik'eh Hózhǫ́ continue to become manifest, in various forms, in Navajo songs and ceremonies. Witherspoon explains: "Ritual language does not describe how things are; it determines how they will be" (34). What Witherspoon calls ritual language, Northrop Frye calls hieroglyphic language, the first stage of language (associated with religion and its mysteries), which uses "words as signs." Frye says that "the word evokes the image: it is an active force, a word of power, and there is a magic latent in it which can affect, even control, some of the operations of nature." In hieroglyphic language, words are "concrete" tangibilities, not "verbal abstractions."[20]

Whether we call it ritual language or hieroglyphic language, this is the sacred language of the ceremonies, not the everyday language of communication. There is yet, however, a vivid sense of the powerful "medicine" of daily speech. Unlike writing, speech is wedded to breath (which is often thought of as spirit). In Lawrence Evers's videotape "Songs of My Hunter Heart: Laguna Songs and Poems," an elderly Laguna woman speaks softly to a gathering of family and friends. Laguna poet and singer Harold Littlebird explains that tribal elders speak gently because they respect the words and what they have to say *"that* much."[21] For Native Americans, language is not an arbitrary sign system. Even if "[l]anguage is not a neutral medium," even if "it is populated—overpopulated—with the intentions of others" (Bakhtin 294), it creates and maintains personal and tribal meaning. To speak, then, is to reveal, to make manifest one's spirit. To speak one's life is to give forth the spirit of one's life, and if others join in the telling, the result is a mingling of breaths, of lives, of spirits.

It is clear, then, that although there are tribal variations about these ideas, pre-contact Native American concepts of self, life, and language were somewhat different from those shared by Europeans. For pre-contact indigenous people (and often for contemporary Native Americans as well) there is the sense of a communal identity, often dynamic, but always linked intimately with the land and therefore with natural cycles; there is a sense of an individual life that is shaped by event, community, and place, and that, in turn, helps to shape tribal life; and there is a sense of language as sacred, filled with the potential to create and shape reality, and of sign systems such as pictographs that can be "read" by tribal members. Considering these distinctly Native American ideas about the nature of self, life, and language, the word *autobiography* is inappropriate unless redefined to end the ethnocentric exaltation of the written word. A more suitable term might be *communo-bio-oratory* (community-life-speaking), since its roots reflect the communal and often oral nature of early Native American autobiographical expressions.[22]

At the 1985 International Symposium on Autobiography and Autobiography Studies, Georges Gusdorf lamented what he termed "autobiophoneme." He interpreted the fact that it is "no longer necessary to write a life, because you can speak it (into a microphone)" as a fall from "graphe" to "phoneme,"[23] a reversal of the Western model that posits continual development from the spoken to the written word. Gusdorf overlooked the connection between the two. Both writing and speaking into a microphone are means to record, and today we have oral-history projects and multimedia libraries that preserve information in oral and visual as well as written form. This is a far cry from earlier oral traditions, which Kiowa author N. Scott Momaday reminds us were "always but one generation removed from extinction."[24] Speaking one's life is not a new phenomenon; people have been speaking their lives since they discovered their voices, themselves, and their communities.

The Web of Self-Narration:
Native American and Euro-American
Autobiographical Traditions

So far, discussion has focused primarily on Native American understandings of self, life, and language, in contrast to Western assumptions about self, life, and writing. Certainly, in some ways Native American and

Euro-American traditions of autobiographical expression are distinct from each other. There are, however, not only differences; there are similarities as well. Such similarities are most apparent in the notion of a communal self found in tribal and oral societies (and sometimes in female communities). Karl J. Weintraub suggests we examine historical self-conceptions to better understand the development of autobiography. In his discussion of the history of the Western idea of self, Weintraub begins with tribal societies: "In tribal societies, where kinship ties have extraordinary strength, where the individual is firmly embedded in the enveloping social realities, where only a very limited degree of functional differentiation prevails, the personality conception tends to be but a prolongation of fairly pervasive social realities."[25] Although Weintraub is referring to ancient Greek tribal societies, using examples from Hellenic and Roman conceptions of personality, at least several of his descriptions of classical self-conceptions and their subsequent self-expressions parallel those of early Native Americans. H. David Brumble has noted the similarity between pre-contact Native American self-conceptions and self-expressions and those of ancient Greeks and Romans. Like the ancient Greeks and Romans, early Native Americans had powerful kinship relations and a strong collective identity, rather than an "individuality" that might distinguish one from the tribal community (Brumble 2–3).[26]

According to Weintraub, as a result of this "lack" of "individuality," ancient Greeks and Romans had little "genuine autobiographical activity" or "self-searching" (*Value* 2).[27] For many scholars of autobiography, this holds true for Native Americans as well. Brumble, however, sees parallels between Weintraub's categories of ancient autobiographical expressions—accounts of "great deeds done (res gestae)," "memorable events," and "philosopher's Lives"—and those of early Native Americans—"coup tales," "memoirs," and "shamans' Lives" (3). Likewise, Brumble finds Weintraub's comments on the ancient reticence " 'to [open] up their souls in the inwardness of true autobiography' " to be true of early Indian informants whose reserve was "widely remarked upon" (3). Brumble's brief comparison of Western classical and American Indian ideas of self suggests that what seems to be culture-specific self-conceptions may be history specific as well.

Like pre-contact Native American and Western classical traditions of personal narrative, contemporary rural Irish storytelling traditions tie the listener "into a web of responsibility."[28] Using Dell Hymes's model for

recording a storytelling performance in its social context, anthropologist
Henry Glassie discusses the stories of Ballymenone, many of them
personal narratives or community tales, which define and unite community members. According to Glassie: "When the sun shines, they work.
When night falls, they assemble in the kitchen and talk. The nighttime
gathering of neighbors is called a ceili (pronounced kaylee). Its center is
held by stories" (33). For the people of Ballymenone, then, stories are
entertainment, education, and self-expression. Beginning and ending in
conversation, "the usual ceili tale," according to Glassie, "is a celebra-
tory account of an action from the recent past by some individual who
embodies a virtue it is important to consider" (42). Even though, like
many Native Americans, Ballymenone folks are reticent to speak about
themselves, personal narratives form an important part of the network of
community stories. Tales of courage, of wit, and of creative intelligence
gather "energy into a gift to others which pleases them in the moment,
then carries them on to further life" (Glassie 36). Like Plains Indian coup
tales, the ceili tale emphasizes a communal sense of self (celebrating an
individual's achievements *in relation to* the community), uses oral tags
and formulas, and serves to educate and unite community members.
Perhaps, then, the process of oral composition, more than historical or
cultural influences, is responsible for these similarities.

Parallels among early Native American, ancient Greek and Roman,
and rural Irish self-narrations are not the only similarities between
American Indian and Western traditions of autobiography. Feminist
criticism of autobiography offers some provocative ideas about the nature
of self and gender and their expression in a literary work. Keeping in
mind the resistance of many Native American women to the predominantly white, middle-class feminist movement (Paula Gunn Allen
claims, in fact, that "traditional tribal lifestyles are more often gynocratic
than not" and that sexism was imposed by Europeans who brought their
patriarchy along with Christianity, whiskey, and smallpox) and the
different cultural notions of gender (Terry Tafoya, Warm Springs–Taos
healer and psychologist, suggests that, unlike dualistic-minded Westerners, many traditional native peoples may have acknowledged "a third
gender" in the form of a berdache, or man-woman),[29] we can still note
resonances in autobiographical expressions. First, many feminists find
not only the critical apparatus of autobiography but the term itself too
limiting. Domna Stanton refers to women's autobiography as "auto-
gyno-graphy," thus shifting the emphasis from "life" to "female-

ness.''[30] With this in mind, scholars are reclaiming literate and nonliterate traditions of female autobiographical activity. In the process, they have to reenvision the parameters of autobiography. Some insist that so-called female autobiographical forms such as diaries, journals, and letters ''are representations of reality rather than failed versions of something more coherent and unified.''[31] Attention to domestic details reveals the female autobiographer's web of relationships, not her circumscribed mind; short pieces of prose reflect the fragmentation of her life, not the insufficiency of her literary skills. Similarly, for Native American autobiographers, the lack of an autonomous ''I'' suggests a communal self, not an absence of self; the event-oriented tale reflects the rhythms of life and the audience's knowledge and understanding of the speaker, not the lack of narrative development.

In addition, feminist scholars have expanded the realm of literary study to include such nonliterate creations as the ''discourse of American quilting'' and stitchery. For Elaine Showalter, ''piecing, the technique of assembling fragments into an intricate and ingenious design,'' can shed light on ''the forms, meanings, and narrative traditions of American women's writing.''[32] Just as we need new aesthetic models relevant to women's autobiographical expressions, we need relevant native models with which to consider the oral and artistic traditions of Native American autobiographical narratives. In particular, the narrative possibilities of nonwritten materials and the privileged status of chronology, unity, and closure should be reconsidered.

The desire to expand the term *autobiography* is not the only concern I share with feminist scholars of autobiography. There are a few similarities between how feminists characterize female personal narrative and how I am describing pre-contact Native American self-narration. According to feminist autobiography theory, women's autobiographical narrative, unlike men's, tends to be circular (cyclical) rather than linear, and their autobiographical focus communal rather than individual. Although these women are Westerners, like Native Americans they share a sense of identity that is based on belonging to and participating in a larger pattern—the cultural patterns of family and social relations and the natural cycles of menstruation and childbirth, for instance. With this communal sense of identity in mind, Germaine Brée announced: ''Autobiography in the first person plural is the next to come.''[33] In fact, a communal ''I'' has been here all along in the autobiographical narratives of indigenous people.

Acknowledging oral and pictographic self-narrations as distinctly native forms of autobiographical activity is important not only for claiming a uniquely Native American tradition of autobiography. Such indigenous narratives have consequences for literary discourse in general, and for autobiography theory in particular. Pictographic and oral narratives challenge the Eurocentrism of the American literary canon; they dispute the ethnocentric definitions of self and self-representation assumed by many theorists of autobiography; and they challenge the primacy of the written word. American literature does not begin with seventeenth-century colonists' accounts of New England; it does not even begin with fifteenth-century explorer narratives. It begins in the pre-Columbian oral traditions of indigenous peoples. Similarly, Native American autobiography does not begin with the imposition of European forms on native peoples. Rather, what we can at least call autobiographical activity emerges on its own terms from pre-contact Native Americans. By the nineteenth century, indigenous oral and pictographic forms of personal narrative intersect with Western autobiographical forms, continuing a long tradition of adaptation and development.

Certainly, some might argue against considering oral and pictographic self-narrations, discussed in Chapters 2 and 3, as autobiography. Instead of being written, pictographic and spoken narratives are rendered with the use of a set of artistic and oral conventions. Rather than focusing on an autonomous self, they reflect a communal self. They often do not reveal deep self-reflection, but focus instead on action. They are not unified, nor do they depict an entire life—they are fragmented and describe only discrete incidents of a life. With such Euro-American parameters as criteria, traditional tribal pictographic and oral narratives do not qualify as autobiography at all. But expanding the narrow boundaries of a Eurocentric conception of autobiography to include communal notions of self and nonliterate modes of self-construction enriches the study of American literature by acknowledging, illuminating, and affirming its inherent plurality.

2 / Pre-Contact Oral and Pictographic Autobiographical Narratives: Coup Tales, Vision Stories, and Naming Practices

Of the more than 250 pre-Columbian native languages in what are now the United States and Canada, none was written. Such nonliteracy has been used as one of many rationales for dispossessing Indian people of their land. Indians were "primitive," European explorers and settlers assumed, since they had no writing and, conveniently, no written record of their ownership of the land. Early contact between Europeans and indigenous peoples, then, was "not so much a communicative exchange" as "a juxtaposition of two opposing world views"[1] "neither of which ever understood the other."[2] Since most Europeans had fabricated ideas of Indian people, defining their "civilized" selves in opposition to the "savage" Other,[3] it is not surprising that most Euro-Americans did not perceive indigenous oral traditions or forms of literacy such as narrative wampum belts, quillwork, and pictographs. Oral autobiographical narratives told to family, friends, and community members; pictographic personal narratives painted on animal hides, tipis, and shields; and even narrative names were all means to construct and narrate a personal identity. Because such indigenous oral and pictographic narratives have generally been examined (if at all, in English Departments) from routinely Eurocentric assumptions with which they were never meant to conform, they have been devalued or overlooked.

Coup Tales

Stories were important as a means to entertain, to educate, and to unite tribal members. Mythic stories, trickster tales, and personal narratives all played a vital role in maintaining a sense of identity—individual and tribal. Myths and the historical stories associated with winter counts (winter counts were "a method of historical record-keeping" often painted on animal hides)[4] helped to define and express a communal identity, while personal stories told to family and tribal members helped to clarify and enhance an individual sense of self within the tribe. One type of autobiographical narrative is the coup story of the Plains Indians, an example of communo-bio-oratory. Among the tribes of the Plains was "a set of graded war honors." They included killing or scalping an enemy, performing a coup, stealing horses or other valuable articles, and rescuing a comrade.[5] Derived from the French word "to touch," a coup meant "to touch a live enemy with the hand or with a special coup stick and get away without being harmed"[6] and was one of the highest rated acts of bravery (Driver 323). Often, humiliating the enemy was superior to destroying him. On returning from battle with fellow warrior-witnesses to vouch for his words, the warrior would narrate his martial accomplishments to his community. This was a way to keep the community informed about its warriors and for the narrator to articulate his personal experience and his new standing within the tribe. Since in many traditional communities one's status depends on one's lifetime achievements, the recitation of a warrior's accumulated martial accomplishments might serve to inform a gathering that he has earned the right to be heard, the right to participate in the event at hand.

Red Eagle's Oral Coup Tale

According to James W. Schultz, a Euro-American "fur trader from 1878 to 1904" who lived among the Blackfeet, married a Piegan woman, and took a Blackfeet name, the one subject that interests old Blackfeet men is the "reminiscences of their youthful days."[7] As Brumble suggests, "We should probably regard Schultz's editions . . . as careful redactions by a man who lived on intimate terms with the people whose stories he is retelling."[8] Gathered together in one lodge to smoke and to talk, several old men would take turns telling stories of the old days and their deeds. Schultz recorded the medicine-maker Red Eagle's humorous and exciting story about restealing horses stolen by the Crow. The most striking feature of this account is that, although it is supposed to be the reminiscences of one old man, it is told in the first- and third-person plural. Red Eagle does not glorify himself and his individual actions by using the first-person singular, "I." Instead, he refers to fellow warriors impersonally as "they" or collectively as "we," in a sense erasing himself from his own story or at least replacing an autonomous "I" with a communal "we."

In another reminiscence, Red Eagle uses the first-person singular and the first-person plural to describe the time his friend Nitaina tamed a wolf puppy, and they all went on the "war trail . . . bound for the country of the Sioux" (Schultz 184). Red Eagle provides exact details of the geography along the way: "We followed the stream down to where it joins the Missouri," he explains, "and there cut across the plains for the western end of the Bear Paw Mountains, traveling only at night. We were one night, and part of another from the river to the pines on top of the westernmost butte of the range" (Schultz 184). Such precise and realistic descriptions of the landscape are sound educationally and narratively. Those who listen can follow Red Eagle's travels just as if he were tracing his route on a map, and they can learn about predominant landmarks, plentiful hunting grounds, and dangerous enemy country. Likewise, the listeners may be convinced of the authenticity of the story because of such realistic detail.

Instead of the Sioux for whom they were looking, Red Eagle and Nitaina found a series of predicaments. They were attacked by a grizzly, almost discovered by enemy Crows, and chased by angry Sioux. From all these misadventures, the wolf pup, Laugher, saved them. On returning to camp, Red Eagle and Nitaina recounted their coups. In a humorous variation on this form, Nitaina spoke for his tame wolf, Laugher, the real hero of the trio:

> "Friends," he went on, "Laugher is going to count his coups. He does not speak our language so I shall be his interpreter. Now, then, listen." And raising his voice he shouted: "Laugher. That is me. That is my name. I went on a raid with Nitaina and Red Eagle. On a bare rock butte of the Little Rockies I discovered the trail of the enemy and gave warning, and saved the lives of my two men. Later, I helped them round up and drive off a band of Sioux horses. Still later, while I alone was awake, I saw the enemy running to kill my sleeping men and take the horses, and again I gave warning, and assisted them to escape. There. I have said." (Schultz 192–193)

Although the "speaker" is somewhat unusual, this is a good example of the basic form of the coup tale. This brief personal narrative begins with announcing one's name; then proceeds to identifying one's associates, locating one's self geographically and strategically, and listing one's brave achievements; and finally ends by stating a formulaic conclusion ("There. I have said."). This form serves as a basic outline for the story or stories that will later be told when tribal members gather in a comfortable lodge. Before the fully embellished narrative is heard, however, there is an immediate audience reply to the narrative. In response to Laugher's coup story, the narrator notes that the "great crowd of people shouted," calling Laugher "a chief," while "the waiting drummers whanged their big drums" (Schultz 193). The seed of the coup narrative is not germinated until it has achieved such a potent response from the tribal members, who thus share in the creation of a new self-image and a new personal narrative for the one recounting coups.[9]

Mah-to-toh-pa's Pictographic Buffalo Robe

Male Native Americans not only told the stories of their personal deeds of bravery, but portrayed them in various visual forms. These artistic representations were often painted on tipis, shields, cloth, or skins. As Helen H. Blish notes, nineteenth-century ethnographer Garrick Mallery called such personal records "bragging biographies" and "partisan histories,"[10] since they are individual records of one person's exploits. One famous example is the robe of Mah-to-toh-pa (Four Bears), a Mandan chief (Figure 1). George Catlin wrote that Mah-to-toh-pa wore "a robe on his back, with the history of all his battles on it, which would fill a book of themselves if they were properly enlarged and translated." According to Catlin, Mah-to-toh-pa's robe, which "was made of the skin of a young buffalo bull, with the fur on one side, and the other finely and delicately dressed; with all the battles of his life emblazoned on it by his own hand," was "the chart of his military life." Catlin recorded the stories behind these drawings as told and enacted by Mah-to-toh-pa and translated by Joseph Kipp, an Indian trader. Catlin asserted that since Kipp, "a gentleman of respectability and truth," vouched for the truth of the stories, and that since he is in a country where "men are the most jealous of rank and of standing" and where the community is so small even the smallest child knows the truth about a warrior's deeds, Mah-to-toh-pa's battle record should be considered "historical fact."[11]

FIGURE 1. *Four Bears, Second Chief in Full Dress* by George Catlin, 1832. (Courtesy of the National Museum of American Art, Smithsonian Institution, Gift of Mrs. Joseph Harrison, Jr.)

George Catlin painted this portrait of the Mandan chief Mah-to-toh-pa (Four Bears). Four Bears wears a full warbonnet of eagle feathers and buffalo horns, porcupine-quill moccasins, and his buffalo-hide robe painted to depict his war deeds. Such a pictographic robe was used as a mnemonic device for recounting war exploits. In one hand, Four Bears holds his lance, which is decorated with eagle feathers to symbolize his martial achievements.

Mah-to-toh-pa's pictographic robe identifies the hero, the traditional beginning of coup tales, in a couple of ways. Since each event is drawn on Mah-to-toh-pa's robe, it is obvious the action refers to the owner of this robe. For a warrior to adorn himself in the depiction of the brave deeds of another would be unthinkable, like a European military officer wearing another officer's medals. Also, sometimes the warrior is identified by a characteristic symbol of himself. For instance, in one picture on the robe, Mah-to-toh-pa is "known by his lance with eagles' quills on it" (Catlin 149).

In contrast to the oral version of coup stories, in pictographs geographic location is not always revealed, in part because geographic details would be difficult to draw adequately in the space available. Strategic position, though, can easily be pictured. In particular, each drawing reveals the warrior's relation to his enemy (behind, in front, surrounded by, etc.), the weapons used to kill the enemy, and the number of opponents (often represented by their tracks, arrows, or bullets rather than by their bodies). The oral formula signifying completion of the story is not pertinent in pictographs. The picture scene is complete in itself, a visual narrative of a personal and a tribal history of battle. To be vitally complete, however, this pictured narrative must come to life as speech and action, as when Catlin tells of Mah-to-toh-pa, who "sat upon the robe, pointing to his painting" of the battle, "and at the same time brandishing the identical knife which he drew from his belt, as he was shewing how the fatal blow was given; and exhibiting the wounds inflicted in his hand, as the blade of the knife was several times drawn through it before he wrested it from his antagonist" (152). This dramatic rendering of the episode is more exciting than hearing the original battle report or looking at the pictures that serve as a mnemonic device for the warrior–storyteller, as a personal and historical record for the individual and the tribe, and as a monument to individual bravery and achievement.

A similar garment is the Crow robe made of elk skin that tells "the story of ten episodes of Crow warriors" (Blish 18). "These two robes," explains Blish, "are not unique in either purpose or execution. They are specimens of an art widely practiced among the Plains Indians . . ." (18). The Mandan and Crow robes, then, are not indications of aberrant individual self-indulgence within a communal society. Rather, they are examples of a "widely practiced" form of artistic personal history. Such "personal records . . . are quite common, especially among the Plains Indians. In fact," says Blish, "these are the most frequently found pictographic records'' (21). Painted buffalo robes can be seen as the "ultimate form of imagery upon which tribal aspirations, tribal lore, and personal aggrandizement could all be concentrated.'' Most often, these "pictographic designs were the work of men boasting about their exploits . . ."[12] Such fierce insistence on individual achievement confounds the often quoted generalization about Native American communal identity. It is not the tribe that achieves and narrates such fearless feats, but individual warriors. But just as Ben Franklin, although representative of Euro-American culture, is still an individual man, Mah-to-toh-pa, although illustrative of Mandan society, is yet a distinct person. Each man distinguished himself within his society and culture, thus setting himself apart from other members of it but also ensuring his place within it.

Kiowa and Kiowa–Apache Pictographic Tipis: Narratives of Spiritual Visions and Martial Accomplishments

Not only did important male Indians paint animal-hide robes, but the Kiowa and Kiowa–Apaches, if they were "prominent tribal leaders," painted their tipis.[13] From 1891 to 1904, ethnographer James Mooney collected "small-scale models of painted tipis" described by the oldest Kiowa and Kiowa–Apaches who remembered and owned these tipis and painted by Kiowa artists—Paul Zotom, Charley Ohettoint, and Silverhorn (Ewers 10). Since a painted tipi was a sign of status within the tribe even before 1870 (before the buffalo were exterminated), "less than one-fifth" of all Kiowa tipis were painted. These "earliest mural artists in North America" obtained designs and colors for their artwork through personal visions, brave war deeds, inheritance, or marriage. Since "designs were handed down generation to generation" within one family, a tipi was closely associated with the individual owner and often with his family (Ewers 8). In fact, "some owners came to be known by the names of their tipis—such as Red Tipi Man, Black-Striped Tipi Man, and Turtle" (Ewers 8). These tipi designs often originated in a dream or vision of one man. Thus a tipi painting was an emblematic personal narrative of one individual's spiritual experiences or aspirations. Turtle most likely received his vision and its power ("turtle medicine") from a "turtle spirit," thereby acquiring his name and his tipi design (Figure 2). The upper part of Turtle's tipi is painted green (a color associated with water), interrupted only by a "red crescent moon" in the center back; the

FIGURE 2. Turtle's tipi. (Courtesy of the Department of Anthropology, Smithsonian Institution)

Using conventional Kiowa symbols, Turtle has painted his tipi to reflect his spiritual life—in this case, his turtle medicine. All the symbols refer to "water powers": the composite turtle/thunderbird in the back center of the tipi (note the turtle-shell body of the bird figure); the two beavers facing each side of the door; and the two rainbows (two sets of parallel lines of various colors) encircling the upper and lower edges of the tipi.

lower portion is painted yellow. Between the green and yellow sections is a large unpainted area of buffalo skin that is bordered by a colorful rainbow symbol ("parallel lines of green, yellow, red, and blue"). At the center back is a painting of "a composite figure" combining "both a turtle and a thunderbird in blue and green"—with a peace pipe perched atop each of the thunderbird's wings. Just above the bottom rainbow, facing each side of the doorway, is "a small black beaver with a yellow belly." A buffalo tail hangs from the center of the back. All the symbolism of Turtle's tipi refers to "water powers—i.e., the turtle, the beaver, the thunderbird, and the rainbow," as well as the color green (Ewers 27–28). Both the design and the colors, then, are personal expressions rendered in a set of conventional symbols, what James Mooney referred to as "Kiowa heraldry."[14] From these symbols one could read about Turtle's interior life—his spiritual aspirations and attainments.

Most of the painted Kiowa tipis had their origin in an individual's personal vision. Chiefs, war leaders, and holy men composed the prestigious minority that envisioned and enacted these striking tipi designs. The tipi owner–dreamer would call together "twenty or thirty of his friends" (Ewers 7) to assist him in the project of making his personal vision manifest. As in the house raisings or the sewing bees of nineteenth-century Euro-American culture, Native American men joined forces to expedite the completion of the project, in this case an artistic autobio-graphical impulse. This tribal cooperation in bringing forth individual expression is a precursor to the Indian–white collaboration of later ethnographer-collected life histories. However, pre-contact tribal collab-oration was equitable, whereas post-contact collaboration was often, as noted by both Arnold Krupat and Thomas Couser, a textual reenactment of Anglo domination.[15]

Turtle's tipi design expressed his inner life and his particular connec-tion to the spirits of power. Other designs often included pictographic coup tales that are more obviously narrative. Although the design for Black-Striped Tipi was dreamed of by Black Cap, a Kiowa holy man, the black and red stripes that encircle the tipi might well have "reference to successful war expeditions" (Ewers 41). Thus not only might the spiritual life of an individual be portrayed, but his secular life could be narrated as well.

Not all such tipis were based on an individual's vision or expressed only one person's achievements. Little Bluff's Tipi with Battle Pictures is an interesting combination of individual and tribal, of pictograph and symbol (Figure 3). The Cheyenne chief Sleeping Bear gave the tipi to Little Bluff, a Kiowa chief, who in return gave him some fine horses. Thus a strong bond of peace was forged between the two formerly warring tribes. When Little Bluff received the tipi, the north half of it was painted with a few battle scenes, and the south side was decorated with some horizontal yellow stripes representing successful Cheyenne raids.[16] Little Bluff and his Kiowa colleagues took great pains to embellish this lodge with their own personal accomplishments. On the south side, Little Bluff added black stripes, to alternate with the yellow ones already in place. Each of these fifteen dark stripes represents "a war party he had led that had brought back one or more enemy scalps" without the loss of any of his own warriors. Down the center of the back, Heart Eater, "a noted

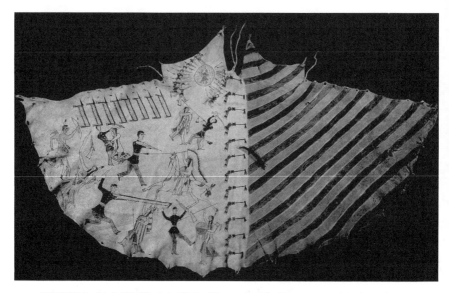

FIGURE 3. Little Bluff's tipi, 1890s. (Courtesy of the Department of Anthropology, Smithsonian Institution)

The Cheyenne chief Sleeping Bear gave this painted tipi to the Kiowa chief Little Bluff, in exchange for some fine horses. When Little Bluff received the tipi, the north side (the left side of the illustration) was painted with battle scenes, and the south side (the right side of the illustration) was decorated with horizontal yellow stripes representing successful Cheyenne raids. Little Bluff and his colleagues embellished the tipi with their own drawings of their collective martial accomplishments. Next to the yellow stripes they alternated fifteen black ones to represent their own successful raids. The Kiowa warrior Heart Eater painted twelve tomahawks down the center back, and Sitting Tree drew eight decorated lances along the length of the door flap, each representing a coup. On the north side, they added pictographic narrations of their battles, thus creating a pictorial anthology of autobiographical narratives.

Kiowa warrior who derived his name from his custom of eating a small piece of the heart of each enemy he killed,'' painted twelve tomahawks. To the north side of the tipi, the Kiowa embellished the few Cheyenne battle pictures with many of their own, often updating the scenes each year with each tipi renewal. The upper section was reserved for a circle picture in which a single warrior in a brave defensive posture was depicted. Next, Sitting Tree painted eight horizontal decorated lances, lining the edge of the door, to represent ''the coups he had counted with his feather-and-red-cloth decorated lance'' (Ewers 15). Finally, as on most painted tipis, a buffalo tail hung from the center back and buffalo hair graced the top flaps of the tipi (Ewers 15), a decorative reminder of one's connection to the life-sustaining earth. Thus Little Bluff, Heart Eater, and Sitting Tree narrated their martial accomplishments using Kiowa symbols and Plains Indian pictography.

The manner of construction of this unique tipi was basically similar to that of the others. Men—those who had the visions and/or had performed the deeds and those who painted the visions and deeds as directed—gathered together to paint and to advise, being fed and housed by the tipi owner during the process. Little Bluff's Tipi with Battle Pictures is different, however, in that instead of recording one individual's war deeds, it records several individuals' battle experiences. This was not an attempt at small-scale tribal history. This is early collaborative auto-biography. At the very least, this "mural in the round," as Ewers refers to it, is an artistic anthology of autobiographical accounts. Since these tipis were generally renewed every year, there was an opportunity to re-create one's most recent autobiographical moment if desired, rather like writing an annual report or updating a résumé or keeping a journal. The Native American sense of life as process is evident here. Most tipi designs, however, did not change so casually as Little Bluff's, but were patterned as closely as possible after the original, suggesting the value of continuity over innovation.

Even though "the painting was always done by men" (Ewers 7), the process of designing Little Bluff's Tipi with Battle Pictures may be analogous to the process of piecing together a quilt. Women from the community gathered together, bringing with them scraps of cloth from home and their own personal styles, designs, and imaginations. Working cooperatively, stitching their individual bits of material together, they united the differences in print and fabric in the overall design. Like early pioneer women's quilts, Little Bluff's tipi is an aesthetic and functional wholeness imagined, designed, and created by many hands and sensibilities all being directed by one person. A major difference to consider, however, is the class difference. The tipi painters were prominent men in the tribe, whereas the quilt makers were most often average women in the community.

Other Artistic Personal Narratives

Just as Kiowa and Kiowa–Apache men decorated their tipis, many Native American men used a variety of materials to narrate their personal exploits artistically. In the Southeast, for instance, indigenous men sometimes ornamented their bodies with pictographic tatoos. "The most elaborate designs," explains Harold Driver, "were worn by warriors and chiefs, who recorded their valorous deeds in this symbolism" (143). Native men in the Southeast tatooed their brave exploits onto their bodies, literally inscribing the self. Similarly, Plains Indian men painted their spiritual and martial experiences on personal shields. According to Frederick J. Dockstader, the "narrative type" of shield is a good example of the artist's personal symbolism and his "ability to tell a story in pictures."[17] Like the pictures rendered on tipis, the designs on personal shields might reflect a man's clan relationships, spiritual visions, and martial activities.[18] In general, then, one's painted shield indicated one's status within the community.

While women did not carry shields, they often decorated parfleches and articles of clothing with symbolic geometric designs. A woman might note, for instance, her clan or family affiliations or spiritual symbols in porcupine quillwork or beadwork. Among the Crow, "some informants claimed that the number of horizontal bands of beadwork on a woman's leggings might represent the number of coups her husband had counted in battle."[19] A woman's identity, then, was defined in part by her relationship with her family (her spouse, in particular) as well as by her own personal characteristics and accomplishments. Thus women, as well as men, expressed themselves in artistic autobiographical forms, sanctioned by the tribe but developed individually. Because, at least in the Plains area, women depicted symbols and not representative figures, they did not narrate their personal experiences of daily life but their relationships to family, community, and tradition.[20] Certainly, women's geometric designs do not convey or even imply explicit personal narratives, as do men's pictographic depictions of heroic actions. The symbolism of women's porcupine quillwork or beadwork is more akin to the abstract designs of Navajo women's woven blankets—personal versions of the tribe's self-defining symbols—than to consciously constructed self-narrations about one's personal life. This is not to imply that Native American women were oppressed by tribal expectations that limited their personal expression. On the contrary, women were considered the upholders of tradition and thus held honored positions within the community. Perhaps, though, Native American women had fewer avenues for individualistic personal narrative because, unlike Plains Indian men who were encouraged to seek individual glory, women were supposed to be modest and stable.[21]

Oral and pictographic autobiography meet in dramatic self-narration or performance. Three common dramatic autobiographical forms are dance, ceremony, and storytelling.[22] When an individual received or took a new name, he or she might announce it and acknowledge the occasion at a public event. When a warrior performed a brave deed, he would recount his coup—recite his actions to the gathered tribe, often reenacting the scene through his storytelling performance and, later, his dancing prowess. If he were an especially decorated fighter, he might wear his pictographic robe or beaded garments. For many Plains Indian tribes, when an individual had a vision it was considered necessary to enact the vision before the tribe in order to instruct the people and gain tribal recognition and support for fulfilling the vision. In this case, many community members might participate in dramatizing the vision, just as Black Elk's colleagues helped him perform the Horse Dance (an enact-ment of part of his large vision), preparing ritual paraphernalia—uniting song, design, color, and ritual action in a tribal pageant that narrated the personal experience of a specific individual and, at the same time, consolidated the spiritual energies of the entire tribe. At this point, oral, pictographic (or artistic), and dramatic dimensions of autobiographical narrative come together. Actually, these three forms of self-narration are not discrete categories. Each form converges on the others so that the oral recounting of a coup or narrating of a vision may be artistic and dramatic as well.

Nineteenth-Century Plains Indian Names and Autobiography

While autobiographical narratives in speech and pictography convey crucial aspects of one's identity, nothing is so fundamental to self-construction as one's name(s). Any representation of self is a linguistic, cultural, and historical construction as well as a personal one. According to Philippe Lejeune, "Everyone is . . . aware of this indeterminacy of the first person, and it is not an accident that we attempt to resolve the indeterminacy by anchoring it to the proper name."[23] In fact, Lejeune insists, "the passion for the name . . . expresses the cry for existence of personal identity itself. The deep subject of autobiography is the proper name" (209). As problem-ridden as it may be, the proper name highlights both a unified self (a conflation of speaker–author and narrator) and a multiple self (a contiguity of the many voices embedded in

language). Our names, then, reflect both a personal and a social identity
and serve at least two semantic functions: referential and expressive.[24]
"Most of the thinking done by philosophers and linguists about the nature
of proper names," insists linguist Marianne Mithun, "has been limited to
Indo-European names, especially English, or to philosophical constructs
based on English names."[25] This section will discuss nineteenth-century
Plains Indian names as they have been translated into English. This, then,
is not a linguistic analysis, but a theoretical consideration of the autobiographical dimensions of serial naming as practiced by nineteenth-century
Plains Indian men and recorded by Euro-American authorities. The focus
is on men's names for two reasons. Generally, men acquired more names
than women, each name reflecting an accomplishment or life transition.
Second, when Euro-American officials of the United States government
(with the assistance of some assimilated Native Americans) compiled the
tribal enrollment lists in the late nineteenth century, they routinely
insisted that men be listed as heads of households. Just as early ethnographers concentrated their attention on men and their activities, census
takers focused on men and their names. The result is that there is a more
substantial record of men's names than of women's.[26]

Like many other indigenous peoples, nineteenth-century Plains Indian
tribal members shared a sense of a collective identity. Such a relational
self reflected deep connections not only to one's people, but to the land
and its natural cycles as well. Nineteenth-century Plains Indian men,
however, displayed a particularly lively sense of individuality. While
Plains Indian women were encouraged to be the educators and tradition
bearers, ensuring the continuance of the nation by teaching the young
people, men were expected to provide for the well-being of the people by
hunting, warring, and obtaining spiritual visions. Prowess in martial
exploits and distinction in spiritual endeavors were ways to earn individual prestige and community affirmation. Men were encouraged to perform such exploits and were often expected to narrate them afterward.
Oral and pictographic autobiographical accounts of brave deeds, known
as coup tales, were common, and a man's names were often determined
by his accomplishments and the community's affirmation of them.
Although proper names may not have been designed as autobiography
(that is, as a self-consciously constructed narrative of the physical and
spiritual events of someone's life), they reveal a great deal about the

person's character, they narrate key transformations, and they can be examined as a fundamental type of autobiographical activity.

Considering nineteenth-century Plains Indian names as serial but nonlinear "autobiographical acts," to use Elizabeth Bruss's term,[27] raises a number of issues. Certainly, native notions of the metonymic function of the proper name challenge the postmodern insistence on language as an arbitrary set of signs. For many Native Americans there is, indeed, an intimate connection between the word and the world, a link further enlivened in ritual, where language is thought to reconfigure reality. Also, examining names in light of autobiography confounds the Eurocentric insistence that "true" autobiography should present a unified story narrated by an older person who reviews an important life in its entirety.[28] In contrast, Plains Indian proper names can be more aptly likened to the seemingly discontinuous autobiographical narratives of Euro-American diaries and journals. Diary and journal entries narrate the immediacy of discrete moments rather than reflections of the past shaped into a unified and chronological narrative. Since names are often conferred by others, the very process of identity construction agitates Euro-American ideas about self-invention, self-representation, and self-narration. If names are bestowed by someone else, how can they be *auto*biographical? A relational identity, though, depends for its existence, and to a certain extent for its expression, on others. When this is so, being given a name by one's community constructs and reflects one's identity just as accurately as inventing one's own name might in individualistic societies. Besides, if what Bakhtin suggests is true, the "I" in any culture is inherently polyvocal, and the construction of a unified subject is always a collaborative social activity.[29]

In Plains Indian traditions, the proper name might reflect accomplishments of the past, aspirations for the future, or connections to geography, to family, to clan, or to the spiritual world in the present. Proper names may embody personal anecdotes, family stories, and tribal myths as well as the dynamic relationship among them. Names, then, can be profoundly narrative as well as descriptive. Finally, traditionally among Plains Indian tribes, individuals, particularly men, were given (or sometimes took for themselves) several names over a lifetime, revising their life narratives as they lived them. Generally, men acquired many more names than women, reflecting their personal secular and spiritual accomplishments. Women, however, sometimes took new names at transitional moments, such as puberty or marriage. Pretty-Shield, a Crow Indian woman, was given her name by her paternal grandfather—the owner of a particularly handsome painted warshield. According to Crow custom, explains Pretty-Shield, "a woman's name never changed unless, when she was very young, she did not grow strong." In that case, parents "sometimes asked one of [the child's] grandfathers to change her name to help her."[30] The idea is that altering one's name (one's fundamental self-representation) reshapes one's life. Such differences in the naming practices for men and women suggest cultural gender roles. Whereas changing male names reflect men's protean activities, relatively stable female names mirror women's roles in preserving tribal traditions. By the time some of these (mostly male) names were recorded by Anglo officials in the late nineteenth century, Euro-American appellations had been added, reflecting bicultural identities imposed by colonialism.

Categorizing, Conferring, Keeping Secret, and Acquiring Names

Using Red Cloud's 1884 pictorial census, the 1884 Oglala Roster, and pictographic names from "winter counts [i.e., tribal histories] of The-Flame, The-Swan, American-Horse, and Cloud-Shield" as sources, nineteenth-century ethnologist Garrick Mallery divided Plains Indian personal names into four categories: objective, metaphoric, animal, and vegetable.[31] Objective names might also be called descriptive names. They include such straightforward appellations as Long-Hair, High-Back-Bone, Left-Handed-Big-Nose, and Squint Eyes. With such names as The Stabber, Licks-with-his-Tongue, and Knock-a-Hole-in-the-Head, there is an implicit narrative as well as a description embedded. We wonder about the story behind how Licks-with-his-Tongue got his name, for instance. It is as though one's name presents one key event of a segment of one's life rather than the fully developed story of one's entire life. Certainly in a small community where everyone knows one another's personal stories, there is no need for an elaborated autobiographical narrative. Everyone can fill in the details.

Metaphoric names, Mallery's second category, are also descriptive, of course, but through comparison of the person with someone or something else. "Wolf-Ear," according to Mallery, "probably refers to size, and is substantially the same as big-ear" (453). Similarly, Tongue is not strictly descriptive, but is a derisive or humorous metonym for someone who "mouths off." Although Mallery made them distinct categories, animal and vegetable names are certainly metaphoric. Mouse, Badger, or Spotted-Elk may refer to the characteristics of the animal that the person has acquired or aspires to acquire—diligence, prowess, or swiftness, for example—or to some spirit animal seen in a vision. The name Badger, for instance, may belong to someone who fights like the feisty beast. Some animal names borrow characteristics from objective names, such as Bear-Looks-Back, which is a bear-in-action, a metaphoric representation of a personal narrative. Although less common, vegetable names exist. The name Tree-in-the-Face sounds as though it might present an exciting story of a tree climber or a falling tree, but according to Mallery it simply describes the painted face of the person. Here Mallery suggested a static description rather than a narrative moment frozen in paint. The tree-painted face itself, however, might be decoded as the man's spiritual symbolism.

Colors added to names—Black Elk or Red Cloud, for example—are based on "a mythical or symbolic significance attributed to colors" (Mallery 446). Such names are often earned or received due to one's spiritual aspirations or accomplishments, rather than one's worldly achievements. The "symbolic significance" of color may differ from tribe to tribe, or even, sometimes, from person to person. The Lakota holy man Black Elk provides a detailed explanation of the color symbolism of his vision, while Lame Deer describes a slightly variant version of the symbolism of Lakota colors in his autobiography. Both Black Elk and Lame Deer agree, however, that certain colors are associated with specific cardinal points, which, in turn, are associated with certain characteristics. Thus Black Elk, whose power is from the Thunder-Beings in the West, has an appropriate name (passed down to him from his father), since black is the color of the West—the place of introspection and the origin of storm clouds.

Charles Alexander Eastman, a Santee Sioux who earned a degree in science from Dartmouth College and a medical degree from Boston University in 1890, wrote numerous books to educate Euro-Americans about Indian life and beliefs. In *The Soul of the Indian* (1911), he categorizes "Indian names" as nicknames, deed names, birth names, or names with "a religious and symbolic meaning."[32] A name reflects the nature of the individual. For example, a "man of forcible character" will usually have "the name of the buffalo or bear, lightning or some dread natural force," while a more peaceful man "may be called Swift Bird or

Blue Sky" (Eastman, *Soul* 44). Women's names are often associated
with "the home" and include adjectives like " 'pretty' or 'good' " (*Soul*
44). "Names of any dignity or importance," notes Eastman, "must be
conferred by the old men," particularly if the names have "spiritual
significance" (*Soul* 44). A spiritual name was "sometimes borne by
three generations, but each individual must prove that he is worthy of it"
(*Soul* 45).

A proper name, a reflection of one's individual characteristics and
aspirations, can reveal a great deal about one's traits, achievements, and
goals. This and the belief in the sacred nature of language may be part of
the reason many indigenous people traditionally do not address others by
their personal names, but by kinship terms or family endearments. Many
have noted the reticence, if not outright refusal, of native people to speak
their personal names. In his 1902 autobiography, *Indian Boyhood,*
Charles Eastman explains that "Indian etiquette" requires "avoiding the
direct address." Instead of one's personal name, a "term of relationship
or some title of courtesy was commonly used . . . by those who wished
to show respect."[33] Although Everard Thurn studied the Indians of
Guiana, Mallery believes that what he says about a person's name given
at birth is true of the indigenous people of North America as well:

> But these names seem of little use, in that owners have a very strong
> objection to telling or using them, apparently on the ground that the name is
> part of the man, and that he who knows the name has part of the owner of
> that name in his power. (444–445)

For many traditional indigenous people, one's first given name is never
spoken, since it is a sacred connection to the spirit world. Such a name is a
gift of essential being that, like an ever-developing embryo, must be
nurtured continuously in the private realm of the womb, there to give
birth to new manifestations of self.

Because of this traditional reticence to speak (or write) about oneself,
talking about oneself unduly or speaking one's name is considered bad
manners or, at the very least, inappropriate behavior. Eastman makes this
clear in his second autobiography, *From the Deep Woods to Civilization*
(1916), when he describes his first day at school. When the Euro-
American teacher asked him what his name was, Eastman did not
respond. "Evidently [the instructor] had not been among the Indians
long," reasoned the young Eastman, "or he would not have asked that
question. It takes a tactician and a diplomat to get an Indian to tell his

name!''[34] Of course, the teacher gave up his attempt in the face of such adamant resistance. Only when one has earned a level of status acknowledged by the community can one speak of oneself without being severely criticized as egotistical (or being ignored altogether).

Even more important than categories of names or the secrecy of the first name is the fact that nineteenth-century Plains Indian names changed during the course of life to reflect an individual's spiritual and worldly accomplishments. Traditionally, among the Kiowa and some other Plains Indian tribes, at least three names were given: one at birth, one at adolescence, and one at adulthood. For the Mandans, "until the child received a name, it was not considered a part of the . . . village but of the 'baby home' from whence it had come."[35] A name, then, conferred status as a tribal member. New names were given or acknowledged "at first menstruation for girls, initiation into a sodality for boys, success in hunting and war for boys, and the acquisition of supernatural power in the vision quest for both sexes" (Driver 390). Plains Indian men might acquire "a dozen or more names in a lifetime by performing as many successive deeds of distinction" (Driver 390).

Plenty-Coups, a Crow warrior, and Charles Eastman, a Sioux physician, provide sound examples of the ways such names can function. Plenty-Coups is a name that sounds as though it could have been earned only after a long and successful career in fighting, raiding, and counting coups—all socially sanctioned means to earn status for oneself and one's tribe. Plenty-Coups explains that his name was given to him by his grandfather. "I name him Aleek-chea-ahoosh [Many Achievements]," the grandfather announced to the boy's mother, "because in my dream I saw him count many coups."[36] Since "all the people knew this," Plenty-Coups felt "obliged to excel" (27). "I must live up to my name, you see" (28), explains Plenty-Coups. Such a promissory name serves to inspire the child to fulfill the vision of his name (and of his family's aspirations for him).

In *Indian Boyhood,* Charles Eastman explains how he had "to bear the humiliating name *Hakadah,* 'the pitiful last' " (a name given to him when his mother died shortly after his birth), "until [he] should earn a more dignified and appropriate name" (21). Several years later, after a victory in a lacrosse game, the medicine man Chankpee-yuhah conferred a new name on Hakadah. "Ohiyesa (or Winner) shall be thy name henceforth," he announced. "Be brave, be patient, and thou shalt always win. Thy name is Ohiyesa" (Eastman, *Boyhood* 47–48). It is important that the gathered people witness and approve his new appellation, given "in memory of this victory" (Eastman, *Boyhood* 47). Eastman's first name, Hakadah, recorded the unfortunate circumstances of his birth and his place within his family structure. Ohiyesa, his second name "earned" by communal accomplishment, reflected the band's lacrosse victory, but more importantly his community's belief in his future potential. The "Pitiful Last" became "The Winner." Still later, he would become Dr. Charles Alexander Eastman, taking on a white man's name to reflect what he describes as his transition from "the deep woods to civilization."

Plains Indian Pictographic Autographs

Writing in 1888 for the Bureau of American Ethnology, Garrick Mallery stated that Indian personal names "were generally connotive," and because of their "sometimes objective and sometimes ideographic nature," they can be "expressed in sign language" and "portrayed in pictographs" (442–445). It is revealing to consider the manner in which a name was "portrayed" or "signed." The Plains Indian way to "write" a name was to draw a head with a line coming from the head or mouth, connecting the body and the pictured object that signified the name (known as a name-symbol). Similarly, in sign language, after the sign for the object was gestured, the person passed "the index finger forward from the mouth in a direct line" (Mallery 442–443). Thus, signifying one's name, whether in pictograph or sign language (both pan-tribal languages to a degree), requires a link between an individual (quite literally a head or mouth) and the objectified personal name, paralleling the process of the speaker speaking his or her name (the breath, then, takes the place of the line, connecting self to name). As well as emphasizing the physical connection between the individual and the name, between self and self-referent, the pictographic autograph suggests that the name emanates from the self. The Cheyenne Wuxpais (Daniel Littlechief) displayed this autograph convention for Albert Gatschet when he drew twenty-nine examples (labeled *a* through *cc*) of Cheyenne autographs (Figure 4). Illustrations *a* through *o* show a variety of free-floating heads, each with a line connecting head and name-symbol. In drawings *p* through *cc,* on the contrary, Wuxpais has omitted the heads and simply drawn the name-symbols. Notice how the name-symbol in figure *a* is a man with a head that is too large in relation to

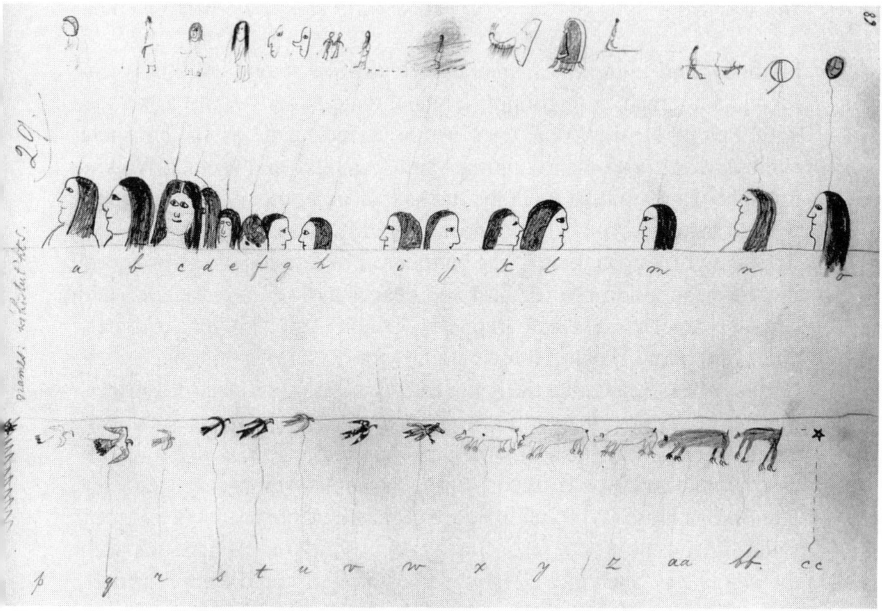

FIGURE 4. Cheyenne autographs from "Cheyenne Drawings" by Wuxpais (Daniel Littlechief), 1891. (Courtesy of The Newberry Library, Chicago)

Wuxpais illustrated a variety of Cheyenne autographs and interpreted them for Albert Gatschet. For the top row (illustrations *a–o*), a line drawn from the top of the head is connected to a name-symbol above. The oversized head on the human figure in example *a*, for instance, translates as Big Head (Makstsiyá); *c* is Red Eye Woman (Ma-eyúkini-i) (note the enlarged and darkened left eye); *e* is Roman Nose (Wō´ xini), with its obvious proboscis; *j* represents the warrior Hair-Arm (Mámishiaxts) (although it resembles the trunk of an elephant, this is the arm of a hair-fringed shirt); and *m* is Kills Across the River (Húxu wina-án) (note the victim has fallen on the far side of the small squiggly line, which represents a river). For the bottom row (illustrations *p–cc*), Wuxpais omits the heads and simply illustrates the name-symbols. In these examples, names are derived from the natural world, especially birds (*p–v*) and bears (*x–bb*). Illustration *w* is half-bird/half-bear, indicating the name Bird Bear (Wíksihi náxku); *q* is Spotted Eagle (Nitchxü-immāsts); *y* is Yellow Bear (Náxkwi húwāsts); and *cc* is Star (Hutúxk). According to Wuxpais, the remaining name-symbols can be translated as follows: *b*, Tied with Belt (Ákutsi); *d*, Red Hair (Ma-owísse); *f*, Pug Nose (Ká-ēs); *g*, Twins (Histá'hk); *h*, Woman Walking About (Ámixtsi); *i*, Woman Walking at Night (Tā-éwiuxtsi); *k*, Big Young Man (Māx uksuá); *l*, Walking High Up (Hiám'htamitsts); *n*, White Shield (Wuxpó hev'ts); *o*, Apple (Máxim); *p*, White Eagle (Nitswúkuma-ists); *r*, Red Bird (Má-owis); *s*, Black Hawk (Muxtáwi ánu); *t*, Black Bird (Hihīn muxtáwast); *u*, Yellow Hawk (Hihúwe-i ánu); *v*, Spotted Bird (Xāx́ki-amin); *x*, White Bear (Wúxpi náxku); *z*, Red Bear (Náxk ma-āsts); *aa*, Black Bear (Muxtá náxku); and *bb*, Tall Bear (Naxk'á îhu-ó-is). During the imprisonment of the Plains warriors, such name-symbols were replaced by costume-symbols and/or writing in syllabary or English.

his body, indicating his name: Big Head (Makstsiyá). Similarly, the second autograph (*b*) highlights a belted tunic to convey the name Tied with Belt (Ákutsi). Sometimes action is indicated, as in the name-symbols *h* and *i*: Woman Walking About (Ámixtsi) and Woman Walking at Night (Ta-éwiuxtsi). Note the tracks indicating movement behind the woman in name-symbol *h* and the darkened sky surrounding the walking woman signifying night in *i*. The bottom row of autographs (*p* through *cc*) illustrates an assortment of bird and bear names, each associated with certain characteristics. Autograph *q* is Spotted Eagle (Nitchxü-immásts), and *u* is Yellow Hawk (Hihúwe-i ánu), for instance, while *w* is a half-bird/half-bear illustrating the name Bird Bear (Wíksihi náxku). Figures *x* through *bb* display an assortment of bear names (*x* is the name-symbol for White Bear [Wúxpi náxku]; *z* is the autograph of Red Bear [Náxk ma-ásts]), while *cc* is Star (Hutúxk). Often the name-symbol is synecdochic, like Roman Nose (Wō´ xini in figure *e*), in which the pronounced profile stands for the entire person, or Black Elk, in which the elk head stands for the whole elk. Such pictographic names bring to mind John Sturrock's early description of ''the new model autobiographer'' who writes associative autobiography that presents a spatial ''diagram of the autobiographer'' rather than a linear narrative description.[37]

It is not surprising that after Euro-American subjugation of Plains Indian people, the pictographic signature changed and, finally, all but disappeared. Such effacement of native names and autographs reflects the Euro-American intent to erase Indian identity altogether. When the last Plains Indian warriors to resist the U.S. invasion of Indian land were defeated, many were sent east and imprisoned at Fort Marion in St. Augustine, Florida (1875–1878). While there, these prisoners of war were provided drawing materials and encouraged to depict their former lives. Autographed pictographic ledger books drawn at this time reveal something of the transformation of Plains Indian pictographic self-representation. At times, the name-symbol dominates with no obvious relation to the head (that is, it is not connected by a line). In Howling Wolf's 1877 sketchbook, for instance, his autograph is a drawing of a seated howling wolf (Figure 5). The wolf's head is thrown back; the lines emanating from the wolf's snout indicate howling. This detailed drawing of a wolf replaces earlier less realistic depictions. Tangible changes in the materials and circumstances of pictographic production (such as colored pencils and paper in place of vegetable dyes and tanned animal hides and ample time due to enforced inactivity) led to more realism in name-symbols and pictography overall.

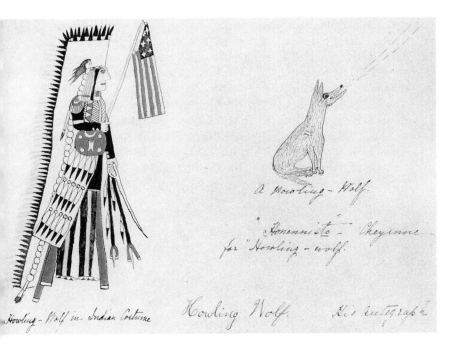

Howling-Wolf in Indian Costume   *Howling Wolf.*   *His autograph.*

FIGURE 5. "Howling Wolf in Indian Costume" by Howling Wolf (Cheyenne), 1877. (Courtesy of the Southwest Museum, Los Angeles, California. Neg. No. 34,653)

Howling Wolf drew this while he was imprisoned at Fort Marion in St. Augustine, Florida. Rather than the traditional pictographic narrative action moving from right to left, this picture is read left to right. On the left is Howling Wolf wearing a feathered bonnet, a bird amulet, and a breastplate. He carries his feathered and painted hide shield (for spiritual protection), a sword, and the U.S. flag. On the right is his name-symbol: a seated howling wolf. With head thrown back, the wolf howls (indicated by the lines emanating from its snout). There is no line connecting the name-symbol to the figure on the left, but beneath the pictographic autograph is Howling Wolf's name written in Cheyenne and English (by Eva Scott, the artist who encouraged Howling Wolf and Zo-Tom to draw and supplied them with art materials during their imprisonment).

At times, the name-symbol is accompanied by the name written in English or syllabary. Sometimes the writing was added by a Euro-American sponsor or friend, as in the case of Howling Wolf. Beneath Howling Wolf's name-symbol, Eva Scott Fényes, who provided the sketchbook and drawing materials, wrote his name: "Honennisto— Cheyenne for Howling Wolf." Sometimes, though, the writing was done

by the artist himself (especially in the Fort Marion pictographic sketchbooks, since the prisoners were taught to write). This was the case with
Packer, who provided what we could call a double or triple signature
(Figure 6). To the right of his head, Packer drew his name-symbol—an
outline of a man with a pronounced back, probably indicating a pack. In
addition, to assist Euro-American readers unfamiliar with Plains Indian
pictographic conventions, he wrote "Packer" in English. He wrote his
name in English a second time directly above his head. At other times the
autograph was translated entirely from pictography to writing. Zo-Tom,
for example, wrote his name in the English alphabet, but still used the

FIGURE 6. "Packer's Triple Signature" by Packer and White Bear (Arapahoes),
May 1875–April 1878. (Courtesy of Hampton University Archives)

Unlike Howling Wolf (Figure 5), who drew his name-symbol and left it to his Euro-
American sponsor to translate it for a non-Indian audience, Packer provided three
distinct autographs. Just to the right of his head is his name-symbol: an outline of a man
with a pronounced back, probably representing a pack. In addition, to assist those
unfamiliar with Plains Indian autograph conventions, he wrote his name in English to
the right of his name-symbol. He added a second signature in English just above his
head. Similarly, White Bear identified himself by writing his name in English above
his picture. For those familiar with pictography and with Packer, the shield he carries
(a type of costume-symbol) might be enough to identify him.

FIGURE 7. "A Class of Indians in Fort Marion with Their Teacher, Mrs. Gibbs" by Zo-Tom (Kiowa), 1877. (Courtesy of the Southwest Museum, Los Angeles, California. Neg. No. 34,649)

Zo-Tom drew this classroom scene while imprisoned at Fort Marion in Florida. His sketchbook was supplied by Eva Scott. Instead of the long-haired, ornamented Kiowa warriors of his earlier drawings, Zo-Tom drew seven short-haired Indian students wearing Western clothing, sitting neatly in a row, studying English. The teacher stands primly before them. Although Zo-Tom wrote his name using the English alphabet, he still drew a line from his head (he is the second man from the left) to the written autograph. He also identified Making Medicine (second man from the right) in the same fashion. Among the drawings by Fort Marion prisoners, the name-symbol almost disappears, replaced by the costume-symbol or the written signature.

pictographic convention of drawing a line to connect the written name to the depiction of himself (Figure 7). Finally, at least among the Fort Marion prisoners, the name-symbol disappeared altogether,[38] perhaps indicating an absence of Euro-American expectations of individual authorship, a transition to writing, or a degree of acculturation to the use of Euro-American drawing materials and conventions. Perhaps also, with prolonged imprisonment and abundant drawing materials, these men had a great deal of time to identify themselves by drawing detailed depictions of their individual dress, ornamentation, and martial accouterments. Such details, known as costume-symbols, served as identifying markers for each warrior and sometimes replaced name-symbols.

The Kiowa chief White Horse, known to whites as "a murderer, ravisher, and . . . general scoundrel" (qtd. in Petersen 118) and to Indians as a heroic warrior and defender of his people, used a variety of autographs in his drawings. His pictographic autographs provide a clear example of the transition from use of a name-symbol to use of a costume-symbol during a time of violent transition. In one drawing (executed sometime between May 1875 and November 1876 in prison at Fort Marion), he depicted himself on horseback (Figure 8). His wife rides on a horse behind, carrying his battle gear. He identified himself most obviously using the traditional name-symbol: a line connects his head with the outline of a white horse above him. In the same drawing, however, he used his costume-symbol, with which he identified himself by depicting details of his dress and adornments. In this case, his costume-symbol consists of "his blue shield with its distinctive pattern and his blue face paint with a white disk" (Petersen 54). In another sketch (drawn sometime between May 1875 and April 1878) (Figure 9), White Horse pictorially narrated his feat of roping a buffalo. This time, his signature is written in English above his head but with no connecting line. It is difficult to determine whether the variety of White Horse's signatures reveals the influence of Euro-American literacy or the considerable flexibility in the conventions of Plains Indian autographs.

Multiple Names in Transition

Ironically, government records provide much of the available information about the multiple names of Plains Indian warriors in the late nineteenth century. Since "the Crow Indians are the only Plains tribe with matrilineal descent" (Driver 37), the imposition of a Euro-American patriarchal naming system on Plains Indians by U.S. officials was not entirely alien to native practices. Tribal enrollment lists—catalogues of tribal members compiled in the late nineteenth and early twentieth centuries—routinely listed only one of a man's several names. Prison records, though, noted what officials referred to as the "aliases" of Indian prisoners of war. The Cheyenne and Kiowa men described below were all labeled "ringleaders" for fighting against U.S. encroachment on Indian land; all were imprisoned at Fort Marion as a result. Each of them had a variety of names, both Native American and Euro-

FIGURE 8. "Cheyenne or Kiowa Indian while at Ft. Marion in St. Augustine, Florida," from "Drawing Book" by White Horse (Kiowa), May 1875–November 1876. (Courtesy of Joslyn Art Museum, Omaha, Nebraska, Gift of Mrs. J. Barlow Reynolds, 1949)

The Kiowa chief White Horse, also imprisoned in Fort Marion, used a variety of autographs in this picture, providing a good example of both a name-symbol and a costume-symbol. On the top left of the page, his name-symbol—an outline of a white horse—is connected by a short line to the top of his head. A costume-symbol identifies him in a second way. The distinctive pattern on his blue shield (carried by his wife, on the right) identifies him as White Horse.

American. The Cheyenne Cohoe's name was derived from "the Spanish 'cojo,' meaning lame."[39] This was the name with which he autographed his pictographs. But Cohoe was also known as Mapera-mohe (Water Elk or Moose) or Mohe (Elk) (Hoebel and Petersen 4). Lieutenant Richard H. Pratt, commonly referred to as Captain Pratt, listed Cohoe's name on the Fort Marion prison records as Broken Leg. In 1879, after he was freed

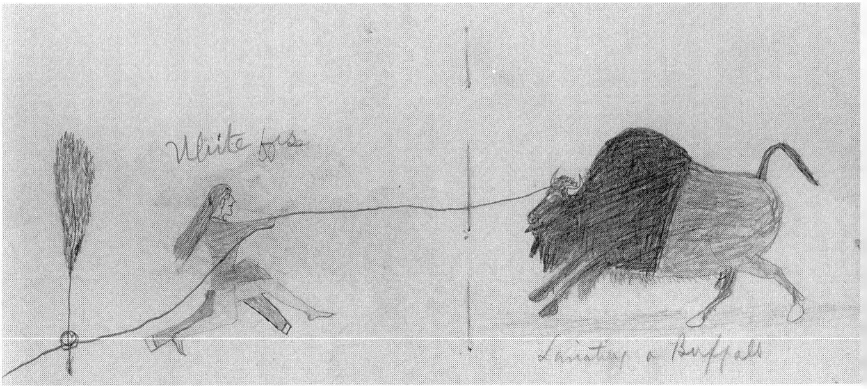

FIGURE 9. "Lariating a Buffalo" by White Horse (Kiowa), May 1875–April 1878. (Courtesy of the Yale Collection of Western Americana, Beinecke Rare Book and Manuscript Library)

Rather than the convention of right-to-left flow of action, this drawing is symmetrical. On the right is an enormous buffalo. On the left, having tied the rope to a tree, White Horse runs toward the buffalo, which he has lariated. His flowing, unbound hair and arched legs indicate fast motion. In contrast to his name-symbol and costume-symbol in Figure 8, White Horse wrote his name in English above his head, but with no connecting line to his figure.

from prison, Cohoe went to Hampton Normal and Agricultural Institute, the school for free black students that opened its doors to Indians in 1878. There he was baptized Cohoe, but "acquired a dignified Cheyenne equivalent" of the name as well: " 'Nohnicas' or 'Cripple' " (Hoebel and Petersen 6). After he returned to his reservation, he added yet another name. Probably due to his Euro-American contact, he became known as William Cohoe, taking on a Euro-American first name and using his Native American name as a surname.

Other imprisoned Plains Indian warriors, such as Bears Heart, Making Medicine, and Ohettoint, followed a similar pattern. Like Cohoe, Bears Heart (a translation of the Cheyenne Nockkoist) was imprisoned for three years at Fort Marion. In 1878 he attended Hampton Institute, where he was baptized Bear's Heart. (Both Captain Pratt and the clergy recorders were careful to add the apostrophe.) By 1880 Bears Heart "first signed his names with the prefix 'James,' " which Petersen suggests was a "compliment to Hampton's 'oldest trustee' " (102), James A. Garfield, whose presidential inauguration Bears Heart attended. A third Cheyenne,

Making Medicine (a translation of the Cheyenne Okuhhatuh), had two aliases: Bear Going Straight and Noksowist. However, he was baptized David Pendleton, taking the surname of his clergyman benefactor. According to Petersen, Oakerhater (which sounds like an Anglicization of Okuhhatuh) was sometimes added to his new surname. Similarly, Kiowa warrior Ohettoint's names included High Forehead, Charley Buffalo, and Padai (Twin). (He had a twin brother named White Buffalo.) He was baptized Ohettoint in 1879, but he "was enrolled in the police under an Irish-Kiowa version": Charles O'Hetowit (Petersen 169). After several variations of this name, he became "Oheltoint in 1894, and the name stuck" (Petersen 169). At the same time, though, he was still known as Charley Buffalo. What is evident here is the traditional multiplicity of Plains Indian proper names, the Euro-American lack of understanding of such protean naming practices, and, despite the move of the owner of the names toward adopting a single Christian name, the persistent vitality of his many names. For such men, their new white men's names did not necessarily erase their Indian names. Instead of transforming Cohoe, Bears Heart, Making Medicine, and Ohettoint into white men (or assimilated Native Americans), their Euro-American names (William Cohoe, James Bear's Heart, David Pendleton, and Charley Ohettoint) were absorbed into the dynamic identities reflected in their existing configuration of names. Thus names directly reflect a historical crisis more than, as Lejeune suggests, an identity crisis. But this historical upheaval challenged the very conditions of personal identity as configured by Plains people.

Nineteenth-century Plains Indian naming customs, then, differed markedly from Euro-American naming traditions. In typical Euro-American naming practices, a child receives a given name, a middle name, and a surname (identifying the father's family), which will be his or hers throughout life. Taking a husband's name or acquiring a title such as M.D. indicates a change of social, economic, or legal status. In nineteenth-century Plains Indian cultures, a child received a "secret" or "war" name at birth, the given name (perhaps it reflected a family or clan name, embodied the family's wish for the child's future, or described the child's physical appearance) (Mallery 442–445). Then throughout life, the individual acquired new names to document personal achievements and transitions. Although the nineteenth-century Plains Indian practice of serial naming contrasts with Euro-American formal naming traditions (except, as Leigh Gilmore suggests, in the case of women who remarry periodically and take on sequentially each new husband's name),[40] it is similar to the more informal and flexible Euro-American practice of taking nicknames. Like Euro-American nicknames, Plains Indian names change several times throughout life, reflecting important transitions, events, and achievements. Similarly, like nicknames, Plains Indian names are generally given by family and community members. Plains Indian serial names and Euro-American nicknames alike do not function in a rigid linear chronology. Just because Little Susie grows up to become Susan does not necessarily mean that family and friends replace the childhood cognomen with the more adult name. It is more likely that both names commingle (at least in memory) as part of a complex sense of identity. Unlike nicknames, though, some Plains Indian names, particularly spiritual names, were conferred in much more serious circumstances. Naming ceremonies provided community affirmation of one's new identity, a type of secular and spiritual transformation.

A name, then, was an oral and/or artistic symbol of the individual, a representation that could be modified to reflect the changes that person had undergone. The Plains Indian process of recurrent naming suggests an acknowledgment and affirmation of an ever-changing self and history. As the individual traveled through life, he or she received new names, reflecting the important deeds and events of that life—both a life and an identity that were in process and that, like Coyote, the trickster culture hero, were continually moving about. In his autobiography, *The Names,* N. Scott Momaday tells us that the Kiowa storyteller Pohd-lohk "believed that a man's life proceeds from his name, in the way a river proceeds from its source."[41] We might amend Momaday's sentence to say that for a nineteenth-century Plains Indian male, life proceeded from his names, each new name joining the others before it, creating a changing but continuous personal history—a palimpsestic configuration of the self. It is important to keep in mind that such recurrent naming was not a linear process of a new name replacing the one before it. Rather, all the names existed in dynamic relation to one another.

Nineteenth-century Plains Indian names, considered *individually,* are similar to diary entries. Just as the Western forms of diaries and journals reflect the daily cycles of an individual's life over an extended period, the Plains Indian autobiographical form of serial naming provides continual updates on a person's life. According to Felicity Nussbaum, the form of the "diary works against a fixed identity" by allowing one to record the minute fluctuations of the self in the process of daily living.[42] In the same manner, while not a daily record of personal experience, progressive naming, by oneself and others, highlights and transcribes individual achievements in the context of community. Taken *collectively,* such serial names are like miniature autobiographies, organizing an individual's life story by documenting the pattern of physical and spiritual events that shape that life. One's collection of names is not a linear, chronological chronicle of one's life, however. One's birth name is a private identity, a spiritual substratum of the self, that is not spoken by even the most intimate family members. New names do not replace earlier names, but add new interpretations of earlier identities, altering the onomastic configuration of one's self.

Such progressive naming, as noted earlier, reflects a fluid rather than a fixed sense of identity. This perplexed already suspicious Euro-American authorities, who throughout the latter part of the nineteenth century were trying to remove, round up, and restrain native peoples. The General Allotment Act (also known as the Dawes Act) of 1887 provided for the allotment of reservation land to individual Indians. This was an attempt to, once and for all, force Indians into farming and ranching; to instill in them a sense of property ownership and, consequently, to eliminate the reservation and encourage assimilation into the Euro-American population; and, ultimately, to free leftover reservation land for takeover by whites. To accomplish this, an accurate list of names of tribal peoples was necessary. Euro-American officials, of course, were leery of such changing, not to mention "unspellable," names. Often Indians took a "white" name for such "official" business with the Bureau of Indian Affairs. Fixing a name, an often alien one at that, on the page reflects the predominant nineteenth-century Euro-American impulse to freeze, in print if not in fact, native peoples. Imposing a relatively unchanging naming system on more dynamic native naming systems was one strategy to accomplish this.

Nineteenth-century Plains Indian serial naming was, to use Elizabeth Bruss's term, an "autobiographical act," an illocutionary act that constructed and narrated personal identity. One's current name allows others to learn about a specific event or exploit; one's accumulated names, like a collection of letters or a set of diaries, reveal a more detailed personal narrative than any one name, letter, or diary entry can provide. Like diaries, journals, or letters, such a configuration of names allows for "articulating a multiplicity of contestatory selves" (Nussbaum 132), for documenting the transformative moments of one's life, or for narrating one's community-endorsed accomplishments. Such name(s) might be spoken or depicted in pictographs, providing a multidimensional (rather than a strictly linear) autobiographical narrative that reflects both individual and tribal, worldly and spiritual, and past and present possibilities. Nineteenth-century Plains Indian names, then, are not merely labels, but compact personal and tribal histories. In addition, names are profoundly narrative; stories nestle within names—personal, historical, and mythical. A name thus evokes one's connection to one's tribe, one's place (in time and space), and one's universe—all of which create and narrate a vital sense of self that struggles against indeterminacy.

Pre-contact Native American oral, artistic, and dramatic forms of personal narrative, defined in part as communo-bio-oratory, can be considered autobiography if we acknowledge non-Western ideas of self, life, and language: a relational identity; episodic narratives of spiritual experiences and martial events; and spoken, painted, and performed self-narrations. Although these appear to be alien to the Western impulse of autobiographical writing, in fact they are not. At the very least, pre-contact Native American forms of personal narrative such as serial names, coup tales, and spiritual narratives spoken, performed, and painted on tipis and shields may be considered, to borrow a phrase from anthropology, the "functional equivalent" of autobiography. These pre-contact modes of personal narrative, modified as they would be by Euro-American editors or acculturated informants, found their way into the life histories of the late nineteenth and early twentieth centuries. From intracultural collaboration to bicultural collaboration, from communo-bio-oratory to collaborative autobiography, the movement of Native American autobiographical narrative paralleled the historical struggles of a people to maintain an identity. The roots of Indian autobiography, then, are not merely in the Western written tradition, but in the pre-contact Native American traditions of orality, art, and performance. These are all means by which one narrates one's life or self in order to assert one's individuality—one's distinction within the tribe or one's relation to the spirits—and to confirm one's place within the cultural and cosmic realms—both at the same time. This paradoxical tension, after all, is what motivates the autobiographical impulse in many traditional communities.

3 / Pictographs as Autobiography: Plains Indian Sketchbooks, Diaries, and Text Construction

When scholars talk about Native American autobiography, the assumption is that they mean the ethnographer-collected life histories of the late nineteenth and early twentieth centuries. Because autobiography has been considered a distinctly Western impulse emphasizing individuality and has been defined as the story of one's life *written* by oneself, pre-contact personal narratives *spoken, performed,* and *painted* by communal-oriented indigenous peoples have generally been overlooked. Even thoughtful critics like Arnold Krupat insist that "Indian autobiography has no prior model in the collective practice of tribal cultures."[1] But long before Anglo ethnographers came along, Native Americans were telling, performing, and painting their personal histories. One potential tribal model of autobiography, at least among Plains Indian males, is the pictographic personal narrative. The symbolic language of pictographs allowed pre-contact Plains Indians to "read" about one another from painted robes, tipis, and shields. According to Helen H. Blish, pictographic hides were a "widely practiced" form of artistic personal history. Such "personal records" were "quite common . . . among the Plains Indians," and, says Blish, "these are the most frequently found pictographic records."[2] In the Great Plains, in particular, pictography was highly developed and "universally employed and understood."[3] Such picture writing was used to convey everyday messages—announcements, rosters, personal letters, business and trade transactions, and geographical directions and charts (Blish 20; Petersen)—as well as tribal histories (known as winter counts) and autobiographical narratives.

By the late nineteenth century, such Plains Indian pictographic traditions of personal history began to intersect with Euro-American autobiography. When Native Americans began to share their life stories with persons outside their cultures, their self-narration encountered new challenges. Often personal narratives were solicited by an ethnologist, a historian, or another "friend of the Indian." Always the teller had to negotiate the difficult terrain of translation—from a native language to English, from an oral or a pictographic to a written form, from a Native American culture to a Euro-American culture. The resulting process of "bicultural composite composition," noted by some critics to be "the principle constituting the Indian autobiography as a genre" (Krupat 31) or as its "most distinctive characteristic,"[4] holds true for nineteenth-century pictographic personal narratives as well as for "as-told-to" life histories. These "bicultural documents"[5] reveal the artistic/literary traditions of two distinct cultures. Indian narrators seem to have told their life stories in their traditional oral or pictographic forms, which then were modified to suit a new audience, purpose, and setting. Personal narratives that affirmed one's place within the community now became self-narrations to explain one's culture to others. Generally, Euro-American editors took considerable liberty in reshaping native oral life histories. Such editorial colonialism is less evident in pictographic narratives, but certainly the introduction of Euro-American art supplies and artistic conventions altered an already dynamic artistic tradition. My purpose here is to consider traditional nineteenth-century Plains Indian pictographic personal narratives and their changes due to the introduction of Euro-American notions of art and texts. Between 1830 and 1890, Plains Indian pictography changed as a result of pictographic autobiographers shifting from indigenous to Euro-American materials, from painting with earth paints on buffalo hides for oneself or one's tribe to painting with commercial paints on paper for oneself, one's tribe, or, all too often, one's oppressor.

Sketchbooks of the Late Nineteenth and Early Twentieth Centuries

In the late seventeenth and early eighteenth centuries when the Sioux, Cheyenne, and Arapaho were chased from the woods of central Minnesota to the Plains by French-armed Cree and Ojibway, they soon became horse-riding, buffalo-hunting, tribe-raiding warrior societies—the epitome of what would become the stereotypical "wild Indian" of the frontier West. Among the Plains Indian tribes, each man could earn war honors by performing such brave deeds as counting coup (striking or touching an enemy in battle), rescuing a fallen comrade, and stealing horses. In fact, notes art historian Dorothy Dunn, from these "deed honors there arose a sort of heraldry which was one of the principal sources of Plains art."[6] Plains Indian men narrated their deeds in speech and artwork, painting their martial exploits, spiritual visions, and personal symbols on buffalo (or elk) hides, tipis and tipi linings, clothing, and shields.[7] Such "portable art" (Dunn, *American Indian Painting* 143), convenient for people on the move, recorded and narrated individual male military and spiritual accomplishments.

Pre-contact Plains Indian men not only *told* the stories of their personal exploits in hunts and battles, but *portrayed* them in various artistic forms.[8] Pictographs were often painted on tipis, shields, cloth, or hides. As Helen H. Blish notes, nineteenth-century ethnographer Garrick Mallery called such personal records " 'bragging biographies' and 'partisan histories,' " since they are individual records of one person's exploits (21). Such "picture-writing" was meant to record and communicate more than to please aesthetically. Before 1830, these pictographic narratives were a type of shorthand. In fact, according to Plains Indian art historian and one-time Smithsonian ethnographer John Ewers, the "characteristic features of this art style" included "little interest in anatomical details," "relative scale," or "perspective."[9] Although a few Indians learned of Euro-American artistic techniques earlier, according to Ewers, it was not until "the decade of the 1830s that a few Indians began to draw and paint in the white man's medium of pencil and watercolors on paper for whites" (Intro. 9). One well-known example is the pictographic robe of the Mandan chief Mah-to-toh-pa (Four Bears) (Figure 1). On a visit to the Mandans in 1832, George Catlin painted "the chart of [Mah-to-toh-pa's] military life," his personal narrative painted on buffalo hide.[10] On his robe, Mah-to-toh-pa uses most of the basic characteristics of early-nineteenth-century hide painting: horse and warrior in action; horse depicted with "long, arched neck, small head, long body, legs spread before and behind"; warrior "shown in profile but with shoulders broadside"; stylized details of costume; "distant objects placed behind or above nearer ones, but not progressively smaller or less distinct"; no landscape or background; outlined figures "filled in with bright, flat colors"; and right-to-left flow of action (Petersen 57). In addition, he presents the traditional pattern of coup tales. He identifies himself, his strategic position, the weapons, the number and identity of the enemy, and his brave deeds. In particular, each drawing reveals the warrior's physical proximity to his enemy, the weapons used, and the number of opponents (represented by their tracks, arrows, or bullets). The pictographic scene is a synecdochic visual narrative of a personal and a tribal battle history. That is, a few conventional details represent a much larger story. Mah-to-toh-pa, it is said, would sit on his painted robe and reenact his great battles for an enthusiastic audience, bringing his pictures to life in performance. The pictographs, then, serve as a mnemonic device, an autobiographical narrative, and a historical record. Whether painted on buffalo robes, tipis, or treebark, the pictographs use a set of conventional symbols (Ewers, Intro. 10) with which the people were conversant. Pictographic literacy was widespread.

During the 1830s, some Plains Indians began to paint with "pencil and watercolor on paper for whites" (Ewers, Intro. 9), probably a direct result of George Catlin's 1832 visit to the Upper Missouri, where he painted Indian portraits and impressed the native people, according to his own account, with his lifelike human figures. Catlin was followed by the Swiss artist Karl Bodmer, who, in 1833/1834, distributed paper, pencils, and watercolors to Plains Indian tribes and taught Mah-to-toh-pa about "realistic portraiture" (Ewers, Intro. 9). These well-known artists were followed by others in the mid-nineteenth century who shared illustrated books, conventions of Euro-American painting, and art supplies. As early as 1840, "the hide robe was out of style" among some Plains Indian tribes (Petersen 22) and by the 1870s painted buffalo robes had been replaced by trade blankets (Ewers, Intro. 11). On the one hand, the shift from pictographic buffalo robes to decorated trade blankets was due to increased trade with Euro-Americans and the ever-growing prestige of wool blankets; on the other hand, it was due to the necessity born of oppression: the desperate attempts to escape the U.S. Army (which meant traveling light and fast) and the decimation of the buffalo.

Other pictographic personal narratives were painted on tipis by certain accomplished Plains Indian men. Before 1870, among the Kiowa and Kiowa–Apaches, decorated tipis were used to signify the elevated status of an individual within the tribe and to narrate the details of spiritual visions or martial achievements.[11] Since personal designs were inherited, a tipi design was closely associated with its owner and his family. Since designs were portrayed using a set of conventional symbols (Ewers, *Murals* 10) with which the Kiowa were conversant, the literate tribe could "read" the pictographic text and "interpret" its meaning.

Between 1891 and 1904, after the Kiowa had been removed to reservations, James Mooney, the ethnologist for the Smithsonian Institution, collected "small-scale models of painted tipis" (Ewers, *Murals* 10) reconstructed by Kiowa artists and elders. Although the pictographic tipis survived primarily in the memories of the tribal elders, younger men, like the Kiowa artist Zo-Tom, would use Euro-American materials to preserve a record of traditional Kiowa pictographs.[12]

Zo-Tom and Howling Wolf

With domination by Euro-Americans, the lives of native people changed dramatically and rapidly. By 1870, Euro-Americans had exterminated the buffalo and, along with these sacred animals, the physical and spiritual sustenance of the indigenous peoples of the Plains. Hostilities between Plains Indians and Anglos often flared into warfare. According to Indian art historian Dorothy Dunn, "[p]ainting and drawing now became an urgent personal record of dying days"[13] rather than the earlier heraldric expressions of self. Plains Indian men continued to paint pictographic personal narratives, but now the materials, the occasion, and the audience had been altered abruptly. It is not surprising that "[m]uch of the new art emerged in army prisons—Fort Robinson, Fort Omaha, Fort Sill, Fort Marion, and others in which the Indians had been confined" for protecting their own homelands (Dunn, Intro. 7). According to Petersen, a specialist in the work of Fort Marion Indian artists, there are "847 extant pieces of art done by twenty-six Plains Indian warriors" who had been imprisoned in Fort Marion (ix).

Two such examples are found in the 1877 sketchbooks of Zo-Tom, a Kiowa, and Howling Wolf, a Cheyenne, who were held prisoners at Fort Marion in St. Augustine, Florida. Like many Indian prisoners, Zo-Tom and Howling Wolf sketched and painted on whatever material was available to them. After seeing their drawings, Eva Scott (who became Eva S. Fényes), an artist herself, ordered art pads for them and asked them "to fill the two sketchbooks with colored drawings" (Dunn, Intro. 11). It was not until 1969 that Fényes's daughter, Leonora Scott Muse Curtin, published reproductions of these drawings because they "provide a rare and fascinating opportunity of seeing the Indians as they saw themselves in bygone times" (Dunn, Intro. 12).

Of the two artists, Howling Wolf is the less explicitly autobiographical. Although he begins his sketchbook with depictions of his personal activities, he shifts his focus to portrayals of tribal life.[14] Plate 1

(Figure 5)[15] is a drawing of Howling Wolf in full Cheyenne warrior regalia. He wears a long warbonnet, breechcloth, breast plate, silver hair plates, and a bird war charm tied in his hair. He carries his personal shield, sword, coup sticks, and, ironically (from some contemporary perspectives), a pendant U.S. flag. In addition to these innovative details of costume, he reverses the traditional flow of action. Instead of the narrative action moving from right to left, as it does in the conventions of earlier hide paintings, we "read" this picture from left to right. Rather than the conventional Plains Indian autograph, in this instance, a shorthand sketch of a howling wolf above or below Howling Wolf with a line connecting the pictographic autograph to the person, Howling Wolf includes a somewhat realistic drawing of *honennisto,* or a howling wolf, without the connecting line. Petersen notes that at least "within Fort Marion, the name-symbol device became obsolescent"; it was used in fewer than 20 out of 460 drawings (53). Howling Wolf uses it, but with innovations. In Plate 2 he presents a picture of himself as a small boy with his father and mother—all dressed in traditional Cheyenne clothing. After this brief presentation of his parents, Howling Wolf's personal account turns into an artistic tribal documentary as he depicts people in ceremonial garb—chiefs, warriors, medicine men, and brides and grooms—and tribal activities—hunting, fishing, singing, dancing, drumming, riding, fighting, and counseling. It is important to remember, however, that in pre-contact times one's individual identity was linked intimately to one's tribal identity. Personal and tribal history were often one and the same. Certainly, however, Howling Wolf was responding to the interests of his Euro-American sponsor also.

Zo-Tom's drawings, on the contrary, are more consistently autobiographical, since he focuses more persistently on his personal narrative. Read from start to finish, his pictographs reveal some of the changes he underwent in this transitional period. Although the drawings are not strictly chronological, they do tell a story of change over time. On one narrative level, the drawings depict his journey from the freedom of the Plains to his imprisonment at Fort Marion in Florida. On another level, they reveal his journey from the old Kiowa ways of life (represented by scenes of hunting, fighting, moving, trading, gambling, and celebrating) to his new Euro-American way of life (in this case, represented by a drawing of Zo-Tom studying English).

Zo-Tom's first drawing depicts a Kiowa camp with nine men and women pursuing assorted activities among the painted tipis. Zo-Tom's Plate 2, entitled by the editor "Chief Receiving a Stranger of Importance," shows the respectful Kiowa reception of a white military officer. After this initial intercultural encounter, there is no more mention of Indian–white interaction until Plate 18, in which the Kiowa prepare to surrender to Captain Pratt. Plates 3 through 17, like Howling Wolf's, deal with Plains Indian daily activities—dancing, chasing Navajo, gambling, trading, sleeping, celebrating, cooking, eating, marrying, burying, moving, hunting, and fighting other tribes. After Plate 18, "Surrender at Mt. Scott," Zo-Tom depicts the journey to Fort Sill in Oklahoma and from Fort Sill to Fort Marion in Florida, with a few flashbacks depicting the old days. In Plate 23 (Figure 10), Zo-Tom presents himself

FIGURE 10. "Zo-Tom Coming to Capt. Pratt with Flag of Truce in '71" by Zo-Tom (Kiowa), 1877. (Courtesy of the Southwest Museum, Los Angeles, California. Neg. No. 34,709)

Carrying a flag of truce, the Kiowa Zo-Tom meets Captain Pratt. Instead of the traditional right-to-left movement of hide paintings, the two men meet face-to-face in the center of the page. Both men extend their right arms in a peaceful greeting, but hold weapons in their left hands. Zo-Tom depicted details of ornamentation for both his and Captain Pratt's martial attire as well as for their horses. Above his figure, Zo-Tom wrote his name using the English alphabet.

as the warrior carrying the flag of truce to Captain Pratt in 1871. Like Howling Wolf, Zo-Tom ignores the traditional right-to-left movement of hide paintings. Instead, he draws Captain Pratt and himself meeting face to face in the center of the page. Both extend their right arms in a peaceful greeting. In his left hand, Pratt grips a sword, while Zo-Tom holds a rifle and carries a quiver of arrows. Traditionally, a mid-nineteenth-century pictographic painter would depict details of the enemy's costume, enough at least to identify tribal affiliation and rank. Accordingly, Zo-Tom provides numerous details of Captain Pratt's military uniform, including buttons, stripes, boots, and spurs. He provides comparable details of his own outfit—what looks like an army jacket adorned with Kiowa designs, leggings, moccasins, breast plate, and shield. This extended treatment of his own costume may be due to the fact that using Euro-American art materials (paper and pens rather than hide and bone) allowed for more detailed treatment of subjects. As a result, notes Petersen, the "name-symbol device" was replaced by "a costume-symbol" (54). The horses, too, are rendered in detail. Pratt's horse is large and brown with horseshoes, while Zo-Tom's is small, spotted, and unshod. Also Zo-Tom's horse has been adorned with feathers (signifying brave escapades) and has had his tail tied (perhaps indicating recent participation in battle). One final innovation to the conventions of pictographic painting is even more remarkable. To be certain the viewer knows that *he* is the one dealing with Pratt, Zo-Tom adds one thing. He writes his name in English above the picture.[16]

In Plate 26, "A Great Battle" (Figure 11), Zo-Tom provides a detailed pictographic narrative of Kiowa warriors and the U.S. Army engaged in battle. This pictograph "in basic respects, in scheme of composition and style of life figures, corresponds to mid-nineteenth century hide paintings" (Dunn, Intro. 17). He uses the main conventions of hide and tipi painting: front view of torso with the rest of the body seen from the side; detailed ornamentation of the enemy; wounds depicted as dark spots with blood streaming from them; and movement depicted from right to left. He also uses some of the basic formats of the coup narrative: he indicates the affiliation and status of warriors and soldiers by providing details of costume and horses, and he presents the strategic positions of both sides. Note how the United States soldiers are barricaded together on the left, while the Indian warriors are attacking from the right. Zo-Tom, however, does not rely entirely on such conventions; he also "extends precedents developed in hide painting" (Dunn, Intro. 19–20). His new additions

FIGURE 11. "A Great Battle" by Zo-Tom (Kiowa), 1877. (Courtesy of the Southwest Museum, Los Angeles, California. Neg. No. 34, 650)

This pictograph follows the artistic conventions of mid-nineteenth-century hide paintings: front view of human torso with the rest of the body viewed from the side; detailed ornamentation of the enemy (in this case, U.S. soldiers); wounds depicted as dark spots with blood streaming from them (note the wounded horse on the bottom right); and narrative movement from right to left. Zo-Tom's artistic innovations include his treatment of the military barricades, the wagons, and the overall representational nature of the drawing. With their horses' tails bound in preparation for battle, the warriors ride swiftly from right to left. Several wounded soldiers lie on the ground in front of the barricades.

include his treatment of the military barricades and wagons and his use of a style "more representational" than that of the older hide paintings (Dunn, Intro. 17).

Following this battle scene, Zo-Tom proceeds to draw the dreary exterior and interior of Fort Marion in St. Augustine, Florida, in the penultimate two plates. His final drawing, "A Class of Indians in Fort Marion with Their Teacher, Mrs. Gibbs" (Figure 7), completes his account of his personal journey and serves as the climax to his cultural conversion narrative. Instead of the long-haired, brilliantly attired and ornamented Kiowa warriors of his earlier pictures, he draws seven clean-cut Indian students in blue pants and snug black coats who sit, lining a long school bench, at a long desk. Mrs. Gibbs, the teacher, stands, prim and pleasant, to the left. Dutifully, the Indian students read names from flashcards. Zo-Tom has written his name above one student, and Making Medicine's above another. Each name, written in English, is connected by a line to its owner (a modification of a traditional Plains Indian autograph). Zo-Tom's name appears again, more discreetly, on the flashcard held by the student next to him. Thus Zo-Tom has become a new person and a new subject—literally. In this new life, he is an object of study not only for Eva Scott, but for himself as well.

To a certain degree, Zo-Tom and Howling Wolf use mid-nineteenth-century Plains Indian artistic principles and conventions in their personal narratives, but they also introduce new elements, such as an occasional written word to aid in explanation, more realistic depictions of animals and people, and frequent drawings of landscape. The original purpose— to describe one's personal heroics—is still accomplished, but in forms modified to be comprehensible to a Euro-American audience. Further- more, a new purpose—to translate one's culture—has been added. The collaborative nature of these drawings continues from pre-contact Native American collaborations in painting tipis and hides, but now there is only one collaborator: a Euro-American sponsor. Eva Scott did not sit with Zo-Tom and Howling Wolf and advise them about how to draw, nor did she edit their final pictures. She did, however, add two major contribu- tions.

Scott added the descriptive titles for each drawing and the general titles for each sketchbook. Her selection of titles is revealing: "The Life of the Red-Man, Illustrated by a Kiowa Brave" (Figure 12) and "Scenes from Indian Life, Drawn by Howling Wolf" (Figure 13). Such titles disclose her interest in depicting a generalized presentation of Indians, rather than the personal artistic interpretations of individuals. This approach was shared by many ethnographers who were interested in presenting a picture of "some representative . . . individual," rather than in de- scribing the personality of a "definite personage."[17] As well as inventing the titles, Eva Scott created the calligraphy and design for the title pages, leaving a space in the center of each for a picture of the Indian artist.

As mentioned earlier, Scott provided the sketchbooks. Thus it is no accident that Zo-Tom and Howling Wolf each have twenty-nine pages of drawings (although Zo-Tom used the back of one page to make the two- page drawing "A Great Battle," and Howling Wolf occasionally drew two related pictures on one page, thus modifying the available space). The very size, shape, and texture of the medium influenced how the artists would proceed. Thus the European artistic sensibilities of their sponsor determined, in part, the artists' output. Such a seemingly casual collaboration is far less intrusive than the more active involvement of many ethnographer–editors, who often rearranged their Indian infor- mants' recorded oral narratives, imposing a strict chronology and excis- ing "tedious" repetitions. Without such direct interference, the tradi-

FIGURE 12. Eva Scott's title page for Zo-Tom's sketchbook, 1877. (Courtesy of the Southwest Museum, Los Angeles, California. Neg. No. 34,651)

As well as providing sketchbooks and drawing materials, Eva Scott prepared the title page for Zo-Tom. She entitled the book "The Life of the Red-Man. Illustrated by a Kiowa Brave," emphasizing Native American life in general, rather than Zo-Tom's life in particular. In addition, referring to the artist as "a Kiowa Brave" and framing his picture with bows and arrows underscore his warrior past, a popular image for those Euro-Americans who purchased such sketchbooks to learn about the colorful life of the "vanishing Indians."

tional Plains Indian pictographic modes of personal narrative continued with only a few modifications made to enhance their accessibility to a white audience in this "evolving bi-cultural expression" (Dunn, Intro. 25).[18] Petersen points out that Indian adaptation of European materials did not begin in prison. In fact, "blank or partly used ledgers, army rosters, daybooks, memorandum books, and sheaves of paper often found their way into Indian hands through gift, trade or capture" (Petersen 25). Even before the buffalo were exterminated, many "warriors adopted the white man's materials for recording the pictographic history of their brave deeds" (Petersen 25).

FIGURE 13. Eva Scott's title page for Howling Wolf's sketchbook, 1877. (Courtesy of the Southwest Museum, Los Angeles, California. Neg. No. 34,652)

As she did for Zo-Tom, Eva Scott provided the sketchbook and drawing materials as well as designed the title page for Howling Wolf's picture book. Like her title for Zo-Tom's, her title for Howling Wolf's sketchbook ("Scenes from Indian Life. Drawn by Howling Wolf") highlights a representative Indian rather than an individual Cheyenne. In the center of the page, she placed a photograph of Howling Wolf (actually half of a photograph that originally was of Howling Wolf and his father, Minimic, taken at Fort Marion between 1875 and 1878). Howling Wolf wears a feathered bonnet and holds his painted and ornamented shield.

White Bull

A more conspicuously modified pictographic personal narrative was composed over fifty years later by White Bull (Pte San Hunka), a Teton Dakota chief who, like Zo-Tom and Howling Wolf, fought whites in the 1870s. He claimed to have killed General George Armstrong Custer at the Battle of the Little Bighorn. White Bull's 1931 written and pictographic personal narrative is clearly influenced by the request and expectations of his solicitor–editor. Chief White Bull's narrative was commissioned by Usher L. Burdick of North Dakota, who paid him fifty dollars for a "Sioux History Book." White Bull wrote part of his account in the Dakota syllabary and drew part of it in traditional pictographs in a business ledger, using "a combination of ink, lead pencil, and colored crayon."[19] Editor James H. Howard begins White Bull's personal narrative with a letter (from White Bull to Burdick) that reiterates the arrangements made with Burdick, at the same time encouraging a more generous payment. White Bull writes:

> Friend, you have asked me to send [return] something and I have done as you wished. What you say is so, but I would like to say this. My war record, as I have written it, is accurate and I have written it for you. You said you would give me fifty dollars for it and that is all right, but I would like to earn more, and as you see I have written much more. (Howard 1–2)

This letter makes it clear that White Bull was not writing for his own edification, but for a monetary compensation. His "personal narrative," then, was not merely solicited, it was purchased. Such considerations may help explain, in part, what White Bull included in his narrative.

After the letter of explanation, White Bull begins his narrative with a brief account of several buffalo-hunting expeditions. After the traditional hunting stories, he presents his genealogy. Following this brief personal reckoning (1–3),[20] White Bull devotes pages 4 through 8 to his winter count (which he purchased from Hairy-Hand)—a pictographic Dakota history covering the years 1764/1765 to 1816/1817 and 1835/1836 to 1930/1931. White Bull, however, recorded events in writing, not in pictographs, even transferring Hairy-Hand's pictographic versions of events painted on hide to his own written versions on paper.

From tribal history, he returns to his personal history, which focuses on hunting and warring. After another set of hunting stories, this time for buffalo and bear, and a political genealogy, White Bull's personal narrative indeed becomes a "war record." He devotes pages 11 through 46 to his war honors, arranging them by type: counting coups in battle (11–32) (Figure 14), rescuing fallen comrades (33–38) (Figure 15), and stealing enemy horses (39–46) (Figure 16). For these he includes traditional Dakota pictographs, but adds to them copious labels and explanations written in the Dakota syllabary. In Figure 14 (Plate 8), White Bull, on the right, chases down and counts coup on a Flathead who fires a gun at him (note the curlicue lines coming from the gun, which indicate gun smoke). Traditional nineteenth-century hide-painting con-

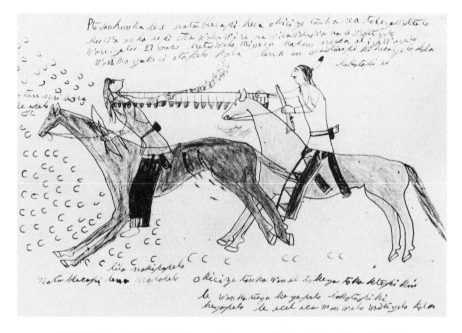

FIGURE 14. "White Bull Counts Coup on a Flathead" by White Bull (Teton Dakota), 1931. (Courtesy of the Chester Fritz Library, University of North Dakota, and the University of Nebraska Press)

On the right, White Bull chases down a Flathead, touching the enemy with his feathered banner. Riding a wounded horse (note the blood streaming from the wounds), the Flathead turns and fires his gun (note the curlicue smoke coming from the weapon). Hoofprints indicate the number and direction of warriors on horseback. To aid a Euro-American audience in understanding the pictographic narrative, White Bull added descriptions written in Dakota syllabary.

ventions included flow of movement from right to left, hoofprints to indicate number and direction of warriors, small heads and elongated bodies of horses, and wound marks (note the two dark spots dripping blood on the enemy's horse's side). White Bull's "feathered banner," notes Howard, was "commonly associated with the Strong-heart and Crow-owners warrior societies" (42). According to Howard, the text above the Flathead's horse's head may be translated as "They were charging me from this direction" (42). This is obvious to a reader of picture writing because of the hoof marks leading in that direction. The Dakota text at the bottom right reiterates the basic information: "There was a big fight and this was the first man killed. Because of it I was highly praised by the Lakotas. It was a glorious fight, my friend'' (Howard 42).

In Figure 15 (Plate 27), White Bull, wearing a full warbonnet, rescues a wounded Cheyenne. (That the wounded man is Cheyenne is indicated by the salamander war charm tied in his hair. Note also the wound in his side.) This is an especially brave deed, since one can see the hoofprints, gun smoke, and flying bullets (indicated by short lines). In a kind of pictographic synecdoche, one gun barrel, on the left, represents a full collection of warriors. The Dakota writing above identifies White Bull and his Cheyenne friend, Sunrise, and describes the action, the enemy, the witnesses, and the battle location (Howard 66–67). In Figure 16

FIGURE 15. "White Bull Rescues a Wounded Cheyenne" by White Bull (Teton Dakota), 1931. (Courtesy of the Chester Fritz Library, University of North Dakota, and the University of Nebraska Press)

Wearing a full warbonnet, White Bull pulls a wounded comrade to safety amid flying bullets (represented by the short lines around them). On the left, the curlicues represent gunsmoke. In a pictographic synedoche, one gun represents a group of enemies. The writing in Dakota syllabary identifies the participants and describes the action for an audience that is not literate in pictography.

FIGURE 16. "White Bull Steals Crow Horses" by White Bull (Teton Dakota), 1931. (Courtesy of the Chester Fritz Library, University of North Dakota, and the University of Nebraska Press)

For nineteenth-century Plains Indian warriors, one honorable way to earn war honors was to steal horses from enemies. Here White Bull steals nine fine horses from a Crow camp (represented on the right as a circle of thirteen tipis). Hoofprints in and around camp indicate the action. White Bull provided a second narrative in writing. Using the Dakota syllabary, he narrated his exploit and labeled the worth of each horse (e.g., *le waste* means "a good one").

(Plate 29), White Bull is shown stealing nine horses from a Crow camp. The camp, on the right, is depicted as a circle of thirteen tipis. In the middle of the circle is the Dakota label Howard translates as "This is the Crow camp" (69). Hoofprints within and around camp indicate the original position of the horses. The squiggly line above camp denotes a stream. The writing above provides basic information about the exploit, while the brief labels near each horse describe their worth. "Four of the adult horses are labeled *'le waste'* ('this was a good one')," explains

Howard, ''and the two colts are labeled *'cincala,'* meaning 'young ones' '' (69). Just as Zo-Tom's pictographic narrative is clarified by the addition of an occasional word, White Bull's drawn personal history is clarified and developed, at least for a Euro-American audience, by the additional detail provided in his written narrative.

In contrast to his numerous drawn and written depictions of his early life, White Bull includes only two written accounts (conspicuously lacking pictographs) of his later life at the agency. In these accounts, he catalogues his titles and achievements obtained in his new life. He served as an Indian policeman, a tribal judge, a chairman of the tribal council, a catechist, and so forth. Finally, White Bull ends his personal narrative with three of his updated pictographs (pictographs that include written commentary) in which, rather than focusing on the present, he returns to his depictions of the past.

White Bull's narrative movement, which fluctuates between personal and tribal foci, may highlight his traditional sense of tribal identity. Perhaps, though, his inclusion of tribal history (especially the winter count) arises from Burdick's desire for a ''Sioux History Book'' or White Bull's own desire for a longer account, which might mean a more financially profitable endeavor. If White Bull's narrative moves liberally between personal and tribal history, it also roams freely between past and present, dwelling heavily on the past. Clearly, the expectations of his Euro-American editor shaped White Bull's personal account. Even though White Bull's narrative is organized, in traditional Plains Indian fashion, according to his brave deeds and war honors, it follows a general chronological progression. With such a pattern one might expect his personal narrative to end with his later life at the agency, but White Bull defied such a Euro-American expectation in three ways.

First, he devoted only two pages to this part of his life. Even though he had held many honorable positions and had achieved a respected status in both the Dakota and white communities, and even though he had lived this ''later life'' for more than fifty years, he did not elaborate on his experiences. Such contracted treatment of so many years filled with so much activity suggests a distinct selection principle on White Bull's part. White Bull's minimal description of this part of his life reflects the reluctance of a great many Indian people to talk about their reservation experiences. Zo-Tom and Howling Wolf, we remember, devoted most of their attention to their pre-reservation days of freedom. The Crow chief Plenty-Coups had only this to say: ''[W]hen the buffalo went away the hearts of my people fell to the ground, and they could not be lifted up again. After this nothing happened. There was little singing anywhere."[21]

Second, unlike his depictions of the honors obtained in his earlier life, White Bull drew no pictographs for his later life. Instead, he catalogued his achievements in writing. Perhaps a traditional Plains Indian pictographic mode simply was not suitable to depict his nontraditional actions as a policeman and a tribal chairman and a church catechist. Although his ceremonial dancing, his Custer battle reenactments, and his apprehension of "antagonistic" Utes for the United States government seem to lend themselves to pictographic expression, he did not give them such artistic treatment. Perhaps the detail he bestowed on the pictographs of his hunting and war deeds of the distant past and the sparse catalogue he wrote of his recent past indicate the relative importance he placed on these two sets of events. It is as though his real life ended fifty years before, at the age of thirty-one, when, as he says, he "followed the ways of the whites, as the President instructed" (Howard 76).

If White Bull were to end his personal narrative with his brief written list of achievements since living "the ways of the whites," we might conclude that he diminished his treatment of his later life because he gloried in his adventurous past, that he yearned for his lost youth, or that he simply ran out of time due to a deadline for his work and so brought it to a hurried conclusion (also explaining the lack of pictographs for this stage of his life). White Bull, however, did not end his personal narrative with his reservation life. He included three final pages, each with a pictograph accompanied by a written explanation. What is striking is that these pages focus once again on the distant past, a third way White Bull confounds a sense of chronology. In Plate 37, White Bull drew a picture of his tipi. On the next page (in Plate 38), he drew "The Ceremonial Camp of the Circle of the Miniconjou," labeling several items and explaining about life "a long time ago" (Howard 80).

The final plate (39) (Figure 17) shows White Bull in "the full ceremonial costume of a Teton chief" (Howard 81). This is not, however, a depiction of White Bull as a young warrior. Rather, it is a picture of the contemporary White Bull (the eighty-one-year-old autobiographer) in the costume he wore "on festive occasions," "at the gatherings of the Lakotas," or "riding in parades" (Howard 81). Thus the two penultimate pages of White Bull's personal narrative return to "a long time ago" when he lived in a tipi and the Miniconjous came together

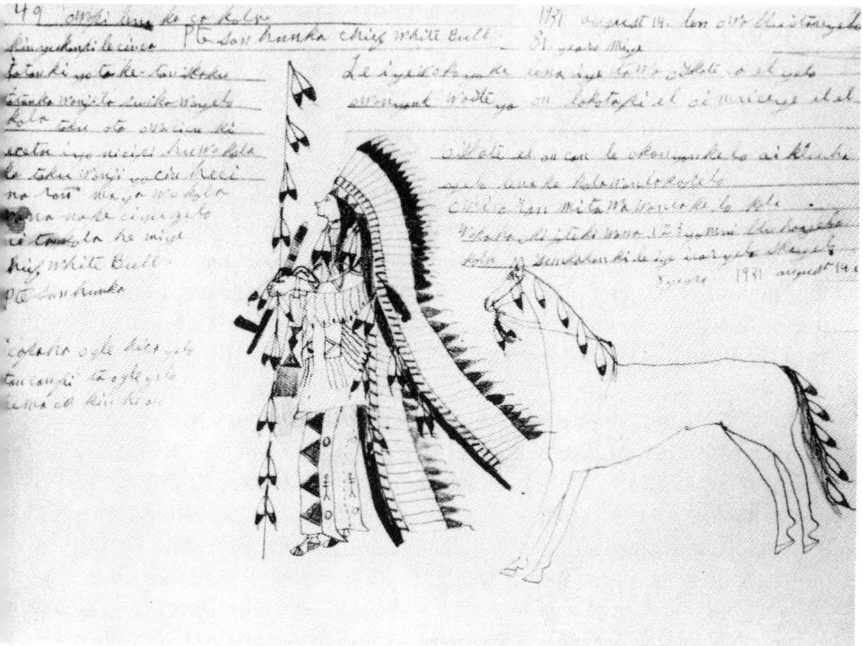

FIGURE 17. "White Bull in Full Dress" by White Bull (Teton Dakota), 1931. (Courtesy of the Chester Fritz Library, University of North Dakota, and the University of Nebraska Press)

White Bull ended his pictographic autobiography with a picture of himself as an eighty-one-year-old (some forty years after his warrior days) in full ceremonial dress, the outfit he wore at dances, ceremonies, and educational programs to inform non-Indians about the Dakota. He holds a pipe and a feathered lance, and his horse is adorned with feathers.

for ceremonials. His final pictograph, however, unites (for the first time in his account) the distant past with the present. The present-day White Bull is shown in his "long-ago" ceremonial clothing in which he reenacted and/or recalled historical deeds for a contemporary audience.

White Bull's narrative is a fascinating example of transitional Plains Indian autobiography in that his personal narrative was solicited and purchased by a Euro-American history buff. It was both drawn and written, thus combining Native American and Euro-American autobiographical forms. White Bull's written explanations and labels themselves suggest a white audience (a Plains Indian audience would need no explanation) and thus reveal an attempt at a type of translation from one cultural code to another. White Bull's personal narrative was also translated, edited, and published by James H. Howard, a Euro-American scholar. Chief White Bull's narrative, then, has been triply mediated by Euro-American society: Burdick's request and expectations, White Bull's modification of traditional pictographic forms to suit a non-Indian audience, and Howard's translation. Yet a sense of White Bull—courageous, proud, and deeply attached to his tribal past—emanates from his hybird autobiography, which mixes past and present, Miniconjou and white, and pictograph and writing, all of which are representative of the boundary culture in which he lived.[22]

Zo-Tom's and Howling Wolf's pictographic sketchbooks from the late nineteenth century and White Bull's pictographic and written Dakota ledger book from the early twentieth century provide insights into one of the pre-contact Plains Indian male traditions of personal narrative and its subsequent adaptation for a white audience. Relying on earlier artistic conventions of Plains Indian hide and tipi painting, these three artist–autobiographers used new materials and modified pictographic conventions for a white audience. These men were not sellouts. Each of them fought against the encroaching Euro-Americans. Zo-Tom was "in the last group of Kiowa warriors to surrender, February 18, 1875" (Petersen 173). Only two months later, Howling Wolf was arrested at the Cheyenne Agency for being a "ringleader" (Petersen 221). A year or so later, White Bull fought at the Battle of Little Bighorn (1876). Only when they had no alternative did they agree to translate their personal exploits and tribal experiences into pictographic narratives modified for a white audience. Certainly, all were motivated by economic factors. The work of Zo-Tom and Howling Wolf was in great demand by wealthy, curious, or sympathetic Euro-Americans. The going price for a Fort Marion Indian sketchbook was two dollars (Petersen 65), and White Bull, we remember, earned fifty dollars for his "Sioux History Book." Each of them was willing, under pressure, to examine the Euro-American way of life. Years after converting to Christianity, however, all three men returned to native ways. After serving as a deacon of the Episcopal Church, Zo-Tom became a Baptist and finally a member of the Native American Church, which blends Christian and native beliefs and ceremonies with the use of peyote. Howling Wolf and White Bull also gave up "the Jesus road" and, by the end of their lives, joined the Native American Church. Under the harshest conditions, these pictographic autobiographers attempted to communicate in modified Plains Indian forms to their white audience. They provided ethnographic details of tribal costume and custom and personal details of individual accomplishments. These pictographic sketchbooks, then, provide an insight into a distinctly traditional Plains Indian form of autobiography as it was being adapted to colonialism.[23]

A Cheyenne Diarist and Indigenous Text Production

Throughout this period, Plains Indian pictographers' materials changed steadily, influenced now by Euro-Americans as they had been earlier by other tribes. Commercial paints replaced earth paints, just as woolen trade blankets superseded buffalo robes. Canvas and muslin were often used for tipis and tipi liners, providing lighter materials and smoother surfaces for painting. Drawing and painting supplies as well as paper were in demand. By means of "gift, trade, or capture," Indians sought "blank or partly-used ledgers, army rosters, daybooks, memorandum books," and paper, as well as "ink, colored and lead pencils, and watercolors" (Petersen 25). In fact, there is evidence that, even earlier than Zo-Tom, Howling Wolf, or White Bull, many tribal historians had already adopted paper books to record winter counts (tribal histories), in part because such books were more portable than the increasingly scarce buffalo hides. According to pictography historian Karen Daniels Petersen, "Cheyenne war-drawing books were captured" during the Army's systematic destruction of Cheyenne villages in 1868, 1869, and 1875 (25–26). There is no telling how many pictographic hides and books were destroyed by the U.S. Army's scorched-village policy—twenty Cheyenne villages burned to the ground between 1865 and 1875 alone—or how many were buried, according to native custom, with their owners.

Along with new art materials, the audience for pictographic paintings and drawings changed. From personal and tribal records designed for the individual and the tribe, pictographic works were now often composed for a Euro-American audience, particularly Army officials who were interested in Indian perspectives of the late Indian wars. Army officers were especially eager to solicit war drawings from the tribes that "had been most consistently hostile to the whites" (Ewers, Intro. 12)—the Sioux, Cheyenne, and Kiowa, in particular. In fact, the more than seventy Plains Indian warriors who were imprisoned at Fort Marion in St. Augustine, Florida, from 1875 to 1878 were among the most copious producers of pictographic artwork. Of course, these "ringleaders" and "hostiles," as they had been labeled by the United States government, had little to do in prison but draw and paint. Captain Richard Pratt, their sympathetic jailer, provided drawing books and art materials and helped imprisoned Indian artists like Zo-Tom and Howling Wolf sell their work to East Coast Euro-Americans. Such art lovers, in fact, may explain why Fort Marion artists are so well represented in pictographic ledger-book collections. Unlike most of the pictographic paintings created on the Plains, those created in prison were purchased and preserved for posterity.

Inside Fort Marion, the pictographic artistic conventions changed even more drastically, since the materials, the occasion, and the audience had been altered forcibly and abruptly. Instead of drawing autobiographical narratives depicting personal exploits, many artists drew tribal documentaries. In addition, they often used mid-nineteenth-century Plains Indian artistic principles and conventions, but introduced new elements such as writing in syllabary or in English (to translate the picture to a Euro-American audience unschooled in pictography), more realistic depiction of animals and people, and frequent inclusions of landscape. To the original purpose of describing one's personal heroics had been added a new one: to translate one's culture. Two other examples of Fort Marion pictography will suggest the range of tradition and innovation (Figures 18 and 19). The group of warriors in Figure 18 was drawn on paper by the Cheyenne Making Medicine in 1875. Even though he drew on Euro-American materials while in prison, and even though he worked some forty years after Mah-to-toh-pa, Making Medicine used early-nineteenth-century hide-painting conventions described earlier: right-to-left flow of action, detailed ornamentation of warriors, elongated horses, side view, and absence of landscape, to name a few. In dramatic contrast to Making Medicine, the Kiowa Wohaw's 1877 picture (Figure 19) reveals innovation in subject and style. His atypical symmetrical pictograph shows him in the center of the picture, caught between two worlds. Above are sun, moon, and meteor. Innovations include replacement of his name-symbol with its translation into English (Wohaw, or White Man's Spotted Cow) (Dunn, *American Indian Painting* 90), inclusion of landscape, front view of the human figure, and overall symmetry. On his right is the Indian way represented by the buffalo, the tipi, and the woods; on his left is the white

FIGURE 18. "On the War Path" by Making Medicine (Cheyenne), August 1875. (Courtesy of the National Anthropological Archives, Smithsonian Institution)

While imprisoned at Fort Marion in St. Augustine, Florida, Making Medicine continued to use early-nineteenth-century hide-painting conventions such as right-to-left flow of action, detailed ornamentation of warriors to convey identity and rank, elongated horses, side view, and absence of landscape.

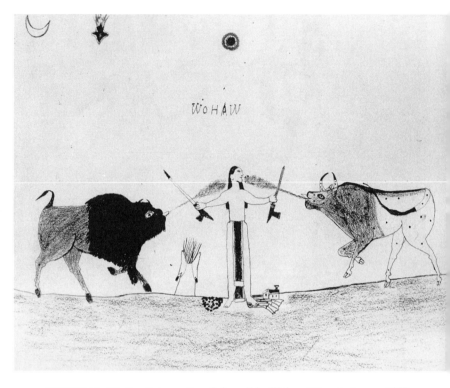

FIGURE 19. ''Indian Between Two Cultures'' by Wohaw (Kiowa), January 1877.
(Courtesy of Missouri Historical Society)

In contrast to Making Medicine's traditional treatment of warriors (Figure 18), Wohaw (also imprisoned at Fort Marion) introduced a new subject and an innovative style. In this symmetrical pictograph, Wohaw stands in the center, situated between two worlds. On his right (the left side of the picture) is the Native American way of life, represented by the buffalo, the tipi, and the woods. On his left (the right side of the picture) is the Euro-American way of life, represented by the cow, the house, and the cultivated land. Although he offers a pipe to both, his left foot is set on the farmland of the Euro-American world, suggesting his cultural conversion. Above are sun, moon, and meteor and Wohaw's name (Spotted Cow) written in the English alphabet.

way represented by the cow, the house, and the cultivated land. He offers a pipe to both, but his left foot is clearly pointed in the direction of the white world. In a single picture, Wohaw told the story of his cultural conversion, a particularly pleasing subject for his captors.

During the time the last resisting Plains Indian warriors were imprisoned at Fort Marion, others continued to draw pictographs in freedom. While the men in prison were supplied with drawing pads and art supplies, the men on the Plains had to trade for, steal, or otherwise locate drawing materials. In a few cases, paper was so scarce that "[s]ome of it was cut into uniform size and sewn together with long stitches into various booklets" (Dunn, *American Indian Painting* 178). One such artist, an anonymous Cheyenne man, constructed a pictographic book sometime after 1877. His unique work was collected in Montana by Captain George L. Tyler. The author–artist collected ten scraps of paper: two one-third sections of a typed letter requesting information about Indian "funereal and other mortuary ceremonies"; a scrap of a handwritten report about Company G, Second Cavalry; a handwritten grocery shopping list; three envelopes (one addressed to "Commanding Officer, Company 'G.' 2nd Cavalry, Montana" and one dated "Dec. 2 '77''"); and others. All were cut into 9.7- by 19.7-centimeter segments, about the size of a business envelope, and then cross- or whip-stitched along the bottom.

Many features distinguish this piece from most other Plains Indian pictography of the period: its subject, materials, construction, function, and audience. Pre-1830 pictographic buffalo robes, we remember, focus primarily on an individual's war exploits. In contrast to tradition, this pictographic autobiographical account emphasizes the artist's love life. Out of sixteen pages of drawings (the other four are written on), only five depict war and hunting scenes. Figure 20, "Hunter, Horse, and Antelope," is one such example. On this envelope, addressed to the commanding officer of Company G, Second Cavalry, the Cheyenne diarist drew a bare-chested man wearing a choker and a blanket and a horse with a noticeable brand on its hindquarter. In the top-right-hand corner, an antelope bounds away, looking over its shoulder. Note the short lines indicating motion beneath its hooves. This is reminiscent of a hunting scene, even though nothing is being pursued.

Eleven drawings, a full two-thirds of the sketches, are devoted to courtship, or "standing-in-the-blanket," as it was called, since the young lovers would wrap a blanket around themselves to converse in privacy—usually within range of a chaperone. Figure 21, "Courtship," shows two pairs of lovers. On the right, the diarist wraps his blanket (with its identifying bar-and-circle border) around his lover as they sit gazing at each other. He wears a breastplate, choker, and hair ornament; she wears beads, and her hair wrapped in braids. A faint squiggly line links her name-symbol to her head. Perhaps her name-symbol translates as Raven

FIGURE 20. "Hunter, Horse, and Antelope" by unknown Cheyenne artist, post-1877. (Courtesy of the Southwest Museum, Los Angeles, California. Neg. No. 37,101)

Since paper was not always readily available, this artist gathered scraps of paper and stitched them together to construct a pictographic book. On this envelope, addressed to "Commanding Officer, Company 'G.' 2nd Cavalry, Montana," he drew a pronghorn antelope looking back over its shoulder as it bounds away, a branded horse, and a bare-chested hunter.

Hair or Evening Woman, since the face on her name-symbol is darkened. The center of this page is torn, revealing the printed text of a letter from someone who is "preparing a memoir upon the 'Burial Customs of the Indians of N— America, both ancient and modern'" and who requests permission of the cavalry commander to visit. On the left is another illustration of probably the same couple. This time, they each wear their own blankets (his the same inlaid design, and hers the striped one). The lovers have come from different tipis. Note the tracks that indicate their movement and convergence.

Perhaps the artist's focus on courtship is due to the unique audience and function of this piece. This was not a drawing to be sold to white

Indian art enthusiasts, like many of the Fort Marion sketchbooks, nor was it a record of personal or tribal achievements addressed to other Cheyenne, like early-nineteenth-century "brag skins,"[24] as the painted buffalo robes have been called. Rather, it is a personal pictographic diary recording this man's preoccupation with his lover. Other pictographs of courtship scenes exist, but usually they are limited to one or a few drawings in a ledger book dominated by numerous depictions of wars, raids, and hunts.[25] Such a focus on martial scenes may be due, in part, to an Anglo audience's desire for details of colorful Indian warfare, safely removed from the frontier to the pages of a sketchbook. But war was a traditional subject for Plains Indian men regardless of the demands of a Euro-American audience. This artist's uncharacteristic expression of inner feelings may be an aberration, or it may be an indication of how

FIGURE 21. "Courtship" by unknown Cheyenne artist, post-1877. (Courtesy of the Southwest Museum, Los Angeles, California. Neg. No. 37,095)

This page of the pictographic diary depicts two scenes of courtship, often called "standing-in-the-blanket," since lovers would wrap a blanket around themselves in order to converse in privacy, usually within range of a chaperone. On the left, a woman and a man meet outside a tipi. On the right, they sit together in his blanket, which is adorned with a bar-and-circle design. Note her name-symbol in the upper-right-hand corner. The ripped section in the middle of the page reveals a previous page of the diary, a printed letter sent to the Second Cavalry requesting permission to study Indian mortuary practices.

little Euro-Americans noted the tender side of Plains Indian men, preferring instead the noble and ferocious warrior stereotype. This unknown Cheyenne was a hunter and warrior, but predominantly, in this work, a lover. Like the hunting scene in Figure 20 the courtship drawing in Figure 22 was drawn on an envelope addressed to the commanding officer of the Second Cavalry in Montana. In "Courtship Scene Drawn on Envelope," "the diarist presents a more fully developed narrative of his courtship. Turning the diary from the horizontal to the vertical, we see two narrative frames. The top drawing (about two-thirds the way up the page) shows the two lovers meeting. Note how he enfolds her in his trademark blanket. Recall, also, how costume-symbols began to replace name-symbols for many sketchbook pictographers. In the bottom scene, the couple has walked from the village (indicated by the tracks coming from in front of and behind the tipi on the right). The wavy line along the bottom represents a river (note the vegetation along the water), a conventional site for courtship. On the ground in front of them are a water bucket and the diarist's feather-decorated sword. Keep in mind that one of the envelopes in his self-constructed book is dated December 1877 (Figure 22), only one year after "eleven hundred cavalry men . . . burst into the Cheyenne village of Dull Knife and Little Wolf," killing people and burning "their tipis, clothing, and winter food supply," and only several months after most Cheyenne and Sioux surrendered to military agencies.[26] With the disintegration of his way of life, perhaps he retreated from the social expectations of Cheyenne men to the personal desires of the heart.

What is even more striking than the shift in subject is the materials and their construction. In "Indigenous Text Production" (Figure 23), the artist has again used an envelope, this time the back of one. In the bottom right corner, we see the faint date "Dec. 2, '77" written in fountain pen. Again, the focus is on courtship. This time the lovers meet under a parasol, and on the left, they are accompanied by friends or chaperones. Since this is the final page of the diary and the outside back cover, it is considerably smudged and worn. This is probably one of the earliest examples of indigenous book production, a self-published Plains Indian author. Note how the diarist has stitched together the pages. Clearly, the artist–bookmaker has an *idea* of pages bound in a book, rather than the large circular surfaces of hides and tipis, in mind. This is not a book for *public*-ation, however, but a private journal, a place to record personal memories and musings, an unusual indulgence for nineteenth-century Plains Indians—men or women. Like nineteenth-century Euro-American

FIGURE 22. "Courtship Scene Drawn on Envelope" by unknown Cheyenne artist, post-1877. (Courtesy of the Southwest Museum, Los Angeles, California. Neg. No. 37,103)

The artist drew an elaborate courtship scene on an envelope addressed to "Commanding Officer, Company 'G.' 2nd Cavalry." Turning the envelope vertically, in the top scene, he illustrated the lovers' meeting. In the more fully developed narrative of the bottom scene, he shows how the lovers leave the tipi (note the lines indicating their tracks from the tipi) to meet near the river (indicated by the wavy line and shrubbery along the bottom of the page). The river was a common site of courtship. The suitor's befeathered sword stands at the left. At the feet of the lovers is a water bucket.

FIGURE 23. "Indigenous Text Production" constructed by unknown Cheyenne artist, post-1877. (Courtesy of the Southwest Museum, Los Angeles, California. Neg. No. 37,107)

Constructing his self-narration from the materials of the oppressor, the diarist gathered scraps of paper—in this case, the back of an envelope—and stitched them together in an early example of indigenous book production. A somewhat smudged courtship scene drawn in pencil is the final entry. While the horse waits on the right, the lovers meet beneath a parasol. On the left, the couple continues their visit in the presence of friends or chaperones. Notice the date ("Dec. 2, '77") on the bottom right (written by the sender) and the whip-stitching in sinew along the bottom.

women who created intricately designed quilts from the scraps of everyday life, the artist gathered, sorted, and assembled an identity and a narrative out of the debris of the Plains. This pictographic diary is not, then, simply an indication of an emerging literacy as a consequence of Euro-American domination. This is not a variant of the Indian informant and Anglo amanuensis collapsed into one late-nineteenth-century Cheyenne. Neither is this an interiorized textual reenactment of Anglo domination. This is a pictographic self-narration, an affirmation of a traditional self, constructed from the very materials of the oppressor. Just as persistently as Euro-Americans have written him out of his land and his culture, this Cheyenne autobiographer has written himself anew on the scraps of their military might—Company G, Second Cavalry—creating a palimpsestic pictographic self.[27]

Plains Indian pictography can be considered a type of literacy if we acknowledge indigenous sign systems and do not insist, like some scholars, on the superiority of alphabetic literacy.[28] And pictographic personal narratives can be considered autobiography if we free ourselves from the Eurocentric insistence on such literary conventions as chronology, unity, and closure. Reading these pictographic texts is like reading a diary or examining a photograph album. Each entry-image is discrete, but is related to the others thematically or spatially. Read individually, each captures the immediacy of the moment. Read together, they compose an associational visual narrative. Like Euro-American diaries, journals, and letters, Plains Indian pictographic self-narrations are not "failed versions of something more coherent and unified,"[29] but a culturally constructed graphic mode of autobiography. Such artistic personal narratives compose a discourse of Plains Indian pictography. Men, like Mah-to-toh-pa, constructed autobiographical narratives from the earth and animals of the Plains; and men, like Howling Wolf, Zo-Tom, White Bull, and the anonymous Cheyenne diarist, reconstructed their disrupted life stories from the colonialists' paper and pencils. For us, they picture-write their cultural presence on the scattered remnants of a campaign that sought to write them out of history.

4 / Literary Boundary Cultures: The Life Histories of Plenty-Coups, Pretty-Shield, Sam Blowsnake, and Mountain Wolf Woman

Many Native American oral autobiographies were solicited in the late nineteenth and early twentieth centuries by Euro-American ethnologists, historians, and others who translated and edited the works of native informants. These "bicultural composite composition[s]"[1] reveal the artistic/literary traditions of two distinct cultures. The amanuenses of these collaborative autobiographies often excised "tedious" repetition, imposed chronology, insisted on introspection, and ignored the life-storyteller's communal context. Even though the final shape and content of the life history were determined by Euro-American editors, however, Indian narrators seem to have told their life stories in their native narrative forms—forms that were shaped originally by the cultural patterns of the tribe, but that then were modified according to the needs of a new audience, purpose, and setting.

When examining this bicultural transformation, we must consider not only the narrator and his or her editor, but also the constraints of language on the process of self-narration. Postmodern literary theory suggests that language precedes, in fact creates, identity. Autobiographies, then, are "fictions of the self" rather than "true" representations.[2] Individual identity is itself a fiction, a linguistic construction that is more aptly described as a plurality than a unity. That is, the linguistic and social construction of self necessarily includes the Other. Thus to use language, particularly for autobiographical expression, is to wrestle with the multiplicity and indeterminacy of the first person.[3] If the struggle between self and Other is evident within the "I" of the individual autobiographer, it is intensified fourfold when one individual attempts to express himself or herself with the assistance of an amanuensis (thus collapsing two "I"'s into one). When these two individuals come from different cultures and speak different languages, the situation is compounded again. Not only is there an interaction between two individuals with their respective senses of self and Other, but there is an interplay of two linguistic communities with their differing assumptions, preconceptions, denotations, and connotations as well. How, then, does a Native American express a genuine sense of self when that self is mediated not only by his or her own language, but by the language of another? How does one define a self in a hostile world? Is the act of expressing one's self in the language and forms of the "oppressor" an attempt at communication, an indication of negotiation, or an act of capitulation?[4]

Pre-contact forms of personal narrative often focused on a communal self. Nineteenth- and twentieth-century solicited autobiographies, however, are concerned not only with a cohesive tribal identity, but with that identity in conflict with Euro-American culture. With this in mind, the anthropological theory of acculturation offers an apt model by which to consider these transitional texts. Rather than a unidirectional process (a "dominant" group absorbing a "minority" group), acculturation involves an exchange between both. In this case, the point of contact or locus of interaction between two distinct cultures, Euro-American and Native American, results in a third culture, what Robert F. Murphy calls "a boundary culture."[5] This is an anthropological model akin to Bakhtin's notion of "heteroglossia" in which a single voice reflects the polyphony of community, in this case the cacaphony of two distinct cultural communities. We can think of late-nineteenth- and early-twentieth-century Native American autobiography as a type of literary "boundary culture" where two cultures influence each other simultaneously. Such a model modifies Arnold Krupat's notion of the composite autobiography as "the textual equivalent of the frontier" (33) by shifting the emphasis from Euro-American domination of Native American voices to Native American resistance and creativity in the face of oppression. Although the focus of this chapter will be how this border encounter changed Native American forms of oral personal narrative, it is vital to remember that Euro-American notions of narrative were challenged as well.

These Native American collaborative autobiographies can be thought of not only as cultural border skirmishes, but also as miniatures of those treaty conferences that, according to A. M. Drummond and Richard Moody, were "our first American drama."[6] The resulting collaborative, "bicultural document" (Brumble 11) might be seen as a personal treaty—an attempt to negotiate between one's individual/tribal identity and a new dominant culture. Native American autobiographies are interesting, then, not merely for what they tell us about the cultural, religious, and historical aspects of an individual and his or her tribe, but for the dramatic way in which they record the human encounter with change, with new and threatening circumstances. If we accept the assumption that we reconstruct ourselves through language, we can examine the development of some patterns of Native American autobiography in which we see individuals who not only attempted to re-create themselves in language, but also tried to refashion themselves in a foreign language for an alien audience.

As well as transitional autobiographies that combine traditional Native American pictographic forms with Euro-American written explanations (discussed in Chapter 3), there are those that combine oral narrations, which are then translated, edited, and organized by a white editor. Such life histories of indigenous people abound. L. L. Langness divides the anthropological "life history," which he defines as "an extensive record of a person's life as it is reported either by the person himself or by others or both, and whether it is written or in interviews or both," into three historical periods: pre-1925, 1925 to 1944, and post-1944. Before 1925, ethnographers, historians, and other interested parties collected stories of native people that "took the form of nonprofessional biographical and autobiographical studies of a sentimental, romantic kind." Generally, they claimed to present a true picture of the "vanishing American" and appealed to a popular audience. From 1925 through 1944, concerns for careful methodology and for the study of the individual (as opposed to culture alone) began to replace the earlier popular romantic autobiographies. For the most part, anthropologists, trained primarily by Franz Boas and motivated by their sense of the urgent need to document rapidly disappearing cultures, collected and recorded ethnographic data but spent little time analyzing it. Conversely, after 1944, claims Langness, personality became an important subject for anthropologists, but without a corresponding commitment to the arduous work of collecting and editing life histories.[7] Along with this post–World War II ethnographic activity came an increasing self-awareness. Certainly, many anthropologists today are acutely self-conscious about the personal and cultural assumptions they bring to their examinations of other cultures. As James Clifford points out, it is no longer possible to behave as if there had not been a "pervasive postcolonial crisis of ethnographic authority."[8] It is no longer acceptable to speak for a cultural Other without acknowledging the difficulty, if not impossibility, of "objectivity." An anthropologist who narrates the life story of a native Other narrates his or her own life as well. In this regard, H. David Brumble offers a useful distinction between the point of view of two kinds of Euro-American amanuenses of Native American autobiography: "Absent Editors," who "create the fiction that the narrative is all the Indian's own" (75), and "Self-Conscious Editors," who attempt to "preserve the point of view" and "mode of telling" of Indian narrators (82–83).

This chapter will focus on two sets of life histories collected from 1920 to 1958, overlapping the three periods of ethnographic life-history collections delineated by Langness. Two unrelated Crows from the same generation, Plenty-Coups and Pretty-Shield, told their stories to trapper–hunter Frank Linderman in 1928 and 1930, respectively. Sam Blowsnake (alias Big Winnebago and Crashing Thunder) wrote his conversion narrative in Winnebago syllabary for anthropologist Paul Radin around 1920, while almost forty years later (1958) Mountain Wolf Woman, Blowsnake's sister, narrated her life story to her friend and adopted niece, anthropologist Nancy O. Lurie. All these individuals lived during a period of violent transformation in the boundary culture created as a result of Indian-Anglo interaction, but all focused their self-narrations on their former ways of life. Most agreed with Pretty-Shield, who conceded: "I am living a life I do not understand."[9] All told their life stories using native autobiographical modes modified for new circumstances. In addition, the pairing of a man and a woman from the same tribe and historical period reveals something of the role gender plays in how an individual constructs an identity and narrates a life.

Two Crow Life Histories

Plenty-Coups

In 1885, at the age of sixteen, Frank B. Linderman left his family in the East to hunt, trap, and live the roaming life of a cowboy in Montana. There he lived and worked among native people, making friends and being adopted into three tribes: ''the Blackfeet, who called him Mex-skim-yo-peek-kinny, meaning Iron Tooth; the Crees, who gave him the name Co-skee-see-cot, which means The Man Who Looks Through Glasses; and the Crows, who named him Mah-paht-sa-not-tsasa, mean-ing Great Sign Talker.''[10] On one otherwise uneventful hunting trip in 1888, Linderman met the Crow chief Plenty-Coups, who was then ''in his forties, a perfect specimen of manhood.''[11] Together they conversed, partly in Indian sign language, about battles with the Flatheads. The two men remained friends, and it was Plenty-Coups who gave Linderman his name: Sign-talker. Forty years later, in 1928, Linderman visited Plenty-Coups in order to record the old warrior's life history. During his interviews with Plenty-Coups, Linderman's room was provided by Reverend John Frost, a ''half-blood Indian,'' and his board was supplied by women working in the mission. Two ''Eastern ladies'' were staying at the mission also, and each night Linderman would ''relate the particulars of [his] day with Plenty-Coups'' for their entertainment (*Montana* 181).

''Old Indians have always impressed me,'' explains Linderman, who often sought out full-blood Indian elders to hear what he believed were the most accurate accounts of tribal history and philosophy. Recording the authentic voices of ''real Indians'' was a key motivation for Linder-man's pursuit of Plenty-Coups' life history. In *Montana Adventure,* his own autobiography, Linderman explains:

> I have tried to break down that something which separates me from them by thinking as old Indians think, perhaps with only imagined success. And yet I believe that I understand many points in their philosophy of life that I cannot yet express in words. Perhaps I shall never learn; certainly not from the offspring of these warriors, who know next to nothing about their people's ancient ways. Now it is too late to learn. The real Indians are gone. (*Montana* 183).

Linderman's nostalgia for a lost past is evident in his work as an amanuensis of Crow autobiographies and in his own autobiography as well. He begins his autobiography with his excitement as a young boy yearning to live a free life in the Far West and ends it with his resignation as an old man. In the final scene, he describes his trip to New York City, where, in the dingy concrete streets, he sees little boys, ''little campfire-builders,'' playing Wild West—a West that now exists only in the imagination (Linderman, *Montana* 197). Linderman's autobiography, then, like those he writes on behalf of Plenty-Coups and Pretty-Shield, begins with hopeful promise and ends with loss. "The real Indians are gone," he laments, and with them the old way of life in the West. Before the Indians and their way of life "vanished," however, Linderman sought to help them as much as possible. He was well loved and respected among Indian people, for instance, for helping to ensure that a reservation was established for "the homeless Crees and Chippewas" (Merriam 206–207). As well as such activism, Linderman sought to preserve traditional native ways in writing.

Linderman thought of himself as a writer and hoped to be accepted as one. Although he received a great deal of encouragement from admirers and friends, he was disappointed that he never became a popular western writer. Writing Plenty-Coups' story "proved to be a difficult piece of work" for him (Linderman, *Montana* 184). Even though he "wrote it twice from beginning to end" (Linderman, *Montana* 184), Scribner's was not interested. As Linderman explains: "Scribner's continued to send me such modest royalty check [*sic*] that I began to feel thin ice beneath my literary moccasins" (*Montana* 167). At this point, the frustrated Linderman gave up on Scribner's and arranged for Plenty-Coups' life story to be published by the John Day Company. Originally entitled *American: The Life Story of a Great Indian,* the book included over forty black-and-white illustrations of Plains Indian life by artist Henry Morton Stoops and was dedicated to Linderman's grandson James Beale Waller. The original title, then, focuses on Plenty-Coups as an "American" and "a great Indian." Keep in mind that this was published in 1930, just six years after American Indians were awarded U.S. citizenship.

Relying on an interpreter, Braided-Scalp-Lock, and his own knowledge of Indian sign language, Frank Linderman recorded what he referred to as "a genuine record" of the life of Plenty-Coups (Aleekchea-ahoosh), a Crow and "the last legitimate chieftain who had seen much of the old life of the Plains Indian."[12] Linderman convinced Plenty-Coups that telling his life history would help "my people to better understand your people."[13] From the beginning, Plenty-Coups insisted that his old friends, Coyote-Runs and Plain-Bull, join them in their sessions under the cottonwood trees near Plenty-Coups' cabin, explaining, "they will help me remember" (Plenty-Coups 4). Just as in the old days when returning warriors would tell the stories of their personal achievements (see coup stories discussed in Chapters 2 and 3), corroborating one another's experiences, Coyote-Runs and Plain-Bull added, embellished, or confirmed a point made by Plenty-Coups. After one of Plenty-Coups' stories about counting coups on a huge buffalo, Coyote-Runs acknowledged its authenticity: " 'I saw him do that,' he said proudly. . . . 'I was there and saw Plenty-Coups strike the bull twice. No other boy struck him at all' " (Plenty-Coups 31). The earlier Plains Indian tradition of corroboration of brave deeds and collaboration in their narration is evident in this transitional oral autobiography. However, there is no evidence that the elderly Plenty-Coups relied on a pictographic hide to spur his memory. While some may question whether an eighty-year-old man could remember such detail with accuracy, we should keep in mind the acute memories of people in oral cultures.

Although Linderman does not provide an elaborate explanation of his process of putting together Plenty-Coups' autobiography or of what he revised during his two rewritings of the text, the reader can readily discern some of Linderman's contributions and motivations. Most apparent is that he guides Plenty-Coups' accounts by his questions and directions. Even though Plenty-Coups began by asking Linderman why he wanted to write down his words (at least according to Linderman's editorial arrangement), it is Linderman's questions that shape the telling after that. These questions can be divided into two types: specific (such as Where were you born? or How did you get that scar on your chin?) and general (such as What are your earliest remembrances?). Sometimes Linderman has to overcome Plenty-Coups' hesitation or refusal to respond to questions that deal with taboo matters such as speaking the names of the dead and relating details of his power vision. As well as through questioning, Linderman directs Plenty-Coups' stories by encouraging detail and performance. For example, he instructs Plenty-Coups: "Show me how you held your bow and arrow" (Plenty-Coups 14).

For the most part, however, Linderman did not have to encourage Plenty-Coups to enact his stories, especially his war stories. He writes: "An old Indian, interested in his tale, acts his part, and Plenty-Coups' hands and body worked with his words as though the fight were now, and the speaking itself a war-song" (Plenty-Coups 17). Throughout the autobiography, Linderman describes Plenty-Coups' performances. When Plenty-Coups describes joining Three-Stars (General Crook) with 135 other Crow warriors, he becomes excited about the spectacle of the "blue soldiers" with their "fine horses" and their "songs of shining horns and drums" (156). With faces painted and warbonnets arranged, the Crows jumped on their horses, crying the Crow war-whoop and firing their guns in the air, as they raced to join the pageantry. Linderman describes Plenty-Coups in the process of recounting the excitement:

> The old man grew excited. Rising, he gave the war-whoop, drumming his mouth with his open hand. His body was tense, his face working, his hands, signing his now rapidly spoken tale, were swift indeed. How he was riding! His old body swayed from side to side, and his imaginary quirt lashed his horse cruelly. I could fairly see him ride! I wish I might tell his story just as he did. (Plenty-Coups 157)

Thus Plenty-Coups performs, rather than merely tells, his personal narrative, and Linderman attempts to re-create such a vivid storytelling experience in writing.

Linderman also includes his own explanations intended to inform the non-Indian reader about a Crow custom or historical event. After Plenty-Coups says: "I am old and am living an unnatural life. . . . I am anxious to go to my Father, Ah-badt-dadt-deah, to live again as men were intended to live" (78), Linderman explains:

> Ah-badt-dadt-deah literally translated means The-one-who-made-all-things. I have sometimes thought it is more nearly a term than a name, and that to the Crow the name of his God is unpronounceable, as with some of the ancient peoples. However, the Indian—certainly any that I know—will scarcely ever speak the name of his God aloud; and if you pronounce it in his presence you will feel his reverence. (Plenty-Coups 79)

Throughout the book, Linderman provides at least sixty-eight such explanations. Clarification is needed by the popular audience for whom this book was intended, but it is far from the copious academic footnotes found in more stringently anthropological autobiographies. At times, though, Linderman's commentary is intrusive. As well as explaining, Linderman sometimes paraphrases or summarizes a particularly long, detailed story that he does not wish to include in its entirety.

Explanations are not the only interruptions Linderman includes. He halts the flow of Plenty-Coups' narrative to insert conversations or descriptions of people, environment, or landscape. He also incorporates interruptions from visitors. This editorial decision gives the reader a flavor of the actual experience of the interviews; it highlights the oral nature of the stories, reveals the interrelations among the members of the group, and provides a sense of daily life and surroundings that is often edited out of such accounts.

Although Plenty-Coups' narratives are guided by Linderman, he seems anxious to tell his stories in the traditional fashion of early Crow warriors. Apologizing for his disregard of chronology (which would be expected by the Euro-American Linderman), Plenty-Coups proceeds by association, allowing one story to remind him of another. This associative narrative functions on two levels: the tribal and the individual. He describes tribal life, including accounts of wars, visions, ceremonies, and healings. He also narrates in detail two major aspects of his individual life. He shares accounts of his spiritual life, in particular his life-shaping visions and dreams and their interpretations. As well as spiritual concerns, he recounts his martial life, especially his brave deeds as a warrior—stealing or retrieving horses, counting coups in battles, and rescuing bodies of slain comrades.

Thus like Zo-Tom, Howling Wolf, and White Bull (Chapter 3), Plenty-Coups focuses on his martial accomplishments of the past, describing raids against the Crow's ancient enemies: the Sioux, Cheyenne, Arapahoe, and Blackfeet. Unlike these three, however, Plenty-Coups did not fight against the whites, but with them. Plenty-Coups fought with Three-Stars (General Crook) on the Rosebud against the Sioux and Cheyenne, and he is quick to point out that he "never killed a white man" (83).

Although Zo-Tom, Howling Wolf, White Bull, and Plenty-Coups have much in common, since they all lived and fought on the Plains before the buffalo disappeared, their narratives differ radically in their treatment (or lack of it) of whites. Plenty-Coups is the only one of the four to criticize "white men [who] too often promised to do one thing and then, when they acted at all, did another" (227). Perhaps it is more possible to develop specific critical commentary in writing than to depict it in pictographs. Certainly, it is easier for Plenty-Coups to be an outspoken critic in 1928, when he is free on his own land, than it was for Zo-Tom or Howling Wolf in 1877 while imprisoned at Fort Marion for opposing the United States government. Or perhaps, with forty years' experience of Euro-American broken promises, Plenty-Coups was simply fed up. Another reason for Plenty-Coups' criticism of whites and his repeated review of Crow assistance to the United States may have to do with one of his motives for telling his life's story to Linderman. He says: "Remember this, Sign-talker, and help my people keep their lands. Help them to hold forever the Pryor and Bighorn mountains. They love them as I do and deserve to have them for the help they gave the white man, who now owns all" (308). Ironically, it is Plenty-Coups, who helped the

United States government obtain Indian lands, who is most openly critical of whites, not those who fought against the government. According to Plenty-Coups, Euro-Americans insisted that "laws were made for everybody," but "thought nothing of breaking them themselves"; they told Indians "not to drink whiskey," but "traded it . . . for furs and robes"; and they tried to impose their Christianity on Indians, but "did not take . . . religion any more seriously than [they did their] laws" (228). Plenty-Coups makes it clear that the Crow policy of aiding Euro-Americans was based on pragmatic matters (keeping their land and overcoming their ancient enemies), not on any love for whites or any hatred for their foes. Crow alliance with Euro-Americans, says Plenty-Coups, was the only way "to save our beautiful country" (154).

Despite his criticism of the United States government, Plenty-Coups assures Linderman that "whenever war comes between this country and another, your people will find my people pointing their guns with yours" (307–308). Thus even after criticizing the wrongs perpetrated by whites, Plenty-Coups ends on a patriotic note. Still, his patriotism is tinged with sadness as he contrasts his earlier "happy days" with the present: "Now the old life is ended. Most of the men who knew it have gone, and I myself am eager to go and find them" (Plenty-Coups 308). In the Author's Note at the end of the autobiography, Linderman explains in Plenty-Coups' words why "Plenty-Coups refused to speak of his life after the passing of the buffalo": " 'when the buffalo went away the hearts of my people fell to the ground, and they could not lift them up again. After this nothing happened. There was little singing anywhere.' " [14]

Pretty-Shield

Four years later, in 1932, Linderman published the life history of Pretty-Shield (whom he interviewed in 1931). *Red Mother,* as the book was entitled originally, was dedicated to Linderman's granddaughter, Sarah Jane Waller, and published by the John Day Company. As in Plenty-Coups' life history, Herbert M. Stoops illustrated Pretty-Shield's story (including about seventeen black-and-white drawings of camp life). In his autobiography, Linderman describes his first meeting and subsequent work with Plenty-Coups, but he does not even mention Pretty-Shield. Certainly, he interacted more with Indian men than women, explaining in the Foreword that during his "forty-six years in Montana" he had "never, until now, talked for ten consecutive minutes directly to an old Indian woman."[15] Indian women, he says, are "diffident, and so self-effacing that acquaintance with them is next to impossible" (Foreword *Pretty-Shield* 9). In addition, as a diligent "Self-Conscious Editor," he acknowledges the difficulty of a translation that, "coming through an interpreter laboring to translate Crow thoughts into English words, must suffer mutation, no matter how conscientious the interpreter may be," and, he insists, his interpreter, Goes-Together, was conscientious. As well as this verbal translation, Linderman relies on his knowledge of Indian sign language so that the seventy-four-year-old Pretty-Shield both speaks and signs her stories as the three sit together in the schoolhouse on the Crow reservation in Montana.

In the same way that Linderman directed Plenty-Coups' narrative, he shaped Pretty-Shield's accounts, at one time paying her four dollars. He compensated her more fully later. After he returned home to write her story, he sent her numerous deer skins. During the course of the narrative, a couple of Linderman's directives to Pretty-Shield become evident. Several times, for instance, as she prepares to deviate from his request, she reminds him that he wanted "only a woman's story" (118). Another time, she tells Linderman: "You have said that I must always tell you what the weather was like, and I am doing this" (87). This may be an indirect way for Linderman to reveal how he shaped Pretty-Shield's narrative, or it may reflect Pretty-Shield's consciousness of shaping her story to suit the interests of an outsider. As well as directives, Linderman includes questions, generally of two types. He asks initial questions, such as "What did you do when people were bitten by rattlesnakes, Pretty-Shield?" or "Now tell me your medicine dream" (Pretty-Shield 162, 165), as well as follow-up questions and directions such as "Tell me more about . . ." (Pretty-Shield 134). Linderman's directives and questions certainly shape Pretty-Shield's oral narrations as much as his active organization of his notes when he returned home to write her story.

As with Plenty-Coups, Linderman includes explanations of Crow customs, events, and beliefs, as well as interruptions to the flow of Pretty-Shield's narrative. Most notably, Pretty-Shield's grandchildren interrupt on several occasions to ask their grandmother for money, or Pretty-Shield excuses herself to check on one of her nine grandchildren. Her grand-children, in fact, become a convenient device for Linderman to intro-duce, suspend, or conclude Pretty-Shield's storytelling and to emphasize her relational identity. These interruptions, along with the episodic nature of Pretty-Shield's narrative, result in a collection of personal and historical anecdotes rather than a unified life history. This is closer to pre-contact self-narrations, in which the teller assumes an audience familiar with the details of community life, than to Euro-American autobiography, in which the writer generally assumes an unknown readership. Similar to the diaries and letters of nineteenth-century Euro-American women, such an associative rather than a chronological structure emphasizes the importance of a network of relationships rather than a sequence of events.

As well as explanations, Linderman includes some of the small talk among Pretty-Shield, Goes-Together, and himself in order to re-create a sense of their amiable relationship. More than once, he describes his admiration for Pretty-Shield because she is "a strong character, a good woman" (Pretty-Shield 96). Like the letters of support written by upstanding white members of the community and appended to slave narratives, Linderman appends to and incorporates into the text Euro-American endorsements of Pretty-Shield and her story. A letter from federal politician Scott Leavit corroborates Pretty-Shield's description of the twenty-five-foot lock of hair in Plenty-Coups' possession. Similarly, C. H. Asbury (the Crow Agency superintendent) provides a positive (although patronizing) character assessment of Pretty-Shield:

> I do not know how some of these people could have lived without her. She is charity itself. She has mothered the motherless; and when at last old Gabriel blows his horn if Pretty-shield doesn't receive rich reward for her services here on earth the rest of us will be out of luck, I'm afraid. (Pretty-Shield 96–97)

Like the authenticating letters of reference appended to nineteenth-century slave narratives, such a laudation bears witness to Pretty-Shield's character, establishing the legitimacy of the elderly Crow woman for her Anglo readers.

Among the more successful of Linderman's techniques is his description of Pretty-Shield's performance of her stories as well as her audience response. In the midst of her anecdotes about rattlesnake bites, Linderman shares an incident: "Here Goes-Together, who had grown tense, jumped as though she herself had been bitten, nearly upsetting the table. Pretty-shield, now convulsed with laughter, had suddenly reached down and pinched the interpreter's leg. Several minutes elapsed before Pretty-shield could control her mirth" (Pretty-Shield 163). Such interludes

highlight the performance aspect of traditional Native American storytelling, not to mention the fun-loving nature of Pretty-Shield. [16] Likewise, when Pretty-Shield imitated a pouting bear cub angry with his
mother, both Goes-Together and Linderman were "convulsed with
laughter" (Pretty-Shield 108). Linderman also describes Pretty-Shield's
facial expressions ("her dark eyes snapping," 230), her gestures ("she
pressed her fist against her forehead, and bent her head," 235), and her
tone of voice ("her voice had grown louder," 238, or "She said a little
bitterly," 230). Although these are nowhere near the elaborate pro-
cedures for recording Native American storytelling performances de-
vised by Dell Hymes and Dennis Tedlock over forty years later, Linderman's early attempts to re-create the experience of storytelling at least
suggest performance possibilities. [17]

As mentioned earlier, Pretty-Shield's foci are determined to a great
extent by Linderman's directions, questions, and editings. She explains
that her name, given to her by her grandfather when she was four days
old, commemorates her grandfather's handsome war shield, which was
"big medicine" (special power) and was thus a name of honor (19). She
describes her experiences of life on the Plains (especially of her encounters with horses and buffalo), childhood, marriage, children, great
persons, and visions. She also incorporates tribal myths and tales into her
narrative. However, even though she is a "Wise-one," a medicine
woman whose helpers are the ant-people, she does not dwell on her own
healing practices, but discusses the work of others. This may be due to a
taboo concerning public discussion of such matters (although like Plenty-
Coups, she violates taboo by speaking the names of the dead) or to the
direction of Linderman's questioning.

Adopted and raised by an aunt, Pretty-Shield, like most Crow women
of the period, grew up in the midst of a predominantly female community. Certainly men were important, but they were often absent, away on
hunting trips or raids, leaving a community of women (as well as young
boys and men) in camp. Because Pretty-Shield lived among women, and
because the Crow society is matriarchal, females are especially important
to her. Pretty-Shield emphasizes the importance of several female role
models: her mother, her aunt, and especially "Kills-good, a tall handsome woman with a soft voice" (32), whose lodge was always neat,
whose food was always good, whose appearance was always impecca-
ble, and whose manner was always kind. As a little girl, Pretty-Shield
mimicked the women around her, constructing and setting up tipis,

carrying dolls in place of babies on her back, cooking pretend food, and dancing at play ceremonies. In addition, she attempted several traditional male activities. Borrowing a father's lance that was longer than the two little girls, Pretty-Shield and Beaver-That-Passes, with a tremendous struggle and a few wounds, succeeded in killing a big buffalo calf (Pretty-Shield 28).

Just as Pretty-Shield experimented with female and male roles, she emphasizes how a woman's story (what Linderman asked for) cannot be told without a man's, how one individual's story cannot be told without the community's. She explains to Linderman: "I am trying to tell you a woman's story, as you wished. I am telling you my *own* story. The medicine-gun is a part of it, because I was with the boy who found the medicine-gun" (78). She describes how one day at play the children found a half-buried rusty gun that, in the course of play, mysteriously discharged, killing a young playmate. Just because a boy found the gun, a boy was killed, and men dubbed the gun a "medicine-gun" does not mean the story is a man's story. The death of a playmate left a lasting impression on all. Such a mingling of stories underscores how personal and community narratives are often difficult to distinguish.

Even though the stories of men and women intermingle, Pretty-Shield emphasizes how a woman's perspective may alter the telling of personal and tribal history. In contrast to Plenty-Coups and other male autobiographers, who underscore the heroic achievements of battle, Pretty-Shield highlights the devastating effects of war on those who stay behind: "We women sometimes tried to keep our men from going to war," explains Pretty-Shield, "but it was like talking to winter-winds; and of course there was always some woman, sometimes many women, mourning for men who had been killed in war" (167). Besides the emotional hardship of losing loved ones, the loss of men in a war led to economic hardship. In the Crow culture of the period, with its gender-specific division of labor, men were responsible for killing animals for women, who would then process food, clothing, and other necessities.

It is difficult to determine if Pretty-Shield's inclusion of so many stories of women in seemingly nontraditional roles, particularly women warriors, is due to Linderman's early insistence on hearing "only a woman's story" or to her own knowledge of and pride in such female achievements. She seems at ease with her traditional female role until the end of her narrative when, asked by Linderman to discuss the Custer battle, she is adamant about telling the truth even if the men do not like it.

"Did the men ever tell you anything about a woman who fought with Three-stars [General Crook] on the Rosebud?" Pretty-Shield asks Linderman, reversing their roles for a moment. She continues:

"Ahh, they do not like to tell of it," she chuckled. "But I will tell you about it. We Crows all know about it. I shall not be stealing anything from the men by telling the truth.

"Yes, a Crow woman fought with Three-stars on the Rosebud. . . ." (228)

Both The-Other-Magpie and Finds-Them-and-Kills-Them, "a woman and a half-woman," explains Pretty-Shield, performed brave deeds during the battle on the Rosebud. They saved Bull-Snake, killed and scalped a Lakota, and scared off the remaining warriors. Earlier, she describes how another "fight between the Crows and the Lacota [*sic*] was won by a woman" (199). "The men never tell about it. They do not like to hear about it, but I am going to tell you what happened. I was there to see" (Pretty-Shield 202). Strikes-Two, a sixty-year-old-woman, using her root digger as a weapon and singing her song, rode straight into the Lakota warriors, who withdrew speedily in fear. "I *saw* her, I *heard* her, and my heart swelled, because she was a woman," says Pretty-Shield (203). Pretty-Shield's explanation implies male censorship of female contributions to major historical events and traditionally male endeavors. By describing female contributions to predominantly male battles and by telling "a story about Plenty-Coups that he, himself, would not be likely to tell" (Pretty-Shield 208) (about the time he shot a woman during preparations for the Sun Dance, an episode *not* found in his version of his life history),[18] Pretty-Shield revises the male-dominated historical narrative of the Crow.

But Pretty-Shield has more problems with the changes forced on her people by Euro-Americans than she does with the Crow men's lack of public acceptance of female contributions to battle. She tells proudly of how she, the second of three wives (all sisters), was the favorite of her husband, Goes-Ahead:

"But I was the only one who gave him children," she added eagerly. "It was my face that he painted when he had gained that right by saving a Crow warrior's life in battle. And it was I who rode his war-horse and carried his shield. Ahh, I felt proud when my man painted my face," she said softly, her eyes lighted by her thoughts. "After this I had the right to paint my face whenever there was a big feast or a big dance; and I did it because it was only showing respect for my man, Goes-ahead." (131)

A Crow woman, then, gained honor, in part, through the achievements of her husband. Pretty-Shield's painted face announces the personal accomplishment of her spouse. Representing her husband's bravery is a female parallel to gaining war honors.

Reservation life, however, brought new problems that Pretty-Shield refuses to discuss. Linderman explains:

> Like the old men Pretty-Shield would not talk at any length of the days when her people were readjusting themselves to the changed conditions brought on by the disappearance of the buffalo, so that her story is largely of her youth and early maturity. "There is nothing to tell, because we did nothing," she insisted when pressed for stories of her middle life. "There were no buffalo. We stayed in one place, and grew lazy." (Foreword *Pretty-Shield* 10)

Although Pretty-Shield refuses to discuss her later life, she catalogues the ill treatment of the Crow since the end of the buffalo when the people's "hearts were like stones" (250). Like Plenty-Coups, Pretty-Shield is critical of whites who brought violence, sickness, starvation, and whiskey and destroyed the buffalo and the land. Insisting that she does "not hate *anybody,* not even the white man," Pretty-Shield says: "He changed everything for us, did many bad deeds before we got used to him" (249). She punctuates her narratives throughout with the differences between then and now, using the problems with her grandchildren today to contrast with her apparently carefree childhood of old. She ends her account on a nostalgic note for the lost nobility of the old life, which has been replaced by decadent white ways. Such nostalgia for a past that is simpler and purer than the present is not a tone unique to Native American autobiographers, but it is a dominant tone for Indian individuals who, like Plenty-Coups and Pretty-Shield, were old enough to remember "the buffalo days, the days of war and excitement" (Pretty-Shield 251).

As well as a shared sense of a lost past, Plenty-Coups and Pretty-Shield share a cultural orientation to self-narration. Plenty-Coups, like other Plains Indian men of the period, emphasizes martial and spiritual accomplishments. True to Plains Indian expectations for women to perpetuate tradition, Pretty-Shield focuses on family relationships. For Plenty-Coups, the traditional Plains Indian form of relating war honors and power visions is still adequate. For Pretty-Shield, the ageless storytelling—of tribal myth, community history, and personal narrative—still serves her well. Both are accomplished storytellers, providing details and drama, if not a linear chronology, to their shortest anecdotes. By working as what Brumble refers to as a "Self-Conscious Editor," Linderman helped to present Plenty-Coups and Pretty-Shield as individuals with distinctive personalities, experiences, and narrative modes. Other amanuenses of this era were not so inclined to emphasize personality. Rather, they sought to present representative types within a particular cultural group, the goal being to better understand a different culture.

Two Winnebago Life Histories

Sam Blowsnake

According to L. L. Langness, Paul Radin's publication of *Crashing Thunder* in 1926 "marks the beginning of truly rigorous work in the field of biography by professional anthropologists" (7).[19] As early as 1920, in his introduction to *The Autobiography of a Winnebago Indian,* Radin describes the difficulty of "obtaining an inside view" of another culture from a native informant who is, "at best, interested merely in satisfying the demands of the investigator."[20] Besides that, he claims, native people, having never studied their cultures "objectively," have a hard time explaining them when asked to do so by an outsider. Seeing autobiographical accounts as a way "to throw more light on the workings of the mind and emotions of primitive man," Radin states his goal: ". . . the aim being, not to obtain autobiographical details about some definite personage, but to have some representative middle-aged individual of moderate ability describe his life in relation to the social group in which he had grown up" (2).

With this in mind, Radin convinced S. B. (Sam Blowsnake, also known as Big Winnebago, who wrote under the pseudonym Crashing Thunder, his older brother's name) to write his life story in the Winnebago syllabary, which Radin translated with the help of Oliver Lamere. Although Radin was interested primarily in culture, he says that "[n]o attempt of any kind was made to influence [Blowsnake] in the selection of the particular facts of his life which he chose to present" (2). This is quite different from the interview method used by Frank B. Linderman, who overtly directed the autobiographies of Plenty-Coups and Pretty-Shield with his questions and demands. Still, there is some doubt about Radin's awareness of any indirect or unintentional influence he may have had on Blowsnake. Perhaps, according to Arnold Krupat, "this most learned and urbane scientist could be relatively unsophisticated in his understanding of what might constitute influence upon an informant," since Radin admits to doggedly pursuing Jasper Blowsnake (Sam's older brother, the true Crashing Thunder), a reluctant informant, in an attempt to gain information. In addition, Nancy O. Lurie notes Mountain Wolf Woman's (Jasper and Sam Blowsnake's sister) aversion to what she interpreted as Radin's "offhand manner" (Krupat, Foreword xii, xvii). H. David Brumble discusses this problem in general terms: "Even when the Indian wrote of his own volition, without the aid of an editor . . . one could argue that white society plays the role of collaborator. It is the white society which provided the pen and the letters, the questions and the occasion for written autobiography" (Brumble, Intro. 1). Radin, however, acknowledges offering Sam Blowsnake a reason to write his life history, which Blowsnake parrots near the end of his account: "I thought I would write it down so that those who came after me, would not be deceived" (Radin 67, n.203). There is another motivating factor that Radin neglects to mention: Blowsnake agreed to write his story only "when the fee offered by Radin could relieve the financial difficulties in which he found himself at the time."[21]

Overall, though, Radin is more direct in explaining his involvement with Blowsnake's autobiography than Linderman was in discussing his arrangement of the materials generated by Plenty-Coups and Pretty-Shield. While the trapper Linderman did not mention how he organized his collected material, the ethnographer Radin claims that he did not change anything, but merely added headings. While Linderman incorporated commentary into his text, Radin relegated explanations to footnotes. Certainly, Linderman, who wrote several years after Radin first published *The Autobiography of a Winnebago Indian* in 1920, was responding to what Radin termed "the lack of 'atmosphere'" in ethnologists' descriptions of cultures (1), whereas Radin, although concerned with adding "atmosphere" to his study, wished primarily to attain a kind of scientific objectivity.

In Sam Blowsnake's 1920 autobiography,[22] many of the pre-contact tribal modes and themes of personal narrative are evident, but barely recognizable in their diluted forms. The problem in Blowsnake's autobiography and, in part, in his life was that he tried to live up to the expectations of an older, more traditional Winnebago life and then to use

the correspondent modes of self-narration that were no longer appropriate
for early-twentieth-century reservation life, with its dramatic changes
and restrictions. Unlike Plenty-Coups (or Mah-to-toh-pa, Zo-Tom,
Howling Wolf, and White Bull discussed in Chapter 3), Blowsnake had
no experience of raiding, counting coups in battle, stealing horses, or
rescuing his wounded comrades. Born around 1875, he was raised in the
old ways of the Winnebago—fasting to obtain visions and blessings,
moving camp often to follow the seasonal cycle of hunting game and
picking berries, and shooting bow and arrows at play. Yet this traditional
upbringing did little to prepare him for a reservation life in which he
would be subject to the alien expectations and laws of Euro-Americans.

Blowsnake did have experiences of traveling and hunting, but unlike
the other male Indian autobiographers discussed, he does not describe
such actions in detail. Also, while he retains the basic tribal narrative
forms, he alters the subject matter. Now, rather than chasing buffalo, he
"chases up the payment," following the government annuity payments
from one distribution point to the next, squandering his money on
drinking and gambling along the way. He is not alone in this behavior;
many "who liked this kind of life, . . . who used to chase around for
the fun of it," followed this practice faithfully so that the location of the
last payment was "always an extremely noisy place" (Radin 34).

Another version of Blowsnake's "hunting" expeditions involves
chasing women. Always concerned about his appeal to women, Blowsnake likes to think that he lives the life of a "lady-killer." He tries
programmatically to "live with as many women" as possible, obtaining
money as well as sexual favors from them (Radin 26). The intelligence
and prowess necessary to hunt game has been reduced to the cunning and
machismo required to stalk money and women.

As well as telling modified versions of hunting stories, Blowsnake
provides a coup tale. He explains that his father and grandfather had
always encouraged him to seek war honors from the spirits by fasting and
giving feasts. Thus Blowsnake and his comrades decide to obtain "some
external emblem of [their] bravery" so they could "wear head orna-
ments" at the dances (Radin 35). Blowsnake writes:

> We meant to kill an individual of another tribe, we meant to perform an act
> of bravery. . . . We had ropes along, too, for we intended to steal some
> horses as well as kill a man, if we met one. Horse-stealing was regarded as a
> praiseworthy feat and I had always admired the people who recounted the
> number of times they had stolen horses, at one of the Brave dances. That
> was why I did these things. (Radin 35–36)

They do, indeed, find a Potawatomi man and kill him. Blowsnake is the first to count coup: "I counted coup first and I announced my name as I gave a war whoop. I shouted 'Big-Winnebago has counted coup upon this man'" (Radin 36). In the old days, Blowsnake would have returned in victory to his camp, announced and recounted his coup, sung and danced at a warrior dance (where he would be entitled to wear a head ornament), and received the adulation of his people. Now, however, his father congratulates him in private: "My son, it is good. Your life is no longer an effeminate one" (Radin 36). But since they have to be careful of the laws of the whites, no public confirmation of his deed is possible. Even with all their care, Blowsnake is arrested, goes to prison, and stands trial for murder. His attempt "to perform an act of bravery" is regarded as cold-blooded murder by Euro-American law.

Recounting visions is a third traditional autobiographical form that Blowsnake incorporates into his account. Rather than recount a personal vision, its interpretation, and its significance to his life, he tells a shoddy history of his pseudovision. Because he is hungry after fasting for four days and because he wants "to appear great in the sight of the people" (Radin 9), he fakes a vision. Then he proceeds to misuse and finally to reject it, replacing it with his real, drug-induced visions during the peyote ceremony. In another incident before his conversion to peyote, he drunkenly boasts of being blessed by a "Grizzly-Bear-spirit," which gives him the power of being "uncontrollable" (Radin 27). Although he is, indeed, "uncontrollable," Blowsnake insists he was lying again and had never been blessed by such a spirit. Even after initiation into the Medicine Dance, with which Blowsnake is sorely disappointed because of the "deception" of the shooting and rebirth enactment, which he finds is only a ritual drama, he says: "I did not have the sensation of any change in me. All that I felt was that I had become a deceiver in one of Earthmaker's creations" (Radin 21).

Along with a vision, one usually received some kind of medicine, or power. Blowsnake claims to have such medicine; he even ensures a woman of an easy childbirth and succeeds. He also carries with him his courting medicine to help him have success with women. (If sheer number is any indication of success, Blowsnake's medicine is powerful stuff.) In general, though, his strongest "medicine" is alcohol, which, although powerful, is a degraded version of the Winnebago concept of medicine because it leads to deterioration rather than amelioration.

Finally, Blowsnake expresses himself through performance, or at least through descriptions of dramatic enactments. He participates in the

Medicine Dance, a medicine feast, and various ceremonies in which he sings and dances in traditional Winnebago fashion. Later he performs in traveling and/or seasonal shows, playing "Indian" for whites and earning money for drink. Just as his phony vision is a perverted form of a traditional Winnebago mode of personal narrative, his performance for whites is a diminished form of traditional dances. His performance does not link him to the spirits or to the tribe, but to a paycheck. Thus ritual drama for spiritual or social purposes becomes primarily a performance for economic ends.

As well as modifying traditional tribal forms of personal narrative in his autobiography, Blowsnake uses Euro-American forms. In fact, Brumble insists that like a Winnebago St. Augustine, Blowsnake " 'reinvented' the autobiography" since he "articulates an individual sense of the self" (118) and adapts "the confessional forms to the demands of autobiography" (121). Following a tradition of Indian autobiographers like William Apes and George Copway who wrote about their spiritual lives, Blowsnake's autobiography follows the basic Euro-American pattern of a conversion narrative.[23] When he joins the peyote religion, Blowsnake has to denounce the traditions of the conservative Winnebagos, whom he now calls, according to Radin's translation, "pagan Indians" (Radin 65). Thus he cuts his long hair; he gives up his courting medicine, tobacco, and polygamy; and he denounces his past, the Medicine Dance, and all traditional Winnebago beliefs. "Before (my conversion) I went about in a pitiable condition," confesses Blowsnake, "but now I am living happily" (Radin 67). This is the simplistic formula of a religious conversion: what went before is evil; what is now is holy. What is curious is that the peyote religion, which Blowsnake says is "the only holy thing that I have been aware of in all my life" (Radin 61), is a blend of the beliefs and symbols of both Winnebago and Christian traditions. This blend is suitable for Blowsnake, who, raised with the traditional values of the Winnebago, finds them inappropriate in his reservation life, constrained as it is by Euro-American law. The peyote religion, combining as it does Winnebago and Christian beliefs, is a fit emblem of the boundary culture to which Blowsnake found it so difficult to adjust.

Although Blowsnake wrote—not spoke, drew, or performed—his life history, he combines aspects of these more traditional modes of self-narration in his autobiography. In his account, tribal autobiographical forms are modified, if not diminished, since living the old ways is no longer possible in early-twentieth-century reservation life. Although Blowsnake uses the Euro-American pattern of the conversion narrative as his primary structure, he still expresses much of his personal narrative through traditional indigenous forms—stories of hunting, counting coups, pursuing visions, and performing ceremonies—updating these traditional forms to suit his new experience. His modifications often take the form of replacing an old subject matter with a new one (chasing women rather than buffalo, for instance), while retaining the basic narrative pattern. Blowsnake's conversion, then, is not the expected one from "pagan" to Christian, from Winnebago to Euro-American. Rather, his conversion is from an older concept of what it means to be Winnebago to an updated idea that borrows aspects from both traditional Winnebago and Euro-American cultures, transforming them into something new: the peyote religion, which comes to be known as the Native American Church.[24]

Mountain Wolf Woman

In 1958, thirty-eight years after Sam Blowsnake wrote his autobiography in the Winnebago syllabary, his sister Mountain Wolf Woman narrated her life story to her friend, adopted niece, and amanuensis, Nancy O. Lurie. Traveling from Black River Falls, Wisconsin, to Ann Arbor, Michigan, Mountain Wolf Woman stayed with the Luries for five weeks as a visiting relative. During that time, Mountain Wolf Woman spoke her life story in Winnebago into a tape recorder; then she "repeated the entire story on tape in English using the Winnebago recordings as a guide."[25] With the assistance of Mountain Wolf Woman's grandniece, Frances Thundercloud Wentz, Lurie translated the Winnebago into "literary English" (Lurie, Appendix B 94–95). According to anthropologist Lurie, Mountain Wolf Woman did not have the intense problems adjusting to reservation life that plagued her brother. Like him, she had a traditional Winnebago upbringing, and like him, she converted to the peyote religion. Unlike her brother, however, she made the transformation from the old ways to the new ways with apparent ease. According to Lurie, "Mountain Wolf Woman's autobiography is a predictable reflection of the greater self-confidence enjoyed by women in comparison to men in a culture undergoing rapid and destructive changes" (Preface xvi). Mountain Wolf Woman's "greater self-confidence" has to do with "the greater continuity and stability of female roles," as well as her older age at the time of relating her autobiography (she told her story at the age of seventy-four, while her brother wrote his before the age of forty-five), not to mention her favored status as the baby of the family (Lurie, Appendix B 101).

Lurie provides a candid and detailed explanation of when, why, and how she collected Mountain Wolf Woman's life history. In Appendix B, she acknowledges the "element of coercion" involved in the fact that she "manipulated the kinship structure for [her] own purposes" (Appendix B 93), asking her aunt for a favor that could not, because of the Winnebago sense of familial obligation, be denied her. She also describes her relationship with Mountain Wolf Woman, the interview setting (Lurie's home), her own editorial principles, Mountain Wolf Woman's character, Winnebago character in general, traditional Winnebago male and female roles, dominant themes, and Mountain Wolf Woman's storytelling skills. Throughout the autobiographical account, she adds footnotes to clarify meaning, tone, or performance. Mountain Wolf Woman, like Plenty-Coups and Pretty-Shield, was a gifted storyteller and "an accomplished mimic," often taking on the voices of various speakers (Lurie, Appendix B 95). Besides mimicking, she would often "relive events as she recalled them," crying or chuckling whenever she felt moved to do so (Lurie, Preface xvi). Lurie, however, makes no attempt to incorporate performance cues into Mountain Wolf Woman's translated narrative. Instead, she limits her commentary to footnotes, a preface, and an appendix. The familiar pattern of framing the life history of the speaker between the authenticating and expository sections of the editor continues. In Appendix A, Lurie includes Mountain Wolf Woman's first attempt at telling her life story—a very brief account that disappointed Lurie so evidently that Mountain Wolf Woman retold each story in fuller form.[26]

Mountain Wolf Woman's oral autobiography, tape-recorded by Lurie in 1958, relates her experiences of traveling, growing up, marrying, being initiated into the medicine lodge, converting to peyote, joining a Christian church, learning Winnebago medicines from her grandfather, and caring for her family. As Mountain Wolf Woman, whose name was given to her by an elderly woman from the Wolf clan, discusses the domestic details of food collection and preparation and family relations, she intersperses humorous anecdotes and old stories. Mountain Wolf Woman narrates a humorous personal story about how as a little girl gathering yellow waterlily roots with her mother and sisters, she imitated her older sister. Observing her sister tie a waterlily root in her belt (to ward off anything bad that might affect her pregnancy), the little girl did the same—much to the amusement of those gathered. Gretchen Bataille and Kathleen Sands point out that rather than "cast themselves in heroic molds," female Indian autobiographers tend "to concentrate on everyday events and activities and family crisis events" (8).[27] In general, this seems true of Mountain Wolf Woman's narrative.

In contrast to her brother's dramatic cultural and religious conflicts, which shape his autobiography, Mountain Wolf Woman's rather placid autobiographical account is anecdotal. According to Ruth Underhill, "No particular pattern appears other than the slow change from the life of an illiterate Indian food gatherer to that of a responsible church member who lives in a modern house, travels in Pullman trains, and believes in the Christian heaven."[28] Underhill's comments reveal her cultural bias, which assumes an evolution from "illiterate Indian food gatherer" to "responsible church member," as though living in the "modern" world necessarily erases one's Indian identity. Perhaps Mountain Wolf Woman's apparent lack of chronological structure is a more accurate reflection of the pattern of her life, which focused on the smaller fluctuations of daily life and family, rather than on the grander shifts of philosophical awakenings. Theorists of autobiography note a similar associational structure (rather than a linear narrative with identifiable beginnings, middles, and ends) and a similar emphasis on the minutiae of domestic detail (rather than on worldly actions) in the writings of many Euro-American women as well. Rather than assume "no particular pattern" other than the obvious pre-contact/post-contact experience, it is more appropriate to reconsider notions of what constitutes a "pattern." Focusing on the daily fluctuations of family relationships is suitable for a woman who had eleven children, thirty-eight grandchildren, and nine great-grandchildren, especially since she raised many of them herself.

Even though Mountain Wolf Woman focuses on family and communal activities and the domestic rhythms of her life, there are two dramatic personal incidents that she spends more than the usual time narrating. The events are related to each other and, not surprisingly, linked to family. Her education and her first marriage were personal crises for Mountain Wolf Woman. She criticizes her family for disrupting her education and for forcing her to marry an unworthy man. Mountain Wolf Woman explains that at age nine she attended school for two years in Tomah, Wisconsin. Although she enjoyed being there, her parents took her out of school to travel with the family as they followed the harvesting and hunting cycles. Years later, as a teenager, she returned to school. There she met Nancy Smith, an Oneida and "the girl's matron" (MWW 29). Together they cruised around on their bicycles, rode horses, participated in Indian dances, and enjoyed themselves. When her family suddenly removed her from school again, she had no idea why. "Alas, I was enjoying school so much," says Mountain Wolf Woman, "and they made me stop." She did not discover until she returned home that she was going to be married. Her mother explained: "It is your brother's doing. You must do whatever your brother says" (MWW 29). Because she could not embarrass her brother or violate the taboo that might end in suffering for him, Mountain Wolf Woman had to submit to his wishes and to this marriage (MWW 122 n.1). She found out from her mother how this came about. It seems her "older brother had been drinking and was asleep" (MWW 30). When Sam Blowsnake awoke, he found a man fanning mosquitoes from his face. To dispense a debt of gratitude for this kindness, her older brother promised his sister to the solicitous man.

Mountain Wolf Woman conveyed her anger and resentment even as she fulfilled her familial duties. As Mountain Wolf Woman's mother combed her weeping daughter's hair in preparation for her soon-to-be married status, she said: "Daughter, I prize you very much, but this matter cannot be helped. When you are older and know better, you can marry whomever you yourself think that you want to marry" (MWW 30). The dutiful daughter never forgot her mother's words. Throughout her description of the marriage arrangement (an economic exchange), the trials of the marriage, and the divorce, Mountain Wolf Woman refers to her first husband as "that man," refusing even to name him. After two children and several unhappy years with "that man," Mountain Wolf Woman left him. Shortly thereafter, once again with the intervention of a brother (this time her eldest brother, the true Crashing Thunder), and with her consent and approval, Mountain Wolf Woman married Bad Soldier, with whom she lived happily until his death in 1936.

Just as Pretty-Shield's narrative is punctuated by interruptions from grandchildren, an intrusion of contemporary Indian life on the stories of the past, family, particularly grandchildren, permeates Mountain Wolf Woman's story. Family relations in general serve as the central organizing device of her self-narration. Grandparents, parents, siblings, husbands, children, and grandchildren provide the context for Mountain Wolf Woman's life. She ends her narrative with accounts of corresponding with her children now "scattered over great distances" (70), raising her grandchildren, and narrating her life story to her "niece." Family relations, then, determine the scope and nature of her life and even its narration. With her Winnebago sense of relatedness, Mountain Wolf Woman's notion of family extends beyond biological connections. One brief anecdote illustrates this. On a trip to Oregon to visit one of her daughters, she learned that a son of hers had been wounded in Germany. On her train trip back to Wisconsin, she and her granddaughter sat at a table in the dining car with two young men "wearing khaki uniforms" (MWW 76). "I am going to eat with my sons," she said to them. " 'Whenever I see somebody wearing khaki, I always think that might be my son.' The boy across from me got up," she continues. " 'My mother died when I was born. I never had a mother. Now I have a mother,' he said. Then he shook my hand" (MWW 76). The worried mother, far from her Wisconsin home and her wounded son, mothered those who were near.

Mountain Wolf Woman shares certain themes with Plenty-Coups, Pretty-Shield, and Sam Blowsnake. Like them, she discusses her participation in dances and ceremonies. Also, she continues to highlight the differences between the old days and the present. Even though she has adjusted to the new ways and does not seem embittered about such enforced change, she recalls that in the old days, "[w]e respected the old people, but today they do not respect the old people" (17). Since she is now one of "the old people," this change has deep meaning for her personally. Likewise, she speaks wistfully of the days when "Indians were real Indians" (25).

Performance, Ceremony, and Self-Narration

As well as pictographic, oral, and written transitional autobiographies (which often incorporate dramatic forms), there continued to be performances geared toward self-narration. Ceremonies and dances, for a time, continued in traditional ways. When it was no longer possible to acquire certain ceremonial necessities, such as buffalo hides for the Plains Indian Sun Dance, or when ceremonial gatherings were outlawed, modifications of the old ways became a necessity. It is important to remember, though, that such ceremonies were always changing, even in "the old days."

The adaptability of ceremonial traditions was illustrated by anthropologist Claire Farrer, who documented how autobiography can become ritual. In July 1977, Farrer observed "the annual summer girls' puberty ceremony at Mescalero, New Mexico on the Mescalero Apache Indian Reservation." Steve Church inherited the rights to the song and design of one of the Mountain God dance groups, rights formerly owned by Carl Nelson, older brother of dancer Bill. Church's "group of Mountain God dancers always includes at least one clown sporting the long ears" of a mule, notes Farrer. Bill Nelson explained that a joke was embedded therein. It seems that during the 1916 performance, a mule "broke loose and wrapped his rope around a group of dancers," breaking their ceremonial horns and creating chaos. Thereafter, Carl, the dance group owner at the time, "incorporated the mule escapade into the costuming of the clowns he painted." Since 1916, then, his mule-earred clowns have become part of a sacred ritual. Only a few people know the origin of the mule ears. Although these clowns are interpreted variously, what is significant is that "an actual event has moved into ritual and become so much a part of it that most people think of the event as having only a ritual context."[29] Just as ceremonies are sometimes incorporated into native autobiographies, at times autobiographical elements find their way into ceremonies.

One of the most striking examples of such a change in the ceremonies and dances, a kind of tribal self-narration, is their being opened to non-Indian audiences. A related phenomenon is the Indian show, such as Buffalo Bill's Wild West Show, which hired Indians to dress in traditional costumes, perform native dances, sing tribal songs, and reenact historic battles against the whites. Such pageants sometimes served to educate Euro-American audiences about Indian ways as well as to entertain them. Often, though, this "education" presented a romanticized picture of "the noble savage" or a brutal image of "the barbarous red man" or an ethnographic presentation of a historical curiosity.[30] Within the tribes themselves, however, dancing continued, but only in ways that would not threaten white authorities, who tended to fear large gatherings of Indians.

Plenty-Coups, Pretty-Shield, Sam Blowsnake, and Mountain Wolf Woman all lived in the troubled boundary culture of the reservation. The Crows—Plenty-Coups and Pretty-Shield—both elders when they narrated their life stories around 1930, remember pre-reservation life vividly. The Winnebagos—Sam Blowsnake and Mountain Wolf Woman— one an adolescent and one a child during the transition to reservation life, remember pre-reservation life primarily from childhood experiences and family accounts. Unlike the others, who were elders at the time of narrating their personal stories, Blowsnake was only about forty-five years old when he wrote his autobiographical narrative in the Winnebago syllabary. In contrast to Plenty-Coups, who focused his oral narrative on his pre-reservation martial and spiritual achievements, Blowsnake directed his written personal narrative to the post-reservation impossibility of living a traditional Winnebago life. What we know of the life stories of these four individuals is due to the efforts of Frank Linderman, Paul Radin, and Nancy O. Lurie, who were responsible for the published forms of their life histories. Linderman, the trapper, hunter, and dweller among Indians, had assistants to translate the spoken Crow into English, while he translated sign language into English and recorded both translations in writing. As a friend of Plenty-Coups, an acquaintance of Pretty-Shield, and a person familiar with Indian ways, Linderman wrote vivid autobiographical narratives of these two Crow elders. The anthropologists Radin and Lurie both asserted their wishes for a Winnebago life story. Radin pressured the reluctant Blowsnake until economic hardship made writing an autobiographical narrative thinkable, and Lurie asked her adopted aunt for a favor that could not be refused. While all three editors explain the circumstances of collection ,and provide additional cultural information for clarification, it is not surprising that the anthropologists include footnotes, whereas Linderman incorporates such material into his story. The life stories of the four Native Americans solicited, translated, recorded (except in Blowsnake's case), and edited by the three editors illustrate some of the variety of collaborative autobiography from 1920 to 1958. Spoken, signed, and written autobiographical narratives were constructed for Euro-American editors, who were responsible for shaping and publishing the final account.

Read together, the life histories of Plenty-Coups, Pretty-Shield, Sam Blowsnake, and Mountain Wolf Woman provide an interesting intratribal gender dialogue. While Native American autobiographers, in general, seem to narrate a relational identity, the sense of interrelatedness is intensified for native women, who were responsible for sustaining families. This is particularly evident in the female autobiographers' dominant focus on family relationships. Both Pretty-Shield and Mountain Wolf Woman wove the stories of their children and grandchildren into their own narratives. At the same time, they unraveled (or at least reconstructed the pattern of) the male stories narrated before. And both women literally had the last word. Pretty-Shield, who told her story two years later than Plenty-Coups, edited Plenty-Coups' male-dominated tribal history. She insisted on telling Linderman about the women warriors whom the men refuse to mention and about a dramatic incident that Plenty-Coups had omitted from his personal narrative. Similarly, almost forty years after Blowsnake wrote his autobiography, Mountain Wolf Woman recast her brother's heroic story in a more critical light. Both women, then, focused on family relationships, community connections, and revisionist tribal histories.

Traditional Native American modes of oral self-narration continued to be evident in the transitional autobiographies of the nineteenth and twentieth centuries. Often these forms were modified to make them comprehensible to a popular or an academic Euro-American audience. Such Indian self-narrations were supplemented by commentary from ethnographers (like Radin and Lurie) and editors (like Linderman) who were often responsible for the final shape of the autobiography as well as its original solicitation. Thus as Native Americans and Euro-Americans clashed and negotiated historically, representatives of these two distinct cultures interacted textually within the pages of transitional autobiography. As Euro-American editors attempted to translate Native American languages, cultures, and personalities into their own language and cultural framework, one result was a blend of traditional Native American oral forms of personal history and Euro-American written modes of autobiography. Such a life story, ''a self-contained fiction,''[31] is an attempt to refashion one's self. If autobiography is an act of self-construction, Native American transitional autobiography is an act of self-reconstruction in which a Native American conceives of himself or herself anew (often reassembling a fragmented tribal identity) as a result of this boundary-culture encounter.

5 / Oral and Written Collaborative Autobiography: Nicholas Black Elk and Charles Alexander Eastman

Black Elk and Charles Alexander Eastman lived during a traumatic transition period for Native Americans. In the final quarter of the nineteenth century, the last armed Indian resistance to U.S. expansionism was destroyed and Indians were forced onto reservations. During this troubled period, life histories of tribal people were solicited by friends, historians, and ethnologists who then translated spoken native languages into written English. Such oral autobiographies as Black Elk's, with their problems of authority and audience, reflect a dual perspective—the raconteur's and the editor's. Even when the native informant wrote his or her own life history, as did Charles Eastman, he or she reflected a double voice—the Native American and the Euro-American—creating what H. David Brumble calls a "bicultural document." [1] Both oral (often referred to as "as-told-to") and written autobiographies of the late nineteenth and early twentieth centuries record the Indian's encounter with aggressive colonialism, with the conflict between retaining an Indian identity and being coerced into adopting an Anglo one.

Like the pictographic sketchbooks of Zo-Tom, Howling Wolf, and White Bull (discussed in Chapter 3), early-twentieth-century Native American autobiographies often reflect traditional tribal autobiographical forms modified to suit an Anglo audience. The cultural and literary blending inherent in these transitional autobiographies reflects the boundary culture in which a Native American narrator and a white editor work together to give expression to a life. While the literary boundary culture of the resulting text was generally dominated by a Euro-American editor,

Roberta Rubenstein reminds us that "the very concept of boundary itself is fluid." [2] Two of the best known Indian autobiographers of the early twentieth century are Black Elk and Ohiyesa, better known as Charles Eastman. Both were born before 1890 (the date of the Wounded Knee Massacre and the official announcement of the closing of the frontier) and experienced pre-reservation life. Although these two men attempted to negotiate with Euro-American society by telling/writing the stories of their lives and by trying to explain their cultures, they were extremely different individuals with drastically opposing narratives to tell. Black Elk, Oglala holy man and Catholic catechist, focused on pre-reservation life and his great vision, while Ohiyesa, Santee Sioux and physician–educator, described pre-reservation life, but emphasized post-reservation life and his attempt to be acculturated into Euro-American society. Both were influenced by Euro-American collaborators, but in different ways. Black Elk, a non-English-speaking Lakota, relied on John G. Neihardt, the poet laureate of Nebraska, to shape his story in English. Eastman, who was well versed in English, wrote his autobiography in English with the editorial assistance of his Euro-American wife. Together, Black Elk and Charles Eastman illustrate two historical streams of Native American autobiography.

Nicholas Black Elk

Black Elk Speaks (1932) is the most renowned Native American auto-biography ever published. Since its republication in 1961, it has been considered by scholars in anthropology, history, sociology, philosophy, religion, and literature. While Vine Deloria, Jr., calls *Black Elk Speaks* "a North American bible of all tribes" and concludes that "the question of Neihardt's literary intrusions into Black Elk's system of beliefs" does not really matter, [3] many scholars have focused precisely on the nature of the relationship between Black Elk and Neihardt. Robert F. Sayre, the first to write about *Black Elk Speaks* as "Indian autobiography," was interested in "the role of vision and prophecy in culture" and "the process by which the symbols are generated and passed on." [4] After visiting John G. Neihardt and reading part of the original manuscript of *Black Elk Speaks* in 1970, Sayre concluded that relations between Neihardt and Black Elk were "outstanding" and that Neihardt did editorial justice to Black Elk's unique voice.

Seven months later, Sally McCluskey visited the ailing Neihardt. She affirms Sayre's impressions of the relationship between Neihardt and Black Elk, emphasizing Neihardt as "the shaping intelligence and lyric voice of the book."[5] To clarify his role in telling Black Elk's story, Neihardt told McCluskey that *"Black Elk Speaks* is a work of art with two collaborators, the chief one being Black Elk. My function was both creative and editorial" (McCluskey 238). Responsible for the eloquent beginning and ending of the book (the first and last three paragraphs, undoubtedly the most often quoted passages), Neihardt describes his work not as mere translation, but as *"transformation"* (McCluskey 238–239). Unlike most other Euro-American editors, Neihardt insists that Black Elk's story was told not merely *to* him, but *through* him. He claims, then, not only to have reported Black Elk's words, but to have translated Black Elk's Lakota personality and life for a non-Indian audience.

Both Sayre and McCluskey agree that Black Elk's relationship with Neihardt was an exceptionally good one.[6] Unlike most other narrator–editor relationships in which a Euro-American anthropologist or historian solicited a "native informant," Black Elk, so the story goes, seemed to select Neihardt as much as Neihardt chose him. Rather than a working relationship, they had a kinship relationship: Black Elk adopted Neihardt as his spiritual son in order to pass on his knowledge to him. Because of this deeply felt collaboration, Carol Holly feels that *Black Elk Speaks* is a "genuine marriage between native American consciousness and western literary form" and is thus "the first Indian autobiography." Sharing Holly's focus on autobiography, Albert E. Stone discusses *Black Elk Speaks* as "one paradigm of modern spiritual autobiography."[7] Such conclusions, based on the assumption that Neihardt is a transparent gauze through which Black Elk's life is filtered rather than a "shaping force," seem incomplete today. The political implications of an individual from a dominant culture shaping the experience of a member of a "minority" culture are worrisome. It is important to keep in mind the consequences of an Anglo majority creating the Other in the image of its self.

Acknowledging Neihardt's contributions to Black Elk's autobiography, some critics emphasize Neihardt's literary artifice. Kenneth Lincoln, for one, realizes that " 'Black Elk' is an Anglicized character drawn from the living visionary," but he does not object to Neihardt's creation of Black Elk's literary persona. Similarly, Calvin Fast Wolf and Mary Sacharoff-Fast Wolf note Neihardt's "conceptualization of Black Elk's vision," particularly "many things which are not Lakota" and a "Christian overlay,'' but they conclude that Black Elk's account of his life and vision is still evident. While agreeing that Neihardt's literary and philosophical sensibilities dominate Black Elk's story, Arnold Krupat places *Black Elk Speaks* in a Western literary tradition. According to Krupat, Neihardt's telling of Black Elk's life story is ''romantic in emplotment,'' presenting Black Elk not as a tragic character, but as '' 'the typical hero of romance.' '' Thomas Couser, on the contrary, sees Neihardt's editorial decisions as evidence of his ethnocentrism. He accuses Neihardt of seeing Black Elk ''through a gloss, whitely''; he calls the narrative ''an act of ventriloquism''; and he condemns the book as a reenactment of the oppression of Indians.[8]

In a letter addressed to ''Friends'' and dated September 20, 1934, Black Elk reveals a more troubling vision of his relationship with John G. Neihardt. Identifying Neihardt as ''a white man'' who asked him ''to make a story book with him,'' Black Elk explains a monetary arrangement not mentioned by Neihardt in the autobiography: ''He promised me that if he completed and publish [*sic*] this book he was to pay half of the price of each book. I trusted him and finished the story of my life for him.'' When the book was published, Black Elk wrote to Neihardt inquiring about payment, and according to Black Elk, Neihardt claimed he had not ''seen a cent from the book.'' ''By this,'' explains Black Elk, ''I know he was now dicieving [*sic*] me about the whole business.'' In addition, Black Elk says he asked Neihardt ''to put at the end of this story that I was not a pagan but have been converted into the Catholic Church in which I work as a Catechist for more than 25 years. I've quit all these pagan works.'' Black Elk asks that if his request to clarify his Catholicism and to receive his payment cannot be made, that ''this book of my life will be null and void.'' He concludes his letter by stating his concern for his soul, apologizing for his ''mistake'' (presumably in talking to Neihardt about Lakota spirituality) and asking witnesses to affirm his words. The letter is signed ''Nick Black Elk,'' and he emphasizes this by adding a postscript: ''My name is not Amerdian [*sic*] but he is lying about my name.''[9] Fast Wolf and Sacharoff-Fast Wolf believe that this letter was probably dictated by Black Elk, but written for him by his wife. Such an epistle may have been yet another means to appease the concentrated disapproval of the Jesuit priests who did not want one of their catechists to backslide (Fast Wolf and Sacharoff-Fast Wolf 1–2).

With Raymond J. DeMallie's 1984 publication of a synthesis of Neihardt's original stenographic notes and the subsequent typed manuscript of Neihardt's 1931 interviews with Black Elk (both recorded by Neihardt's daughter, Enid), the distinction between what Black Elk said and what Neihardt added, changed, and arranged is somewhat clarified.[10] For instance, Neihardt edited out many of Black Elk's accounts of his warlike achievements and attitudes, his interactions with whites before joining the Wild West Show, and his active Catholicism. Likewise, he deemphasized the importance of the Thunder-Beings in Black Elk's vision and added historical accounts of Sioux battles and religious movements. Even more surprising, as Michael Castro has noted, is that Neihardt invented parts of Black Elk's vision, such as the fourth ascent (89–90). In effect, Neihardt was creating the autobiographical Black Elk, the Lakota seer—brave, but not too warlike; exposed to whites, but not too familiar with them—thereby embedding him in the Euro-American myth of the frontier West. Neihardt was not interested in anthropological facts, however, but in poetic truth. In his 1971 preface, Neihardt explains that "it was not the facts that mattered most"; rather, he wished "to re-create in English the mood and manner of the old man's narrative."[11]

DeMallie's short biography of Black Elk describes Black Elk's active participation as a Catholic catechist and as a performer in Duhamel's Sioux Indian pageant in the Black Hills, thus confounding Anglo expectations of Black Elk as a *wicaśa wakan* (Lakota holy man) and as a spokesman for Lakota tradition. Black Elk's great-granddaughter, Charlotte Black Elk, says she has fifteen letters dictated by her great-grandfather and written down by his relatives. When the time is right, she will make them accessible to the public. There is still much to learn about Black Elk. But a person's factual life is always different from his or her imagined life as shaped and trimmed into an autobiographical mode. Life outside the pages of autobiography has neither the clear beginnings nor the obvious endings that lend life-turned-art found in autobiography such pattern. When one's experiences are translated, arranged, and edited by another person, especially a person from another culture, the "transformation," as Neihardt calls it, from lived to written life is magnified.

Born around 1863, Black Elk was raised as a traditional Oglala Lakota, but through economic, military, and political interaction he and his people were influenced consistently by Euro-American culture as well. Having been shaped by both Lakota and, to a lesser extent, Euro-American cultures, Black Elk synthesized these two different worlds.

Some of this cultural complexity was removed by Neihardt, who wished to create the "genuine" Black Elk, but who created instead a character who sometimes resembles a saintly version of Chingachgook—a literary symbol of the noble, doomed red man. The cultural encounter between Neihardt and Black Elk is reenacted in the literary boundary culture of this collaborative autobiography.

The Black Elk–Neihardt collaboration is more complex than most such joint autobiographical efforts. Sitting on the South Dakota plains with a gathering of family and old friends, Black Elk spoke in Lakota, which his son, Benjamin, translated into English. Neihardt interrupted this process to ask about issues and incidents he wished to have elaborated or explained. Neihardt's rewording of Ben's English translations of Black Elk's Lakota words was transcribed by Neihardt's daughter, Enid, who later typed the transcript. Thus Enid's stenographic notes were not "a verbatim record of Black Elk's words, but a rephrasing in comprehensible English" (DeMallie 32). From these transcriptions, Neihardt organized and edited *Black Elk Speaks*. Such a multilayered dialogic transmission of information compounds Neihardt's mediation of Black Elk's words as well as the complexity of the final form.

Neihardt was not the only one to collaborate with Black Elk. Just as tribal members gathered to corroborate, hear, and participate in coup tales, Fire Thunder, Standing Bear, Iron Hawk, and Holy Black Tail Deer met with Black Elk and Neihardt to modify, add to, and affirm Black Elk's stories. Such a collaborative team underscores Black Elk's tribal identity and, at the same time, substantiates his individual actions. Fire Thunder offers another perspective on important battles, and Standing Bear clarifies Black Elk's accounts of his vision. Although traditional to Lakota oral personal narrative, this collaboration was suggested by Neihardt in a November 6, 1930, letter to Black Elk:

> I feel that the whole story of your life ought to be written truthfully by somebody with the right feeling and understanding of your people and of their great history. My idea is to come back to the reservation next spring . . . and have a number of meetings with you and your old friends among the Oglalas who have shared the great history of your race, during the past half century or more.
>
> I would want you to tell the story of your life beginning at the beginning and going straight through to Wounded Knee. . . .
>
> So, you see, this book would be not only the story of your life, but the story of the life of your people. . . . (DeMallie 29)

Perhaps Neihardt was sensitive to Black Elk's sense of a tribal identity. Perhaps he was simply pursuing his own interests in writing about Sioux history. Or perhaps Neihardt suggested this, as he says to Black Elk later in the same letter, because he wanted "to tell the things that you and your friends know" (DeMallie 29). The collaboration between Black Elk and his old friends, then, was as much Neihardt's idea as it was Black Elk's wish.

What is clear is that Neihardt himself emphasizes the Lakota sense of communal identity. The first three paragraphs of *Black Elk Speaks* are Neihardt's invention, and the first line introduces the Lakota reticence to single oneself out as well as the scope of the autobiography:

> My friend, I am going to tell you the story of my life, as you wish; and if it were only the story of my life I think I would not tell it; for what is one man that he should make much of his winters, even when they bend him like a heavy snow?[12]

On behalf of Black Elk, Neihardt insists that this is not Black Elk's story alone, but the story of all his people. Not surprisingly, Neihardt used a similar phrase in several of his other writings. Employed by the Bureau of Indian Affairs to write "a cultural history of the Oglala Sioux," Neihardt returned to Pine Ridge in 1944. There he interviewed Eagle Elk, an old Lakota man, as well as Black Elk. His interviews with Black Elk make up "a historical summary of Lakota culture," while his interview with Eagle Elk provided him with details of Eagle Elk's life. *When the Tree Flowered,* a "fictional autobiography" based on Neihardt's 1944 interviews with Eagle Elk and Black Elk, "follows the life of Eagle Elk, but incorporates experiences from Black Elk's life as well" (DeMallie 72, 299). In the novel, Eagle Voice, an old Lakota man, sits inside a tipi with Neihardt and begins his reminiscences like this: "It will be good to remember, as you wish."[13] The phrase "as you wish" in *Black Elk Speaks* and *When the Tree Flowered* relieves both Black Elk and the fictional Eagle Voice from any potential criticism of vanity. Both men have told their stories only on request.

In the third paragraph of *Black Elk Speaks,* Neihardt, speaking for Black Elk, writes:

> This, then, is not the tale of a great hunter or a great warrior, or of a great traveler. . . . I know it was the story of a mighty vision given to a man too weak to use it; of a holy tree that should have flourished . . . , and of a people's dream that died in bloody snow. (Black Elk 1–2)

Neihardt offers a beautifully paralleled description of what this tale is *not:* it is not a story of individual worldly accomplishments. He replaces the vacancy left by this negative description with what the story *is:* it is a tale of tribal spiritual destruction.

Neihardt used this imagery and parallelism even earlier in a story included in his 1907 collection, *Indian Tales and Others*. In his first story, "The Singer of the Ache," we see a precursor to the third paragraph of *Black Elk Speaks*. In the fictional voice of an old Omaha, he insists that the story of Moon-Walker is "a story of one who walked not with his people, but with a dream."[14] Having had a wondrous vision, Moon-Walker tells his dream to his parents, who say: "This is not a warrior's dream, nor is it the dream of a Holy Man; nor yet is it the vision of a mighty bison hunter" (Neihardt 5). Just as Neihardt's description of Moon-Walker's dream presents the standard range of role possibilities for an Omaha male—warrior, medicine man, and hunter—his description of Black Elk's autobiography, twenty-four years later, offers several of the common roles for a Lakota male—hunter, warrior, and traveler. Both statements underscore the unique natures of Moon-Walker and Black Elk by making the reader aware of a larger context of Indian activities. The point here, though, is that Neihardt's style of telling "Indian" tales is evident. Despite Neihardt's many contributions, though, versions of Lakota autobiographical forms are found in Black Elk's autobiography. Discussion here will be limited to tracing traditional Lakota autobiographical forms and Black Elk's and Neihardt's modifications of them in *Black Elk Speaks*.

Traditional Lakota Orality:
Mythical and Historical Personal Narratives

From the beginning, the oral nature of Black Elk's autobiography is clear. The title, *Black Elk Speaks,* prepares the reader to *hear* a voice, rather than merely to *read* a text. Neihardt further accentuates the orality of the book when he begins the first chapter, "The Offering of the Pipe," with the note: "Black Elk Speaks." Throughout the book, he identifies speakers much as a dramatic script identifies the lines of each character. Although Neihardt seems merely to identify these speakers, in fact he directs them.

Neihardt begins Black Elk's story with an explanation of the symbolism of the pipe, a necessary service for the non-Lakota reader. Black Elk then proceeds to tell the story of the origin of the pipe and to offer the pipe with prayer. Storytelling—in this case, telling the story of White Buffalo Woman—educates and unites the reader/listener in the mythic origins of Lakota ceremony. Such a story is known as *Ehani Woyakapi* (legend), one of the three traditional Lakota oral forms of narrative. The other two forms are *Woyakapi* (true stories) and *Ohunkakapi* (fiction).[15] Black Elk's life story, then, can be considered *Woyakapi* that incorporates *Ehani Woyakapi*.

Several formulaic phrases reveal the oral nature of Black Elk's words. In telling an *Ehani Woyakapi*, the legend of White Buffalo Woman, he begins, "A very long time ago, they say . . ." (Black Elk 3). The first clause sets the scene in the distant past and begins the story, much like the traditional Western story opening, "Once upon a time. . . ." The second clause, "they say," is a storytelling formula among many Native American tribes. "They say" removes the teller from the role of author to the role of mediator. The story is passed along from those who came before, not created by the storyteller on the spot. Karl Kroeber, describing a Kato story in which *ya'nee* (they say) occurs after almost every sentence, says the term has the following effect: "This is not my story, not a personal report, but a traditional mythological event."[16] Kroeber speculates that the phrase serves also as "a rhythmic marker" (6). Likewise, in Navajo storytelling, the phrase *jiní* (it is said) appears frequently.[17] Since "they say" does not appear in the stenographic notes, it seems likely that Neihardt includes the phrase to enhance the oral dimensions of the book.

In the midst of the White Buffalo Woman myth is a song, another oral component of the work. White Buffalo Woman sings:

> With visible breath I am walking.
> A voice I am sending as I walk.
> In a sacred manner I am walking.
> With visible tracks I am walking.
> In a sacred manner I am walking. (Black Elk 4)

In the stenographic notes, Neihardt records Black Elk's words as follows: "She sang a song as she entered the tipi" (DeMallie 284). DeMallie does not clarify whether Black Elk sang this song or spoke it. But Black Elk's status as a holy man, his singing in the Duhamel pageant and in healing ceremonies, and Neihardt's phrase "this is what she sang" suggest that Black Elk did indeed sing the words. If Black Elk attempted to sing his sacred songs "in a crude wooden gondola seven hundred feet up the mountain on the aerial tramway" to Mount Rushmore, as DeMallie suggests (65), he almost certainly sang the songs as he sat comfortably on the prairie with Neihardt and friends.

White Buffalo Woman's song has many of the characteristics of traditional Native American oral poetry. Repetition of words, phrases, and syntax is one. The present progressive phrase, "I am walking," introduced in line 1, and repeated in lines 3 to 5 (and varied in line 2 to the simple present: "I walk"), emphasizes the self in motion in a perpetual present. In line 1, the prepositional phrase, "With visible breath," modifies the person walking. White Buffalo Woman sings, and from her mouth comes "a white cloud that was good to smell" (Black Elk 4). Her song leads directly to her message to the Lakota and to her gift of the sacred pipe, a means of prayer for the people. This phrase has a parallel in line 4, in which her tracks, rather than her breath, are visible. Line 2 offers rhythmic and syntactic variety in the song, while echoing the idea in line 1 (singing and walking). Line 4 repeats syntactically line 1, but replaces the prepositional phrase with another that emphasizes the "visible tracks" of walking. The final line repeats the third. Instead of Western word rhyme, such repetitious syntactic rhyming serves as a mnemonic device to help the singer remember the words, as a strategy to build poetic intensity, and as an aesthetic principle to please the listeners.

This is not the only song in Black Elk's life story. No fewer than thirty-four songs are included. White Buffalo Woman's song, however, is the only song associated with Lakota legend. Twenty-eight of the thirty-four songs are from Black Elk's vision and/or are used in ceremonies. Four songs deal with battle, and only one with childhood. Black Elk may sing these songs for Neihardt, but they arise from many distinct voices. Everyone sings: the black stallion and the Grandfathers in his vision; the medicine men Black Road, Bear Sings, Fox Belly, and Running Elk; the *heyoka* (sacred clown) Wachpanne; the daybreak star; the warriors after the Custer battle; and occasionally the entire tribe. The weaving together of these songs from so many varied voices provides an oral texture to the book. Neihardt, then, not only directs Black Elk's voice, but also orchestrates an entire choral universe.

Tales of Hunting and Battle

A more secular oral mode is found in Black Elk's *Woyakapi* (true accounts). In particular, Black Elk and his friends—Standing Bear, Fire

Thunder, and Iron Hawk—narrate many stories of hunting and warring. In the process, they offer multiple points of view. The older warriors provide accounts about incidents in which Black Elk was too young to have participated as well as corroborations, explanations, justifications, and alternative perspectives. One key addition to this many-voiced narration is the marked editorials and elaborate justifications directed to white readers. In Chapter 4, Black Elk recalls a bison hunt he observed as a child, but it is Standing Bear who recounts the story as a participant:

> I remember that hunt, for before that time I had only killed a calf. I was thirteen years old and supposed to be a man, so I made up my mind I'd get a yearling. . . . I think I hit his heart, for he began to wobble as he ran. . . . Hunters cried "Yuhoo!" once when they killed, but this was my first big bison, and I just kept on yelling "Yuhoo!" People must have thought I was killing a whole herd, the way I yelled. (Black Elk 57)

This humorous account is a contracted version of the interview record in which it is Standing Bear, not Black Elk, as Neihardt would have us believe, who describes the people preparing for "the making of meat" and the scouts reporting the location of the buffalo (DeMallie 143). Although usually more serious in tone, such hunting stories, like those told and depicted by Zo-Tom, Howling Wolf, and Plenty-coups (Chapters 3 and 4), were shared routinely with family and community. Including them in Black Elk's life story provides a vivid picture of one of the important tribal activities of Lakota men.

More frequently than hunting stories, Neihardt incorporates battle narratives into Black Elk's life story. This reflects Neihardt's interest in Sioux history and an Anglo audience's fascination with Plains Indian warriors as well as the nineteenth-century Lakota warrior culture. The Battle of the Hundred Slain, better known as the Fetterman Fight (1866), is the first of numerous military engagements described. Since Black Elk was only three years old at the time of this battle, he recalls only that "it was a time when everything seemed troubled and afraid" (Black Elk 8). From his present perspective, though, Black Elk offers a rationale for the bloodshed:

> Once we were happy in our own country and we were seldom hungry, for then the two-leggeds and the four-leggeds lived together like relatives, and there was plenty for them and for us. But the Wasichus came, and they have made little islands for the four-leggeds, and always these islands are becoming smaller, for around them surges the gnawing flood of the Wasichu; and it is dirty with lies and greed. (9)

When the *Wasichus* (pronounced Wa-shee'-chu and translated as "white people") built a fort nearby, the Lakota, along with their friends the Shyela (the Cheyennes) and the Blue Clouds (the Arapahoes), "went on the warpath against the soldiers" (Black Elk 10). Fire Thunder, a sixteen-year-old warrior at that time, now an eighty-three-year-old man, describes how they tricked the soldiers into leaving the fort and fought until "there was nobody left of the soldiers" (Black Elk 13). Later, he describes the Attacking of the Wagons, or the Wagon Box Fight (1867), in which the Lakota were defeated because of the soldiers' breech-loading Springfields (DeMallie 108).

Another story of battle, this time told by Black Elk, is the skirmish between his band and some *Wasichus* who were "part of the river of Wasichus that was running into the Black Hills" (Black Elk 93) in search of the "yellow metal" (Black Elk 81). As he describes the incident, Black Elk is careful to note that the whites shot first:

> They shot at our scouts, and we decided we would attack them. When the war party was getting ready, I made up my mind that, small as I was, I might as well die there, and if I did, maybe I'd be known. . . . When the Wasichus saw us coming, they put their wagons in a circle and got inside with their oxen. We rode around and around them in a wide circle that kept getting narrower. . . . While we were riding around the wagons, we were hanging low on the outside of the ponies and shooting under their necks. . . . The Wasichus shot fast at us from behind the wagons, and I could hear bullets whizzing, but they did not hit any of us. . . . This was my first fight. (93–94)

This seems to be a prototypical description of clashing "cowboys and Indians" seen on television Westerns, but Neihardt deemphasizes the violence. Although Black Elk describes reciprocal gunfire, this was a relatively harmless encounter in which no blood was shed on either side.

Just as Standing Bear and Fire Thunder have narrated their battle actions and have commented on their reasons for and methods of fighting, Iron Hawk, a Hunkpapa veteran of the battle with Three Stars (General George Crook) (1876), tells how as a fourteen-year-old he joined the smaller of two war parties. In "a wide valley there at the bend of the river with some bluffs and hills around it" (Black Elk 100), the warriors encountered *Wasichu* soldiers and Crows and joined the fight. After several retreats and advances during this "pitiful, long-stretched-out battle," Iron Hawk says, "[b]y now I was very scared, and I ran for my life" (Black Elk 101). Like the other battle accounts, Iron Hawk's is not a traditional coup tale. Although he identifies himself (''I am a Hunk-papa'') and locates himself geographically (''at the bend of the river''), he does not identify his associates (except as a small war party from the north end of camp). Neither can he describe their strategic position, since the fighting was ''all mixed up.'' Finally, in place of listing his brave achievements, he can describe only his fear.

Certainly the most famous battle Black Elk narrates, and the one he reports most extensively, is ''the rubbing out of Long Hair,'' or the Battle of Little Bighorn (1876), in which George Armstrong Custer's Seventh Cavalry was wiped out. As a young man of thirteen, Black Elk did not participate fully in the battle. Rather, he describes what he saw of the action from his observation point behind some bushes atop a hill:

> The valley went darker with dust and smoke, and there were only shadows and a big noise of many cries and hoofs and guns. . . . The soldiers were running upstream and we were all mixed there in the twilight and the great noise. I did not see much. . . . I was small and could not crowd in to where the soldiers were, so I did not kill anybody. There were so many ahead of me, and it was all dark and mixed up. (111)

Black Elk emphasizes the confusion of battle and his own distance from the violence. Furthermore, later in the book, Neihardt records Black Elk's words as ''people were stripping dead soldiers and putting the clothes on themselves'' (Black Elk 112). In the stenographic notes, however, Black Elk says: ''We stopped on a flat and everyone would get a soldier and strip him and put on his clothes for himself. We took everything they had—pistols, guns, ammunition, etc.'' (DeMallie 183). The shift from the first-person plural (''we'') of the interview record to the third-person plural (''people'' or they) of the autobiography reveals Neihardt's reluctance to implicate Black Elk in such aggressive actions. Even when a Lakota warrior orders young Black Elk to scalp a still-living soldier, Neihardt emphasizes Black Elk's mercy: ''I got off and started to do it. He had short hair and my knife was not very sharp. He ground his teeth. Then I shot him in the forehead and got his scalp . . .'' (Black Elk 112). Black Elk stops in the midst of scalping this soldier to kill him (an act of mercy at this point) before he continues his gruesome task. As well as Neihardt's desire to present Black Elk as a holy man of peace, Black Elk's Christian beliefs may have influenced how this episode was told.

Black Elk's Minneconjou friend, Standing Bear, likewise tells of the ''dust and smoke,'' ''the noise of all those hoofs and guns and cries'' that all seemed "like a bad dream" (Black Elk 116). Unlike Black Elk, however, Standing Bear actively participated in the battle:

> All at once I saw a soldier right beside me, and I leaned over and knocked him down with the butt of the six-shooter. I think I had already shot it empty, but I don't remember when. The soldier fell off and was under the hoofs. There were so many of us that I think we did not need guns. Just the hoofs would have been enough. (Black Elk 116)

Even here, Standing Bear's aggressive fighting is understated. Although Standing Bear fights actively, he does not shoot the soldier. The soldier is killed by falling beneath the hordes of hooves. Standing Bear admits, however, that they "were all crazy," ready to scalp any enemy, and in their frenzy scalping a friendly Cheyenne by mistake.

Iron Hawk was fourteen years old when Custer attacked. He is more straightforward about his battle deeds:

> I met a soldier on horseback, and I let him have it. The arrow went through from side to side under his ribs and it stuck out both sides. He screamed and took hold of his saddle horn and hung on, wobbling, with his head hanging down. I kept along beside him, and I took my heavy bow and struck him across the back of the neck. He fell from his saddle, and I got off and beat him to death with my bow. I kept on beating him awhile after he was dead. . . . These Wasichus wanted it, and they came to get it, and we gave it to them. (Black Elk 123)

This account is more violent than the rest, but the last sentence insists that the *Wasichus* got only what they deserved. While it neglects many of the characteristic components of a traditional Plains Indian coup tale, Iron Hawk's detailed description of how he killed the soldier emphasizes his brave battle accomplishments. Of course, since he is talking to Neihardt, he offers his reason for his actions. He certainly would not have to explain himself to his people, whom he has defended. The addition of such justification serves to educate non-Indian readers.

After the battle, Black Elk and other boys rode down to the battlefield, "shooting arrows into the Wasichus" who were "still alive and kicking" and stealing whatever they could find (Black Elk 125). After scalping a soldier for a little boy and stealing a gold watch, Black Elk says, "I was not sorry at all. I was a happy boy. Those Wasichus had come to kill our mothers and fathers and us, and it was our country" (127). Black Elk offers less justification for his actions in the stenographic notes. Rather, in the notes, he emphasizes the power of his vision. Because of his vision he "knew beforehand that this was going to happen" (DeMallie 194). Here, it seems, Neihardt once again diminishes any suggestion of Black Elk's warlike inclinations. There were considerable complications for Native American men who narrated their battles with Euro-Americans *for* Euro-Americans. An example similar to Neihardt's reduction of Black Elk's war activities is found in a few of the Plains Indian ledger books that some native men kept as war records. Native Americans knew that with the Euro-American reliance on the authority of paper, such books could be confiscated and used as incriminating evidence against them. As a consequence, sometimes the men would alter their pictographic ledger-book narratives to erase or obscure their participation in raids and battles against whites. One such artist–diarist whose work is in the Newberry Library converted square houses into circular tipis and dead white men into murdered Indians from hostile tribes. But the revisions are obvious, and the result is a clear superimposition of the edited image on top of the original. Such a dual narrative is evident to a lesser degree in Neihardt's editing of Black Elk's words.

While Neihardt provides multiple Lakota perspectives on the Custer battle, he presents only Black Elk's on the Wounded Knee Massacre. During the excruciating transition from freedom to reservation life, with its poverty, hunger, and overall deprivation, the suffering of Indian people was immeasurable. In 1889, a Sioux delegation brought their people details of a new religion, a new hope. Begun by the Paiute Messiah, Wovoka (also known as Jack Wilson), the Ghost Dance religion, "a religion of regeneration in the face of desperation,"[18] promised that whites would disappear, dead relatives would come back to life, the buffalo (which had been exterminated systematically by the United States government to ensure that the Plains Indians could no longer continue to hunt for a living) would return, and pre-contact Indian life would be restored. However, "an incompetent and fearful Indian agent began to see the Sioux Ghost Dance as an Indian uprising" (Spicer 92), and after his order to stop the practice of the Ghost Dance was not obeyed, he called for federal soldiers. They, in turn, wiped out three hundred, mostly unarmed, members of Big Foot's band whom they suspected because of their Ghost Dance activities. Black Elk had become involved, reluctantly at first, with the Ghost Dance. In fact, it was because of the Ghost Dance that he had not wanted to fight whites. After the Wounded Knee Massacre (1890), however, Black Elk changed his mind. Seeing the "butchered women and children and babies" (Black

Elk 262) scattered along the gulch had its effect. "After what I had seen over there," he says, "I wanted revenge; I wanted to kill" (264). At this point, he presents an account that is close to a traditional coup tale. He provides specific details of geographic and strategic locations ("We crossed White Clay Creek and followed it up, keeping on the west side. . . . [W]e could see that the Lakotas were on both sides of the creek and were shooting at soldiers, who were coming down the creek," 264–265), and he lists his brave achievements (he rescues Red Willow, Long Bear, and another man). Here, of course, the reader knows why Black Elk is ready to give up his pacifist ways.

In each of these battle accounts, the traditional form of the Plains Indian coup tale has been modified. Generally, there is less straightforward description of battle and more justification for fighting.[19] This is due, in large part, to a new audience, a historical distance, and a Euro-American editor. Because Black Elk, Iron Hawk, Standing Bear, and Fire Thunder speak to Neihardt, an Anglo author (and through him to a wider white audience), they feel the need to explain and justify fighting United States soldiers. Because their war experiences occurred at least half a century earlier, they are not fresh from battle with announcements about their war deeds, but are reminiscing about those long-ago battles. What might have been a coup tale told by a young warrior to his tribe in 1876 becomes, in 1931, war stories remembered by old men for a former enemy. Because Neihardt wishes to make Euro-American audiences sympathetic to Black Elk and because he is intrigued with Sioux spirituality, he emphasizes Black Elk the Lakota visionary rather than Black Elk the Sioux warrior. Finally, Black Elk's own Christian beliefs may have had a great deal to do with toning down the images of violence as well. If, as some scholars believe, Black Elk was, in his later years, a "creative theologian" attempting to integrate Christian and Lakota beliefs,[20] subduing the fierce image of the Sioux warrior may have been a vital part of such a calling.

Spiritual Autobiography: Black Elk's Vision

As well as telling hunting and battle tales, Black Elk presents another type of oral autobiography: the narrative of his vision. Black Elk not only *tells* his vision, however, but *shows* it and *performs* it as well, thus uniting oral, pictographic, and dramatic forms of personal narrative. As Robert Sayre points out, almost one-tenth of the book is devoted to recounting the vision Black Elk had when he was nine years old (516). This figure takes into consideration only his specific description of his "great vision." If we add the pages in which he refers to this central vision (and other lesser visions) and in which he enacts it, at least one-quarter of the book deals with Black Elk's vision(s). If such percentages mean anything, Black Elk's vision is important indeed. Blair Whitney, in fact, believes Black Elk's vision is "completely authentic and achieves the level of myth, prophecy, or revelation."[21]

Whether it is "completely authentic" or not, Black Elk's vision is central to his life and his life history. In Chapter 3 of his autobiography, Black Elk recalls his vision in detail, precisely noting symbols of Lakota cosmology, particularly the four cardinal directions: west (*Sapa*), north (*Ska*), east (*Xa*), and south (*Zi*). With the assistance of the Six Grand-fathers (the powers of the universe: four cardinal directions plus the earth and sky), Black Elk moves toward the goal of a Lakota quest: "to become a relative to all living things."[22] Reciting the vision at this point in his autobiography serves at least two purposes. Since it comes just after a brief chapter on his memories of boyhood (and Black Elk had his vision when he was only nine years old), the story of his vision fits chronologi-cally. The vision also presents the core of his life and the unifying aspect of his autobiography early on. From this point on, every event in Black Elk's life and every account in his autobiography will be measured against his "great vision."

Later, when Black Elk is seventeen years old and at the mercy of a "compelling fear," he tells his vision to the holy man Black Road. Rather than repeat the full account of his vision, Black Elk says, ". . . I told him about my vision, and when I was through he looked long at me . . ." (161). In the interview notes, Black Elk says that Black Road "asked me if I had had a vision and I told him briefly" (DeMallie 214). Telling his vision to an experienced *wicaśa wakan* for interpretation and guidance was the correct procedure for a young Lakota visionary. This would be told in much the same way Black Elk tells the reader about it in Chapter 3. Just as Black Road explains Black Elk's vision in terms of the young man's life, the reader interprets Black Elk's vision in the context of his autobiography.

As soon as Black Road hears about Black Elk's vision, he knows what has to be done. Black Elk must perform his vision in a series of ceremonies. Paula Gunn Allen explains such Native American ceremo-nies in a general way:

> The purpose of a ceremony is to integrate: to fuse the individual with his or her fellows, the community of people with that of other kingdoms, and this larger communal group with the worlds beyond this one. . . . In addition to this general purpose, each ceremony has its own specific purpose. This purpose usually varies from tribe to tribe and may be culture-specific. (*Studies* 10)

For the Lakota, a vision is not complete until it has been enacted in front of the tribe. In fact, Black Elk says that "a man who has a vision is not able to use the power of it until after he has performed the vision on earth for the people to see" (204). Black Elk, then, must bring his vision to life through performance. The people gather not to observe passively, but to participate actively. All the symbols in his vision come to life on earth through the ceremonies he performs. The first is the Horse Dance. In preparation for this, Black Elk teaches Black Road and Bear Sings the songs from his vision; he gathers "the four prettiest maidens in the village" to carry the gifts from the Grandfathers in his vision; he organizes twelve riders and horses, three for each direction; and he selects six old men to represent the Six Grandfathers (DeMallie 215). Since the "people are to appear just the way they did in the vision" (DeMallie 217), such attention to detail is essential. After performing the Horse Dance, everything was better. Black Elk's people "were renewed and happy," the horses were healthier, and Black Elk himself was inspired. Black Elk "was now recognized as a medicine man at the age of seventeen" (DeMallie 225).

Returning to the Oglalas at what is now Pine Ridge, South Dakota, Black Elk discovers that the people there, not having seen his Horse Dance, know nothing of his visions. He says, "The people there did not know that I had power and they were a burden to me and I thought they just had to know it" (DeMallie 227). To remedy this situation and to better understand his vision, Black Elk prepares himself for *hanblecheyapi* (crying for a vision), one of the seven rites of the Oglala Sioux.[23] After experiencing his Dog Vision, he must enact yet another ceremony—the *Heyoka* Ceremony. Once again, the people gathered to help him. In return, the *heyokas,* the sacred clowns, share some of their *wakan* (sacred power) with the people. After this, Black Elk performs his first cure. Later, Black Elk performs the Bison and the Elk Ceremonies and becomes "a success with the Great Spirit" (DeMallie 242).

Although Black Elk describes these ceremonies in words, he emphasizes their performance aspects. The Horse Dance, the *Heyoka*

Ceremony, and the Buffalo and Elk Ceremonies are tribal pageants, incorporating dance, song, and symbol that enact Black Elk's vision, acknowledge and release Black Elk's sacred power, and unite the people socially and spiritually. Oral and artistic modes of individual and communal narrative unite in these ritual dramas. In the Horse Dance, for instance, the participants express themselves not only through song and dance, but through ritual dress and decoration as well. Humans and animals alike are decorated. The riders are painted the color corresponding to the cardinal direction they represent and are adorned with a symbol representative of its gifts. The four riders from the west are painted black with a daybreak star; riders from the north are painted white with red lightning streaks; riders from the east and south are painted red and yellow, respectively, both with black lightning streaks. The maidens are dressed in scarlet, and their faces are painted red. Designs of the lightning and the spotted eagle, symbols of his vision, are painted on Black Elk's horse. Black Elk himself is painted red and, like the others, dressed in ritual paraphernalia. Both clothes and symbolic ornamentation accentuate the performance of Black Elk's personal vision that the community comes together to hear, to see, and to affirm. Thus personal experience is fulfilled in its communal expression.

Standing Bear's Paintings and Pictographs

As well as performances of his vision, Black Elk includes pictographs to narrate his martial and spiritual achievements. Standing Bear draws pictures to illustrate Black Elk's life history, and sixteen of them are published in the 1972 Pocket Book edition of *Black Elk Speaks*. Except for their materials (paper instead of animal hide), several of these drawings are similar in style to the mid-nineteenth-century pictographic paintings found on bison hides and tipis. They also cover similar subjects. One illustration shows a bison hunt in traditional style, while another indicates the Plains Indian way to write a name. Nine of the sixteen pictures present images of Black Elk's vision, attesting again to its importance: six illustrate his "great vision"; one shows details of a rider enacting Black Elk's vision in the Horse Dance; another depicts Black Elk's spirit journey from England to his mother's lodge at Pine Ridge; and the last shows Black Elk teaching others about the Ghost Dance shirt, which was revealed to him in a later vision.

Five of these drawings are pictographic battle accounts—two of the

Custer battle and three of the Wounded Knee Massacre. In the Custer battle pictures, Standing Bear uses traditional pictographic conventions to identify the heroes (this time tribal heroes rather than individual heroes), to reveal the strategic position of the warriors in relation to the enemy, and to catalogue the type of weapons and the number of enemy. Rather than a "bragging biography"[24] depicting the achievements of one warrior like Mah-to-toh-pa or Zo-Tom (Chapter 3), however, it is a tribal history of the Sioux and Cheyenne victory over Custer's Seventh Cavalry.

A series of three illustrations narrate the tragedy of Wounded Knee. The first picture, "U.S. Soldiers Shooting Indians at Wounded Knee" (Figure 24), tells the story of the beginning of the violence against Big Foot's band. On the left, three robed women stand behind three men for protection. A single man sits serenely before them holding a pipe. In the bottom left corner, two soldiers disarm a man. On the right, three soldiers aim their guns at three women who, sitting outside their tipis, are peacefully surrendering their weapons. A fourth soldier stands behind, heavily laden with a collection of weapons—several rifles, an axe, and a knife. The overall mood is one of strained peacefulness.

In the next picture, "The Massacre at Wounded Knee" (Figure 25), the violence is in full force. In the traditional flow of movement, the narrative moves from right to left across the page, following the soldiers' gunfire to the devastation of those dying. Bordering the right side of the page, only the heads of the soldiers are seen, synecdoches of the army troopers and their unit. An assortment of disembodied soldiers' heads float eerily behind the cannon, while the firing of guns is indicated in front of each head. To the left, immediately in front of the cannon, sits a Lakota man quietly holding his pipe. Behind him, near the left center of the page, a Lakota and a soldier fight. Surrounding the two fighting men sprawl dead men, women, and children.

"Black Elk Defying the Soldiers at Wounded Knee," the final drawing of Wounded Knee (Figure 26), shows six disembodied troopers' heads, a hauntingly ironic echo of the Six Grandfathers in Black Elk's vision. From these heads, on the right side of the page, gunfire is pouring down. Black Elk—riding his horse, wearing his Ghost Dance shirt, and raising his lance to the *Wasichus*—is impervious to the bullets streaming all around him. In the far left of the picture, a woman with a baby on her back and two young children on foot run from destruction amid the flying bullets (indicated in traditional mid-nineteenth-century pictographic fashion by short lines).

FIGURE 24. "U.S. Soldiers Shooting Indians at Wounded Knee" by Standing Bear (Lakota), 1930s. (Courtesy of Hilda Neihardt Petri, Trustee, the John G. Neihardt Trust and Western Historical Manuscript Collection, University of Missouri–Columbia)

At John G. Neihardt's request, Standing Bear, a friend of Black Elk's and one of the several Lakota men who confirmed and enhanced Black Elk's narrative, illustrated the events of the 1890 Wounded Knee Massacre. On the right, three soldiers aim their guns at three women who surrender weapons peacefully. A fourth soldier in the center holds a collection of weapons. On the left, three women stand behind three men; one man sits holding a peace pipe; and in the bottom left corner, two soldiers disarm a man. The mood seems to be tense, but peaceful.

Standing Bear's drawings are basically traditional, but like Zo-Tom's and Howling Wolf's pictographic personal narratives (discussed in Chapter 3), some have titles or labels and brief captions in English (added by Neihardt) to help explain them. The sixteen pictures are clearly meant to accompany the written narrative, not to stand alone as they might have at an earlier time. Apparently, Neihardt arranged for Standing Bear to illustrate Black Elk's autobiography, much as he suggested that he interview Black Elk and his "old friends among the Oglalas" (DeMallie 29–30). It is difficult to know what was Black Elk's idea and what was Neihardt's contribution. What is clear is that together they incorporated many traditional Lakota (for Black Elk, that means pre-reservation) forms of personal narrative. They modified these autobiographical forms to suit the purposes of collaborative personal history that attempts to translate the spoken word, the visual image, and the performed act of the

FIGURE 25. "The Massacre at Wounded Knee" by Standing Bear (Lakota), 1930s. (Courtesy of Hilda Neihardt Petri, Trustee, the John G. Neihardt Trust and Western Historical Manuscript Collection, University of Missouri–Columbia)

The relative peacefulness of the scene in Figure 24 has erupted into violence. The dramatic narrative moves from right to left. On the right, fifteen disembodied heads represent U.S. soldiers who have opened fire on the unarmed Lakota people. Gunfire flares forth in flamelike projections. One cannon is aimed directly at the man who, wrapped in his blanket, sits peacefully, clutching his peace pipe. Just left of center, a Lakota man who may be resisting giving up his rifle, struggles with a soldier. Around them sprawl dead and wounded men, women, and children.

FIGURE 26. "Black Elk Defying the Soldiers at Wounded Knee" by Standing Bear (Lakota), 1930s. (Courtesy of Hilda Neihardt Petri, Trustee, the John G. Neihardt Trust and Western Historical Manuscript Collection, University of Missouri–Columbia)

Six soldiers' heads, an ironic echo of the Six Grandfathers of Black Elk's vision, line the right side of the page. From them gunfire spews forth in great smoky clouds. Black Elk on horseback turns and shakes his lance at the *Wasichus,* impervious to the bullets streaming all around him. On the left, two children and a woman carrying a child on her back flee the bullets.

Lakota into a written text for Anglos. In the process, Black Elk and Neihardt challenged and expanded the realms of both Lakota and Euro-American forms of autobiography. Without Neihardt, Black Elk's words would not have reached as many people; without Black Elk, Neihardt would not be remembered as a poetic sensibility of any stature.

Charles Alexander Eastman

When his mother died shortly after his birth (1858) in the woodlands of southwest Minnesota, Hadakah (The Pitiful Last) was raised in the traditional Santee Sioux ways by his paternal grandmother (Uncheedah) and his uncle. A few years later, as an honor for his band's triumph in a lacrosse game, he was awarded the name Ohiyesa (The Winner).[25] In 1862, when Ohiyesa was four years old, the first of three life-changing events occurred. Having been denied their rightful government annuities, factions of the starving Minnesota Sioux killed several hundred white settlers in what is now called the Minnesota Sioux Conflict. Believing Ohiyesa's father, Many Lightnings, had been arrested and executed by Euro-Americans, the rest of the family fled to Ontario, Canada. There Ohiyesa spent the next eleven years in the woods of the Turtle Mountains learning to be a hunter and a warrior in the pre-contact ways of his people.

At the age of fifteen, when Ohiyesa was just about ready to go on his vision quest, Many Lightnings appeared, as if returned from the dead, to take his son back to the United States to learn the ways of the whites. From this time on, Ohiyesa, soon to become Charles Eastman, had to contend with this second major disruption of his life. After attending Beloit College, Knox College, and Dartmouth College and graduating from Boston University Medical School in 1890, he arrived at Pine Ridge Reservation in time to care for the victims of the Wounded Knee Massacre, the third life-altering event of his life. Every idealistic notion he entertained about "the Christian love and lofty ideals of the white man" was strained severely as he tended to the wounded and dying members of Big Foot's band.[26]

At Pine Ridge he met Elaine Goodale, a white New Englander teaching in Indian Territory. They were married in New England in 1891. To support his family of six children over the years, Eastman worked at a series of jobs in various locations: as a physician on and off reservations, as a YMCA representative to Indians, as a Bureau of Indian Affairs employee in numerous capacities, as an attorney for the Sioux in Washington, D.C., and as a writer and lecturer. In 1921, after thirty years of marriage, Elaine and Charles were separated. In the same year, his growing disillusionment with Euro-American Christian values led him to leave New England for a quieter life in Minnesota. In the 1930s, he retreated to a cabin in the semiseclusion of the Ontario forest, retracing his steps back from "civilization" to the deep woods.[27]

During the years of his marriage, Eastman, "always with the devoted cooperation" of his wife, wrote numerous books and articles about native life and Indian concerns (Eastman, *Deep Woods* 185). In the epilogue to her autobiography, *Sister to the Sioux,* Elaine Goodale Eastman, an author in her own right, wrote:

> In an hour of comparative leisure I had urged him to write down his recollections of the wild life, which I carefully edited and placed with *St. Nicholas.* From this small beginning grew *Indian Boyhood* and eight other books of Indian lore, upon all of which I collaborated more or less.[28]

Goodale, then, provided the initiative and the editing for nine of Eastman's eleven books.[29] After their separation in 1921, Eastman continued to write, but he never again published. Eastman's biographers tend to agree that Eastman was responsible for the ideas, while his wife was responsible for the editing. She seems to have been the force guiding his work into print as well.[30]

This collaborative relationship is quite different from the relationship of Neihardt and Black Elk. Filled with nineteenth-century "Friends of the Indian" notions of helping native people assimilate into the mainstream of American life (through education and Christianity), Elaine Goodale spent five and a half years teaching in small villages on what was then the Great Sioux Reservation. She was no idle curiosity seeker. She knew the Lakota language, went on at least one hunting trip with native friends, and was known as "Little Sister" to the Sioux. During this time, she wrote articles about the Lakota for newspapers and magazines in the East. In 1930, she admitted that her "songs of Indian life exhibit a pardonable coloring of romance." But, she added, she wrote "mainly in prose and with serious educational purpose."[31] Some of this "coloring of romance" and "educational purpose" is evident in her husband's two autobiographies: *Indian Boyhood* (1902) and *From the Deep Woods to Civilization* (1916). This may not be due entirely to his wife's editing, however. Eastman himself believed in the Christian humanism he had been schooled in for eighteen years.

While most Native American autobiographers of this period *speak* their tribal stories to Euro-American editors, Eastman *writes* his personal history himself, relying on such Western autobiographical forms as education and conversion experiences. Although Eastman collaborated with his wife–editor, this may be less important than the extent to which he incorporated the collaborative process into himself, combining the functions of both white editor and Indian informant. In addition, Eastman was raised in the traditional ways of the Santee Sioux, but he received a Euro-American education. He worked closely with white Indian reformers who believed that assimilation was the answer to "the Indian problem," but at the same time, he was fiercely attached to traditional Sioux values. This uneasy alliance induced Eastman to attempt to consolidate Christian and Sioux values. Ohiyesa, as the young Eastman was called, whose childhood had been spent in the Ontario woods, became Charles Alexander Eastman, the transformed Sioux who was trained as a physician. One problem for him, then, was how to write about his Indian life for a white audience, how to reconcile truth and romance, how to balance his Sioux upbringing with his Anglo education.

Indian Boyhood

Published in 1902, *Indian Boyhood* covers the first fifteen years of Ohiyesa's life. The narrative is not strictly chronological. Instead, it jumps ahead and back, moving from anecdote to dialogue to ethnological description. Like Black Elk, Eastman incorporates multiple voices into his life history. We hear dialogues with and stories from his grandmother Uncheedah, the "preserver of history and legend" Smoky Day, his uncle White Footprint, and the storyteller Weyuha.[32] It is as though Eastman were re-creating for his children, for whom he wrote the book, the family and tribal storytellers of his youth. Unlike Black Elk, Eastman writes the accounts from his own memory, unaided by those whose voices he re-creates.

Like Black Elk, Eastman relies on the oral and performance aspects of native personal narrative, but he does not include pictographs or drawings of any sort. Eastman includes stories from two of the three traditional Lakota narrative forms: *Ehani Woyakapi* (legend) and *Woyakapi* (true stories). Smoky Day tells the legend "The Stone Boy" and true accounts of the battle exploits of Jingling Thunder and Morning Star. Weyudah relates the legend of his people, while Uncheedah recites the true stories of an Ojibway raid and of the first battle of her son, Mysterious Medicine. After much coaxing by the young Ohiyesa, White Footprint tells him numerous hunting stories, including one about the beautiful female huntress, Manitoshaw. Humorous stories of real misadventures are told by the comic Matogee, and by his friends Chankpayuhah and Bobdoo.

In contrast to the numerous mythological and historical stories, songs are a minor part of the oral component of Eastman's autobiography. He includes three lyrics from three types of songs: a Strong Heart song to be sung in battle, a serenade from a wooer to a maiden, and a lullaby his grandmother sang to him. Together, these few songs give the reader a sense of the variety of songs and their importance to the Sioux; they provide ethnological details rather than insights into Ohiyesa's childhood.

Just as songs are scarce in *Indian Boyhood,* performance cues are few. Eastman does not elaborate on the storytelling styles of the speakers. Although he includes descriptions of the Bear Dance and the Maidens' Feast, he does so to explain them to a Euro-American readership rather than to dramatize the events or to illuminate their effect on his personal life. In so doing, he sounds more like an "objective" ethnographer than an autobiographer. In fact, like an outsider and one acutely cognizant of his Euro-American readers, he criticizes the belief in the Bear Dance as "one of the superstitions of the Santee Sioux" (*Boyhood* 120).

Use of his Indian name, lack of rigid chronology, incorporation of multiple voices that emphasize tribal identity, and inclusion of Lakota narrative forms, all indicate a Native American perspective. There is much, however, that is distinctly Euro-American. *Indian Boyhood* is, in part, the "Indian Education of Charles Eastman" in which Eastman attempts to rectify the Euro-American misconception that "there is no systematic education of their children among the aborigines of this country." "Nothing," he insists, "could be further from the truth" (*Boyhood* 49). Certainly, he is trying to correct mistaken notions about indigenous people and life by describing the elaborate education every Indian child receives. Bo Schöler states that "by writing about his boyhood he wishes to illustrate the way things used to be in order to break down the stereotype of the Sioux. . . ."[33] While this is true to a certain degree, Eastman's purpose and message are not that simple.

Brumble suggests Eastman's complexity when he notes that *Indian Boyhood* is based on "Romantic Racialist and Social Darwinist assumptions fundamental to Eastman's thinking during these years" (148). Like other indigenous people trying to live biculturally, Eastman faced the difficult task of trying to translate Indian life for non-Indians. To counter the stereotypes of bloodthirsty savages killing wantonly, many Indian writers perpetuated the more positive stereotype of the noble savage. Eastman wished to illustrate how it was possible for a "child of the forest" to live with personal integrity and, through education and conversion to Christianity (believed to be a kind of evolutionary development), to live successfully among Euro-Americans. As a part of this impulse, Eastman describes his mother as "the Demi-Goddess of the

Sioux,'' and to substantiate this claim he explains that tradition says she ''had every feature of a Caucasian descent with the exception of her luxuriant black hair and deep black eyes'' (*Boyhood* 21). His mother's beauty, then, is due to her Caucasian physiognomy rather than to her Indian attributes. Perhaps Eastman intends to contradict demeaning popular images of Indians with oversized noses and ungainly bodies. One reviewer of this book aptly points out a parallel issue in African-American literature of the second half of the nineteenth century. At that time, African-American novelists created ''tragic mulatto'' heroines with white features in order to gain the sympathy of their Euro-American readers. In a similar fashion, Eastman describes his uncle who served as his adviser and teacher: ''He is a typical Indian—not handsome, but truthful and brave'' (*Boyhood* 31). In this instance, Eastman may wish to emphasize the interior beauty of his uncle, again contradicting popular stereotypes of Indians as treacherous and untrustworthy. At the very least, his descriptions reflect a tenuous double vision. Eastman reconstructs native people who will gain the attention, sympathy, and respect of their oppressors/white readers.

As well as emphasizing Sioux internal and external beauty, Eastman presents romantic images of the Indian to counteract other predominantly negative stereotypes. He writes that ''[t]he Indian boy was a prince of the wilderness,'' ''a born hunter'' (*Boyhood* 57, 73). Uncheedah, he says, helped her sons develop ''to the height of savage nobility'' (*Boyhood* 82). Elsewhere he talks about ''savage wealth'' and ''savage entertainments'' (*Boyhood* 127). When Ohiyesa has to offer his beloved dog to the Great Mystery, he describes himself from an outsider's perspective: ''To a civilized eye he would have appeared at that moment like a little copper statue'' (*Boyhood* 85).[34] Similarly, he talks of his ''rude home'' and his ''untutored mind,'' and refers to himself as ''the little redskin'' (*Boyhood* 2, 77). In addition, he notes ''the Indian's dusky bosom'' and their ''tawny bodies'' (*Boyhood* 45, 47).

Even more evident than his Eurocentric descriptions of the Sioux is his ambivalence about which perspective is his. His double vision is part anthropological observer (he describes many Sioux customs and ''superstitions'') and part Santee Sioux participant:

> Such was the Indian's wild life! When game was to be had and the sun shone, *they* easily forgot the bitter experiences of the winter before. Little preparation was made for the future. *They* are children of Nature, and

occasionally she whips *them* with the lashes of experience, yet *they* are forgetful and careless. Much of *their* suffering might have been prevented by a little calculation. (*Boyhood* 29–30, emphases mine)

Speaking of his people in the third person is, in part, a linguistic device to distance himself from them, to enhance his position as an "objective" observer and reporter of Sioux people. *He* describes *them* as though he were not one of them himself. At the same time, he perpetuates the stereotypes of Indians as innocent and incompetent "children of Nature" who do not know enough to plan for the future, and who consequently need the Great White Father to admonish and teach them.

Eastman, however, does not consistently use the third person to describe his people. A few pages later, for instance, he discusses *"our* native women" and *"our* food" (*Boyhood* 33, emphases mine). There seems to be no pattern to when Eastman talks about the Sioux in the first-person plural (we) and when he uses the third-person plural (they). What is striking are his abrupt shifts from a Santee Sioux to a Euro-American perspective and back again, a reflection, perhaps, of his own uncertain identity or perhaps his wife's editorial pen. Andrew Wiget comments on Eastman's "ambivalence toward both cultures": "His support of the Boy Scout Indian programs and his public appearance in tribal dress, though they did reinforce the "noble savage" stereotype, were Eastman's attempts to assert the dignity of native culture in terms compatible with the best elements of Christianity in his emerging universalist perspective."[35] The seeming contradictions and the evident tensions in Eastman's pronoun use, behavior, and dress reveal his struggle to reconcile two opposing cultures.

Part anthropological document, part personal narrative, *Indian Boyhood* is important background reading for understanding the more mature Eastman found in *From the Deep Woods to Civilization.* At the end of *Indian Boyhood,* Ohiyesa follows his father to Flandreau, South Dakota. "Here my wild life came to an end," he concludes, "and my schooldays began" (*Boyhood* 192).

From the Deep Woods to Civilization

From the Deep Woods to Civilization (1916) continues Eastman's education from the time he entered the white world. In the Foreword, Elaine Goodale Eastman explains:

> We are now to hear of a single-hearted quest throughout eighteen years of
> adolescence and early maturity, for the attainment of the modern ideal of
> Christian culture: and again of a quarter of a century devoted to testing that
> hard-won standard in various fields of endeavor, partly by holding it up
> before his own race, and partly by interpreting their racial ideals to the white
> man, leading in the end to a partial reaction in favor of the earlier, the
> simpler, perhaps the more spiritual philosophy.[36]

Eastman's 1916 autobiography, then, combines several Euro-American
autobiographical forms. It is part secular conversion narrative (from
"savagery" to "civilization"), part "the Anglo education of Charles A.
Eastman," and part quest.

When his father, Many Lightnings (now Jacob Eastman), explains the
importance of Euro-American education, he uses images of Eastman's
former life. The ability "to think strongly and well," he tells his son,
"will be a quiver full of arrows for you" (Eastman, *Deep Woods* 27). He
compares the whites' "way of knowledge" with the Indians' "old way in
hunting." In both you start with a dim footprint, which, if pursued
faithfully, "may lead you to a clearer trail" (Eastman, *Deep Woods* 29).
To encourage his reticent son, Many Lightnings says: "Remember, my
boy, it is the same as if I sent you on your first war-path. I shall expect you
to conquer" (Eastman, *Deep Woods* 31–32). Prepared as he was to be a
hunter and warrior, Ohiyesa sets out to hunt the white man's wisdom and
to conquer his knowledge.

The young Santee Sioux is out of place in this new world, and in the
beginning pages of *From the Deep Woods to Civilization,* he underscores
this by referring to himself in metaphors of wild nature. He describes the
dramatic change in his life "as if a little mountain brook should pause and
turn upon itself to gather strength for the long journey toward an unknown
ocean" (*Deep Woods* 1). Later, he compares himself to wild ponies
roaming free on the prairie "who loved their freedom too well and would
not come in" (*Deep Woods* 14). He is a "wild cub caught" (*Deep Woods*
23); "a young blue heron just leaving the nest," balancing precariously
on a flimsy branch (*Deep Woods* 36); "a turtle" pulling himself into the
safety of his shell (*Deep Woods* 36); "a wild goose with its wings
clipped" (*Deep Woods* 44); and, to certain whites at Dartmouth, "a wild
fox" in the midst of their chicken coop (*Deep Woods* 68). Such
metaphors emphasize his Sioux identity, and contrast his former free and
natural life in the woods with his current restricted and uncertain life in
"civilization."

Just as he did in *Indian Boyhood*, Eastman often describes his people using the positive stereotypes of Indians commonly used by those sympathetic to native people. He refers to Indians as the "children of nature"—the "sons of nature" and the "daughter[s] of the woods" (*Deep Woods* 176, 183). When he seeks "rare curios and ethnological specimens" from the "wilder and more scattered bands" in Minnesota, he describes the area as "the true virgin wilderness, the final refuge . . . of American big game and primitive man" (*Deep Woods* 166, 173). His collecting ethnological artifacts and considering "big game and primitive man" as dual aspects of the wilderness reveal his Euro-American education or at least his awareness of this Euro-American perspective. Similarly, he exults over his "wonderful opportunity to come into contact with the racial mind" (*Deep Woods* 150).

Eastman does not always write from such a seemingly Eurocentric point of view. He often vacillates between allegiance to the Indians and loyalty to the whites. Although he is critical of Euro-American society, aware of his audience, he is careful to temper his admonitions. Just after describing how he overheard a Beloit classmate call him "Sitting Bull's nephew," who might score a "scalplock before morning," he explains: "It must be remembered that this was September, 1876, less than three months after Custer's gallant command was annihilated by the hostile Sioux" (*Deep Woods* 53). Eastman's choice of adjectives reveals his awareness of his rhetorical predicament. Describing Custer's cavalry as "gallant" and the Sioux as "hostile" and using the highly charged verb "annihilated" echo newspaper accounts of the event and suggest that Eastman was sensitive to his classmates' perceptions of the battle and their consequent judgment of Indian people. Certainly, this is not the story that Eastman's two uncles who took part in the Custer battle would tell. Although this might be read ironically, in context this description seems to be a straightforward explanation. In addition, it reveals Eastman's and his wife–editor's clear awareness of his Euro-American readers.

Eastman tries to strike a balance between Native American and Euro-American concerns in order to mediate Indian perspectives to policy-makers in the East. During the trouble at Pine Ridge in South Dakota in the winter of 1890, the moderate chief, American Horse, asks Eastman for advice about how to deal with his torn loyalties between the "ghost dancers, men of their own blood, and the Government to which they had pledged their loyalty" (Eastman, *Deep Woods* 96). Eastman advises that they "reason with the wilder element" "for a peaceful settlement," but remember their "solemn duty to serve the United States Government" (*Deep Woods* 96). Certainly, such a precarious political position, part of Eastman's bicultural predicament, was difficult, and often dangerous, to sustain.

Nowhere is this bicultural tension more apparent than in his pronoun shifts. As in his earlier autobiography, he shifts his perspective between first-person plural (we) and third-person plural (they). As an attorney for the Sioux, Eastman learns about the treacherous history of treaties between the Sioux nation and the United States. In his description, he refers to himself as one of the Sioux. His pronouns are "we" and "us" until "the frightful 'Minnesota massacre' in 1862" (*Deep Woods* 154). After this episode, Eastman shifts to talking about the Sioux as "them." On the next page, he says he went to Washington with "great respect for *our* public men and institutions" (*Deep Woods* 155, emphasis mine). Here "our" refers to the whites. Later in the same paragraph, "they" refers to the white "political henchmen on the reservations," who abuse the Sioux, and "our" alludes to the Sioux, who have been wronged. Eastman's transitions from first person to third person are rhetorical devices to remove himself from whichever group he is criticizing at the moment. He wishes to identify himself with only the best of both worlds. But later he describes Native Americans in the third person not to excoriate them as "hostiles," but to analyze them from an Anglo ethnological perspective:

> The philosophy of the original American was demonstrably on a high plane, *his* gift of eloquence, wit, humor and poetry is well established; *his* democracy and community life was much nearer the ideal than ours today; *his* standard of honor and friendship unsurpassed, and all *his* faults are the faults of generous youth. (*Deep Woods* 188, emphases mine)

The "original American," then, is a noble savage superior in many ways to the "civilized" white. But Eastman (perhaps with the influence of his wife) clearly aligns himself linguistically with white society. "Our" (i.e., Euro-American) philosophy is not so ideal, he insists. As well as the perspective of ethnographer, he adopts the typically Euro-American pose of generous and tolerant father when he excuses Indian faults as "the faults of generous youth."

At times Eastman *is* ironic. For instance, when he hears about the graft of Pine Ridge officials, he writes: "I held that a great government such as *ours* would never condone or permit any such practices'' (*Deep Woods* 118, emphasis mine). Similarly, he subverts the language usually limited to describing Native Americans and applies it to Euro-Americans. Disillusioned with the failure of white Christians to live their ideals, he describes the ''savagery of civilization'' and the ''warfare of civilized life'' (*Deep Woods* 139, 165). Even Jesus, the embodiment of the Christian ideal, is described ironically. As a YMCA practitioner, East-man travels among various tribes preaching about ''the life and character of the Man Jesus'' (*Deep Woods* 142). At one point, an elderly Indian man responds:

> I have come to the conclusion that this Jesus was an Indian. He was opposed to material acquirement and to great possessions. He was inclined to peace. He was as unpractical as any Indian and set no price upon his labor of love. These are not the principles upon which the white man has founded his civilization. It is strange that he could not rise to these simple principles which were commonly observed among our people. (Eastman, *Deep Woods* 143)

With these words, spoken safely by an anonymous unreconstructed Indian elder, Eastman undercuts the fancied superiority of Euro-American ideals. His very next anecdote is about an Indian who converts a white man to Christianity, overturning expectations that it is the white man who ''saves'' the Indian. Still later, in another role reversal, he has a white guide lead him into the wilderness to seek Ojibway artifacts. By subverting Euro-American assumptions about the language, ideas, and activities of Indians, Eastman overturns Indian stereotypes (just as he seems to perpetuate them elsewhere). In the process, he educates whites and restores humanity to native peoples. Eastman's stance, though, is never absolute, as reflected in his linguistic ambivalence.

In *From the Deep Woods to Civilization,* Eastman includes few traditional Sioux modes of personal narrative. He mentions several *Woyakapi* and paraphrases a few stories, but elaborates on none. Through reconstructed speeches and dialogue, we hear numerous voices and gain a vague sense of performance. In part, the recurring dialogue between his father and grandmother serves to introduce and clarify his argument about the ideals of civilization versus the values of the deep woods. He continues this dialogic device throughout the autobiography, furthering his argument in the voices of others.

Instead of pictographs, Eastman includes sixteen photographs. Six are of individuals important in his life (a white influence: Reverend Alfred L. Riggs; his family: Many Lightnings, Mrs. Frank Wood [his "white mother"], Elaine, and his son Ohiyesa; and one historical figure: Kicking Bear). Five are of buildings (an Indian cabin, tipis, Santee Normal Training School, Chapel of the Holy Cross, and Pine Ridge Agency). He includes three pictures of himself, one of his Dartmouth class, and one of him and his wilderness guide. Like the written narrative, his photographs highlight education, religion, and the difference between Indian and white ways. Unlike narrative pictographs, these photographs do not tell his story themselves. Rather, they enhance his written account, illustrating personal and cultural details.

From the Deep Woods to Civilization as a whole can be seen as a reenactment of the tedious and painful process of Ohiyesa's assimilation into Euro-American culture, his transformation from Ohiyesa into Dr. Charles Alexander Eastman, whom Pine Ridge residents called "the 'white doctor' who was also an Indian" (Eastman, *Deep Woods* 76). This is not the traditional, formalized enactment of tribal ceremony, but the new, undetermined drama of Native American acculturation.

Eastman ends his autobiography with a catalogue of his "civilized" pursuits. Just as if he were recounting brave battle deeds in a coup tale, he recalls his major accomplishments as an author, a public speaker, a representative of North American Indians at the First Universal Races Congress in England, an acquaintance of famous personages, a traveler, a correspondent and editor, and a Boy Scout proponent. Dropping the names of the famous as he proceeds through his list of achievements, Eastman means for the reader to marvel at his wondrous adaptation to the Euro-American world. Yet after this lengthy list, he criticizes the very basis of the culture he has adopted. He reflects on "the Christ ideal"—its potential good, but more important, the "modern divergence from that ideal" (*Deep Woods* 193). He condemns those who "are anxious to pass on their religion to all races of men, but keep very little of it for themselves" (*Deep Woods* 194). "Behind the material and intellectual splendor of our civilization," he declares, "primitive savagery and cruelty and lust hold sway, undiminished, and it seems, unheeded" (*Deep Woods* 194). It is Euro-American civilization, then, not Native American culture, that is primitive, that is savage, cruel, and lustful. Still, Eastman advocates "civilization" for two reasons: it is impossible to go back to the simpler life of pre-contact times, and Christianity is not to blame for the wrongdoings of whites.

In the carefully balanced final paragraph of his autobiography, Eastman's initial tension between Native American and Euro-American cultures remains unresolved:

> I am an Indian; and while I have learned much from civilization, for which I am grateful, I have never lost my Indian sense of right and justice. I am for development and progress along social and spiritual lines, rather than those of commerce, nationalism, or material efficiency. Nevertheless, so long as I live, I am an American. (*Deep Woods* 195)

With several qualifications, Eastman insists that he can be both Indian and American. It is important to keep in mind that this book was published in 1916, just one year before the United States entered World War I (in which many Indian men enlisted) and eight years before Indians were granted citizenship. This prismatic paragraph begins and ends with mirror images asserting his bicultural identity: "I am an Indian"; "I am an American." These are the two opposites he has tried to reconcile in himself, in the United States of the early twentieth century, and in his autobiography that deals with both.

Both Black Elk and Charles Eastman lived during the tumultuous second half of the nineteenth century. In 1890, during the Ghost Dance ceremonies at Pine Ridge, Black Elk was one of the "wilder elements," while Eastman was one of the assimilationists. They shared, however, a deeply felt sense of their Indian identities. In accord with their Sioux heritages, both Black Elk (Oglala) and Eastman (Santee) had visions—visions of personal and tribal renewal. But their attempts to realize their dreams took them in opposite directions, at least for a time. Although it seems that their personal narratives are mirror images of each other (Black Elk looking back to traditional ways and Eastman looking forward to "civilized" ways), the men and their visions are not so simple.

Janus-like, each man looked ahead and behind. From the physical and spiritual decay of reservation life, Black Elk reaffirmed traditional Lakota spirituality informed by Catholicism. From the spiritual barrenness of civilized life, Eastman reclaimed the best of Sioux philosophy, rebuked the worst of Christianity, and tried to reconcile their apparent contradictions. Not surprisingly, both men felt they failed to fulfill their aspirations.[37] Black Elk could not maintain the sacred hoop of his people; Eastman did not find the "Christ ideal" in white society.

Both Black Elk and Charles Eastman felt compelled to tell their stories to the white world. Both collaborated with Euro-Americans to do so. Black Elk's collaboration with Neihardt is now a classic example of oral autobiography. Eastman's collaboration with his wife is less important than the fact that he incorporated the collaborative process into himself. He is both "the racial mind," as he calls it, and the Anglo investigator who gives it voice. By combining the functions of white editor and Indian informant, Eastman continued the autobiographical tradition of Euro-American–influenced native people like William Apes (Pequot, 1798–?) and Sarah Winnemucca Hopkins (Pauite, c. 1844–1891) who wrote their life stories in English without the aid of an amanuensis.[38] Furthermore, Eastman prefigured contemporary Native American autobiographers like N. Scott Momaday and Leslie Marmon Silko (Chapter 6) who write their personal narratives from an eclectic perspective, reflecting both Native American and Euro-American values and forms. Black Elk and Eastman, then, expanded the literary boundary culture of Native American autobiography in different directions. Black Elk spoke his tribal story to Neihardt, using modified versions of traditional Lakota modes of personal narrative. Eastman wrote his life history, relying on such Western autobiographical forms as education, conversion, and quest narratives, and using traditional Sioux narrative modes sparingly. These two divergent but parallel directions of Native American personal narrative (oral/written, tribal/individual) provide two distinct, yet related, models in the historical transformation of Native American autobiography.

6 / Contemporary Innovations of Oral Traditions: N. Scott Momaday and Leslie Marmon Silko

Native American autobiography today is far more politically complex than the oral, pictographic, and dramatic personal narratives[1] of pre-contact times. All three roots of the term *autobiography*—self, life, and writing (language)—are not so easily defined as they were when individuals lived in small tribal units or bands. Today what it means to be Indian is defined in numerous, often contradictory, ways. Whether being Indian depends on genetics (''degree of Indian blood''), culture, residence, community acceptance, tribal enrollment, or spiritual orientation depends on who is defining whom and for what purposes.[2] Certainly the United States government, wanting quantitative indicators in order to determine program budgets, has a stake in emphasizing genetics and tribal enrollment. All too often, though, the federal government, linking Indian identity to a land base that has been diminished or stolen outright, defines Indian tribes out of legal existence.[3] While some tribes, wishing to protect their share of land settlements or their cultural integrity, stress community acceptance as well as ''degree of Indian blood'' and enrollment, some individuals insist that being truly Indian is a way of perceiving the world, some ineffable spirituality that preempts genetic determination or community acceptance. My point here is that in pre-reservation times it would have been unthinkable to question Indian identity—you were or were not Lakota or Hopi or Cherokee on the bases of tribe, band, clan, and family affiliations. With the breakdown of many native communities, the autobiographical activity of self-construction has become especially important.

In many ways, life is more difficult today also. Ironically, pre-contact Native Americans, while seemingly having fewer choices about their individual vocations (Plains Indian males, for instance, might be hunters, warriors, or holy men), had greater possibilities for success. Today, while theoretical opportunities abound, the realities of economic and educational inequities often limit self-development within both reservations and inner cities where urban Indians often cluster. High rates of alcoholism and violence, resulting from and contributing to despair and hopelessness, ravage Native American communities. While the story is not as grim for those who choose to renew tribal traditions or those who obtain college educations (sometimes both at the same time), American Indians still have to grapple with the ponderous questions of personal and tribal identity.

Like considerations of self and life, language is another perplexing issue. While there are ongoing oral traditions in native languages and numerous oral-history projects to record the oral traditions of native-speaking tribal elders, the majority of Native Americans speak English as their first language. The language of the oppressor has become the dominant language of the oppressed. Indeed, in the late nineteenth and early twentieth centuries, an active campaign to coerce indigenous people to speak English was enforced regularly and fiercely at mission schools, where Indian children were punished severely for speaking their native languages. Consequently, most of the literature produced by Native Americans in the twentieth century is in English. This leads to passionate debate about whether Native Americans use ''the language of the colonialists . . . for their own purposes,'' thus resisting colonization, or whether for Native Americans, ''the resistance is often done in one's [native] language.''[4]

A complicated sense of self; the altered, often circumscribed, possibilities for life; and a substitute language contribute to the complexity of twentieth-century Native American autobiography. While the literary boundary culture becomes more complex, the transitional autobiographical traditions of Black Elk and Charles Eastman continue. As was true in Neihardt's and Black Elk's collaboration, anthropologists, historians, and literati still work with tribal elders, converting spoken personal histories into written autobiographies. Richard Erdoes and John (Fire) Lame Deer, for instance, worked together to create an autobiography filled with anthropological data, social satire, and humor. In addition, some editors, like Brian Swann and Arnold Krupat, have solicited personal narratives *written* by contemporary Native American writers, providing primarily the impetus to write autobiographically.[5] Like Eastman, many contemporary Native American autobiographers have collapsed the collaborative process into one person, often consciously combining their Native American traditions with their Euro-American educations. In the works of such authors as N. Scott Momaday and Leslie Marmon Silko, both of these autobiographical directions—"bi-cultural collaboration"[6] and internalized bicultural (or perhaps more precisely, multicultural) collaboration—continue in the redefined literary boundary culture of contemporary Native American autobiography. Three of the most accomplished examples of this modified literary boundary culture are the autobiographical works of N. Scott Momaday and Leslie Marmon Silko.

N. Scott Momaday

N. Scott Momaday was born Navarro Scotte Mammedaty in an Oklahoma Indian hospital in 1934. After his mother, Natachee Scott (one-eighth Cherokee),[7] and his Kiowa father, Alfred Mammedaty (he later changed his name to Momaday), were married, they moved west. Throughout his childhood, Momaday lived in various areas of New Mexico and Arizona: the Navajo reservation at Shiprock; the San Carlos reservation; and Jemez Pueblo, where his parents taught school. In his precollege years, then, Momaday was exposed to Kiowa, Navajo, Tanoan, and Euro-American cultures. On graduating from the University of New Mexico in Albuquerque with a B.A. in political science in 1958, Momaday taught school on the Jicarilla reservation in New Mexico. From 1959 to 1963, he studied under Yvor Winters at Stanford University, where he earned a Ph.D.[8]

Since that time he has been teaching, writing, and drawing. In 1967 he published privately *The Journey of Tai-me,* a collection of stories from the Kiowa oral tradition and the precursor to *The Way to Rainy Mountain* (1969). His novel *House Made of Dawn* was published in 1968 and received the Pulitzer Prize for fiction the following year. In 1976 *The Gourd Dancer,* a collection of poems, and *The Names,* a memoir, were published. He has also written numerous essays and a weekly column for *Viva,* northern New Mexico's Sunday magazine. Since his 1974 stay in Moscow, Momaday has been drawing as well as writing.

Before discussing Momaday's autobiographies, *The Way to Rainy Mountain* and *The Names,* it is crucial to consider his personal and literary

philosophy. In his essay "The Man Made of Words," Momaday
articulates this philosophy. He discusses his Kiowa heritage, his connection to language, his insistence on imagination, his relation to the land,
and the interplay among these. For Momaday, "we are all made of
words," since language is "the element in which we think and dream and
act, in which we live our daily lives."[9] In defining an American Indian,
then, Momaday extends this idea: ". . . an Indian is an idea which a
given man has of himself. And it is a moral idea, for it accounts for the
way in which he reacts to other men and to the world in general. And that
idea, in order to be realized completely, has to be expressed" (Man 162).
This definition of an Indian ignores the generally disputed conceptions of
Indian identity discussed earlier and replaces them with an act of
imagination. That Indian identity is a self-conception (shaped by history
and community) is an idea common to many native people who must
continually define what it means to be "Indian" to non-Indians. Certainly, Momaday does not mean to claim that since an Indian is merely an
"idea," someone without an indigenous genetic endowment can claim to
be Indian. But by granting the imagination such a privileged position,
Momaday may be perpetuating inadvertently the Euro-American literati's questionable claim to universality (a notion all too often assumed to
be equivalent to European male experience) and overlooking the quite
tangible problem of those who would appropriate Indian identity.

Insisting on the primacy and reality of the imagination, however, is a
key idea for Momaday for personal as well as artistic reasons. In 1929, at
the age of sixteen, his mother, Natachee, descended from a Cherokee
great-grandmother, "began to see herself as an Indian."[10] In *The Names:
A Memoir,* Momaday explains: "She imagined who she was. This act of
the imagination, was, I believe, among the most important events of my
mother's early life, as later the same essential act was to be among the
most important of my own" (25). When Momaday was in his early
thirties, like his mother before him, he began to be interested in his
Indian heritage. Due to urgings from his mentor Yvor Winters, as well as
his own personal interest, Momaday embarked on a course of study,
finding out as much as possible about his Kiowa background. He
explains:

> I think of myself as an Indian because at one time in my life I suddenly
> realized that my father had grown up speaking a language that I didn't grow
> up speaking, that my forebears on his side had made a migration from
> Canada along with . . . Athapaskan peoples that I knew nothing about,
> and so I determined to find out something about these things and in the

process I acquired an identity; it is an Indian identity, as far as I'm concerned.[11]

Matthias Schubnell notes "two crucial experiences which initiated [Momaday's] conscious exploration of Kiowa tradition" in his writing: his "encounter with the Tai-me bundle, the sacred Sun Dance fetish of the Kiowa tribe," and his trip to Rainy Mountain Cemetery in honor of his grandmother, where his experience with the landscape provided another link to his background (141–142). Certainly, for many indigenous people "conscious exploration" of tribal traditions is necessary to reconstruct a fractured historical identity.

For Momaday it is not enough to imagine himself independent of his surroundings. Rather, he wants to "come to moral terms" with the environment. He offers Kiowa culture and its "deep, ethical regard for the land" as a model for all Americans who suffer from "a kind of psychic dislocation" (Man 162, 166). "We Americans," he says, "need now more than ever before . . . to imagine who and what we are with respect to the earth and sky." With a collective act of the imagination, based on the Indian "regard of and for the natural world," Momaday envisions "an American land ethic" (Man 166–167).[12] Like Charles Eastman, Momaday aligns himself linguistically with Euro-American society, contrasting "[w]e Americans" with "Ko-sahn and her people" (Man 167). The distinction, however, seems to be more historical than cultural. Ko-sahn lived in the late nineteenth century, before U.S. citizenship was awarded to (or imposed on) Indian people. While this may suggest the romantic stereotype of the ecological Indian, a reverence for the land was and is a traditional pan-Indian perspective. And Momaday, more than any other Native American author, elicits the form and feelings of the landscape he describes so minutely and lovingly in his writings.

Through language, storytelling unites Momaday's concerns for the land, the Kiowa, and the imagination. According to Momaday:

> Storytelling . . . is an act by which man strives to realize his capacity for wonder, meaning and delight. It is also a process in which man invests and preserves himself in the context of ideas. Man tells stories in order to understand his experience, whatever it may be. The possibilities of storytelling are precisely those of understanding the human experience. (Man 168)

Through telling stories, both personal and tribal, Momaday seeks to understand his individual experience in the context of the Kiowa tribal experience. In the process, he transforms the popular Euro-American mythology of the "self-made man."

To tell one's personal story, one must remember past events, one must recall old images, and one must resurrect previous feelings. Memory, then, in conjunction with imagination, plays a vital role in individual and collective self-narration—synthesizing differences and ordering chaos. Through memory and imagination, expressed in language, storytelling helps us to understand human experience. This emphasis on the importance of language reflects Momaday's dual heritage. It is due, in part, to the traditional Native American belief in the sacred, potent nature of the word and, in part, to a traditional Stanford literary education that scrutinizes the beauty and efficacy of language.

The Way to Rainy Mountain

Momaday's belief in the transforming capabilities of the imagination, in the synthesizing potential of memory, in the identity-inducing possibilities of the land, and in the power, beauty, and grace of the word finds its way into *The Way to Rainy Mountain*. The first of his two autobiographies, *The Way to Rainy Mountain* is the more experimental. Many critics, including Momaday himself, have commented on its unique structure and purpose.

Claiming that it defies generic classification, Robert L. Berner refers to *The Way to Rainy Mountain* as "an abbreviated history of the Kiowa people, a re-working of Kiowa folklore, a mixture of legend, historical fact, and autobiography." Not content with these attempts at labeling, he calls it "a kind of prose poem," "an exercise in self-definition," and, most dubiously, "a profoundly civilized work of literature." Similarly, Kenneth Fields writes: ". . . I know of no book like *Rainy Mountain*. . . ." Due to its concentrated and evocative language, it approaches poetry; but also, due to its multiple voices, its form "resembles those ancient texts with subsequent commentaries." Its "real subject," however, "is the recognition of what it means to feel himself a Kiowa in the modern American culture that displaced his ancestors." Not sharing Berner's and Fields's quandary over the work's genre, Thekla Zachrau mistakenly calls it "Momaday's second novel," which can be read "as a variation on the identity theme." Charles A. Nicholas, on the contrary, interprets the work as expressing Momaday's belief in "the essential continuity of myth and poetry and their ability to induce vision and compel belief.'' For Mick McAllister, *"The Way to Rainy Mountain* has the simplicity, and the complexity, of a piece of music,'' and ''is at once a celebration and an exercise in form.'' Roger Dickinson-Brown limits his comments to its ''associational structure'' and its ''almost Jamesian symmetry,'' while Barbara Strelke calls it ''a multivoiced response to the question of personal and cultural creation through imagination and language.'' In his study of the Western literary sources of Momaday's works, Matthias Schubnell states that Momaday's mentor Yvor Winters ''urged Momaday to try a combination of expository writing and fictitious, historical, or legendary narrative. . . .'' The result was *The Way to Rainy Mountain,* which reflects ''Momaday's own exploration of his racial heritage.'' Certainly, Arnold Krupat's recent denunciation of Momaday as the ''Native American writer most committed to hegemonic monologue'' and his insistence that Momaday's ''writing offers a single, invariant poetic voice that everywhere commits itself to subsuming and translating all other voices'' is overstated.[13] In fact, as will be discussed in this section, throughout this unique polyvocal autobiographical narrative, Momaday constructs a communal self. His individual identity comes into being only in relation to the ancient tribal past, the historical Kiowa experience, and the multicultural present.

Momaday himself has plenty to say about *The Way to Rainy Mountain:*

> In one sense, then, the way to Rainy Mountain is preeminently the history of an idea, man's idea of himself, and it has old and essential being in language. . . .
> The journey herein recalled continues to be made anew each time the miracle comes to mind, for that is peculiarly the right and responsibility of the imagination.[14]

This journey, ''made with the whole memory, that experience of the mind which is legendary as well as historical, personal as well as cultural,'' evokes three particular things: ''a landscape that is incomparable, a time that is gone forever, and the human spirit, which endures'' (*WRM* 4). Momaday links the legendary, historical, and personal literally in his journey and literarily in his imagination. After retracing the historical Kiowa migration, Momaday returned to Oklahoma. There, like a Kiowa Neihardt, he ''interviewed a number of Kiowa elders and obtained from them a remarkable body of history and learning, fact and fiction—all of it in the oral tradition . . .'' (*Man* 170). Since Momaday does not speak Kiowa, these oral accounts were translated and added to by Momaday's father, Al Momaday.[15] This collaborative work was then published privately as *The Journey of Tai-me* (1967), which later formed the basis for *The Way to Rainy Mountain*.

The Way to Rainy Mountain is an autobiography in which Momaday constructs and narrates a Kiowa personal identity that can come into being only in relation to Kiowa myth and history. Like many transitional personal narratives, Momaday's autobiographical self is relational and his form predominantly a reconstruction of the spoken word in writing. The multilayered autobiographical narrative is composed of three basic divisions that are preceded by a prologue and an introduction, concluded by an epilogue, and framed by two poems. The two poems, "Headwaters" and "Rainy Mountain Cemetery," which begin and end the work, repeat in miniature the longer narrative of the Momaday–Kiowa journey. Al Momaday drew the eleven illustrations found throughout, and the running title along the bottom of the three main chapters beckons the book designer's reader–traveler like a typographical trail into the journey.[16]

The autobiography's tripartite structure reflects three narrative voices: the mythical, the historical, and the personal, each accentuated by different typeface.[17] The twenty-four three-part narrative units are divided into three larger chapters: "The Setting Out" (sections I–XI), "The Going On" (sections XII–XVIII), and "The Closing In" (sections XIX–XXIV). These three main divisions reflect the historical movement of the Kiowa migration from "the mountains of what is now western Montana," traveling south and east to what is now southwestern Oklahoma (Man 169), as well as Momaday's personal journey in their distant trail. The first chapter, "The Setting Out," tells the story of the beginning of the Kiowas—their emergence into the world through a hollow log, their tribal split, and their "struggle for existence in the bleak northern mountains" (*WRM* 4). This chapter also describes the beginning of their migration south and east across the plains. The primary aspects of the Kiowa religion are introduced as well: the hero twins fathered by the Sun, who came to earth, helped overcome chaos, and metamorphosed into the ten sacred bundles; Tai-me, the sacred symbol of the Sun Dance Ceremony; the Sun Dance; and the peyote religion.

"The Going On," the second chapter, deals with the interim of Kiowa culture, "a time of great adventure and nobility and fulfillment" (*WRM* 3), when, by obtaining the horse, the Kiowa male was transformed from "a half-starved skulker" into "the daring buffalo hunter" (*WRM* 61).

Momaday describes the highlight of the Kiowa Plains culture, and a people who ''had dared to imagine and determine who they were'' (*WRM* 4). We hear stories of the magic of Kiowa language, the arrowmaker, the ''buffalo with horns of steel,'' the hard lives of women, and the everyday life on the Plains.

''The Closing In'' describes the end of the Kiowa Plains culture, which ''withered and died like grass that is burned in the prairie wind'' (*WRM* 3). It is filled with images of constraint and destruction: capture by the U.S. Cavalry; lack of food; extermination of the buffalo, ''the animal representation of the sun'' (*WRM* 3); destruction of the Kiowa's horses; deicide; and, as a consequence of all these, the loss of personal bravery. Despite the dreariness of the subject, the chapter ends with a description of a woman buried in a beautiful elk-tooth buckskin dress—a vision of the timeless connection of the people to the land and of the buried beauty of the Kiowa culture.

Although the overall narrative movement of these three main sections is chronological, Momaday blends the mythic, historical, and personal by an elaborate process of association. The intermixing of these distinct historical periods suggests a kind of timelessness or, at the very least, an intimate and irrevocable connection among the three. McAllister refers to such associations as ''secondary patterns'' that weave the various parts of the work together (20). A more subtle association, though, is the connection between personal and tribal experience, present and past lives united in story.

Reclaimed Autobiographical Traditions

Momaday's experimentation with the structure of *The Way to Rainy Mountain* reflects his familiarity with Western literary conventions and his knowledge of Kiowa oral traditions.[18] Like the Indian autobiographers of the late nineteenth and early twentieth centuries (such as Charles Alexander Eastman and Black Elk), Momaday modifies pre-contact oral and pictographic modes of personal narrative. Unlike those of earlier Native American autobiographers, Momaday's changes are highly self-conscious, not residual forms that innocuously find their way into written expression. Likewise, they are due to his creative imagination, rather than to a political or an ethnological expediency. He wishes to show the evolution from an oral tradition to a written tradition, to show the oral tradition ''within the framework of a literary continuance . . .'' (Man

170). In fact, according to Momaday, who applies an evolutionary model to traditional Kiowa notions of the cyclical nature of life and narrative, the Kiowa tales in *The Way to Rainy Mountain* "constitute a kind of literary chronicle" (Man 170).[19] He dramatizes this evolution in the text when, in the third chapter, he replaces ancient Kiowa myths with family stories now elevated to legendary status: "that is, Momaday is creating myth out of his memories of his ancestors rather than passing on already established and socially sanctioned tales" (Nicholas 154). Similarly, the historical accounts become family memories, and the personal reminiscences become "prose poems containing symbols which link them thematically to the other two, suggesting that all three journeys are products of the imagination" (Nicholas 154), and, I would add, suggesting that the mythical, historical, and personal are all facets of Momaday the autobiographer. Refashioning pre-contact personal narrative is one way he attempts to define his Kiowa identity and to suggest the continuity of Native American traditions, from orality to literacy.

Orality

The oral aspects of personal narrative are focused within, but not limited to, the mythical sections, which, of course, were all originally oral. Momaday emphasizes orality by including dialogues; multiple voices; songs; oral devices such as repetition of words, phrases, and images; and oral formulas, as well as a few variations on Plains Indian coup tales. Throughout the work, Momaday includes a type of one-sided dialogue that allows for many voices to be heard. An enemy appears to a family, demanding, "If you will feed us all, we will not harm you" (*WRM* 44). Although this is a one-way conversation (we hear only the enemy), a response from the listener is implied. Other speakers provide little besides lively choral backgrounds—like the dog (*WRM* 20), the sun (*WRM* 22), the giant's wife (*WRM* 32), Tai-me (*WRM* 36), an invisible voice (*WRM* 54), and the blind hunter (*WRM* 58). Thus Momaday, with economical concentration, provides the feeling of conversation but allows only one person to speak.

More important than unidirectional dialogues (not to be confused with monologues, which require no listener) are the few voices that speak for themselves. Only two people—Aho and Ko-sahn—are allowed to speak for themselves at length. They, of course, are major figures in the entire work. Momaday's Kiowa grandmother, Aho, provides the occasion for the work and its best unifying image. It is her death that compels

Momaday to begin his personal/tribal quest, to return to his people, and to write his book. In the introduction, Aho tells the legend of the creation of Devils Tower (a rock formation in northeastern Wyoming) and of the seven sisters who "were borne into the sky, and . . . became the stars of the Big Dipper" (*WRM* 8). "From that moment," says Momaday, "and so long as the legend lives, the Kiowas have kinsmen in the night sky" (*WRM* 8). This story links earth to sky and humans to both. Also, we discover elsewhere, the story and the place are significant as the source of one of Momaday's names—Tsoai-talee, Kiowa for Rock Boy, a name inspired by Devils Tower (*Names* 55–57, 170).

Balancing Aho's story in the introduction, Ko-sahn's recollections are found in the epilogue. Momaday refers to this "hundred-year-old woman" as the embodiment of the "living memory and verbal tradition which transcends it" (*WRM* 86). For her, at least as she is re-created on the page by Momaday, there is no distinction between individual and tribal memory, between mythical and historical realms (Man 166). Just as Aho is the deceased image of the Kiowa past, Ko-sahn is the living symbol of Kiowa antiquity. Through her memory, reenvisioned by Momaday, the mythical and historical unite in the present. Finally, both Aho and Ko-sahn, as Momaday imagines them, function as literary images of Kiowa heritage rather than as realistic depictions of flesh-and-blood women.

Five brief songs, a second oral component, are included in *The Way to Rainy Mountain*. These five songs parallel Momaday's ideas about the process of literary evolution. The first is sung by a mythical character, Spider Woman, while the song of the wife of Many Bears is clearly grounded in historical experience. Ko-sahn's songs unite the mythical and historical in the personal present. Of course, empowered by myth and history, Momaday is the creative intelligence behind each of these singers. With his belief in the liveliness of the past in the present moment, a tribal past that he tries to resurrect in himself and in his work, he presents *The Way to Rainy Mountain* as the polyphonous song of his Anglo-Kiowa identity, of his individual/tribal self.

As well as multiple voices and songs, Momaday uses the formulas and style of oral composition. His language is simple, and he frequently begins his stories with traditional openings such as "They were going along . . ." (*WRM* 18), "A long time ago . . ." (*WRM* 38), "Once there was a man and his wife . . ." (*WRM* 46), "This is how it was: Long ago . . ." (*WRM* 48), and "Once upon a time . . ." (*WRM* 60).

At times, he inserts the phrase "you know" to slow the pace of the sentence, accentuating the orality of the story and giving it a personal tone.

One aspect of oral style he masters is repetition, which creates an "irresistible accumulation of power" (Woodard 143). In this case he repeats words, phrases, images, themes, characters, and structural units. For instance, the poem "Headwaters" introduces the Kiowa creation myth in which the Kiowa emerge through a "log, hollow and weather-stained." This is echoed in the prologue: "You know, everything had to begin. . . . For the Kiowas the beginning was . . ." (*WRM* 3). This phrase is repeated almost exactly in the first and last sentences of the mythical passage of section I. In the historical part of section I, the ethnological explanation, derived from nineteenth-century ethnographer James Mooney's reports, repeats the previously mentioned notion that *Kwuda* means "coming out." This idea of emerging is again repeated when, in the personal recollection, Momaday writes: "I remember *coming out* upon the northern Great Plains . . ." (*WRM* 17, emphasis mine). Similarly, the end of the prologue is repeated exactly in Ko-sahn's final words in the epilogue. Such resonant repetition is used with images of halves (e.g., the Kiowa haircuts, which are long on one side and short on the other; the tribal split; the twins; and the mirror image), animals (varying images of antelope, buffalos, dogs, horses, and spiders are echoed throughout), and people (e.g., Mammedaty, Ka-au-ointy, Ko-sahn, and Aho). In addition, in the songs particularly, Momaday uses the progressive repetition often associated with oral poetry. It is important to keep in mind, though, that such techniques owe as much to his study of Euro-American modernists as to his examination of Kiowa oral traditions.

Similarly, repeated themes occur often. The three parts of section VIII introduce Momaday's insistence on the importance of language. When the twin warriors are in danger of being killed by giants, they remember Grandmother Spider's advice to say to themselves "the word thain-mom, 'above my eyes.'" They "repeated the word thain-mom over and over to themselves," and the smoke from the giants' fire stayed above their eyes (*WRM* 32). In the historical section, Momaday elaborates: "A word has power in and of itself. It comes from nothing into sound and meaning; it gives origin to all things. By means of words can a man deal with the world on equal terms. And the word is sacred" (*WRM* 33). Momaday completes his ethnographic discussion of Indian language with a discussion of the potency of a Kiowa's name. Then, in his personal account, he remembers that Aho, when she "saw or heard something bad, . . . said the word *zei-dl-bei*, 'frightful' ''—"an exertion of language upon ignorance and disorder" (*WRM* 33).

The theme of the potency of words is repeated in the often quoted story of the arrowmaker (section XIII), in the use of a phrase to pacify the storm spirit (section XIV), and in the anecdote about the "bad woman" who, abusing the power of language, lies to her blind husband and her people (section XVII). Of course, the entirety of *The Way to Rainy Mountain* is testimony to the power of language to create and shape reality, to re-create myth, to recollect history, to recall personal responses, and to unify these imaginatively.

As well as verbal and thematic repetitions, there are structural repetitions. Each of the three main sections ends at Rainy Mountain, as do the introduction, the epilogue, and the final poem, "Rainy Mountain Cemetery." These returns reveal several cyclical patterns within the larger framework of the journey. Rainy Mountain is where Momaday returned to seek his roots, where the Kiowa made their way, where Aho is buried, and where the reader arrives. It represents more than a specific geographic location; it is the localized source and end of our collective seeking.

A final oral aspect that Momaday uses sparingly is a modification of Plains Indian coup tales—accounts of brave deeds generally performed during a hunt or a fight. Basically, Momaday retains only the barest echoes of the "bragging biographies" of the Kiowa, whose contact with horses, according to Momaday, gave them "a taste for danger and an inclination to belligerence [*sic*]."[20] According to legend, on one hunting trip the tribe split in two because of a quarrel over an antelope udder. The historical passage does not glorify a particular hunting exploit, but explains the technique for a great circle hunt. In the personal reflections, Momaday is a poet, an artist, a man of sensibility as he describes not the triumph of catching a fine deer, but the joy of attaining a lovely image—the white rump of a frightened pronghorn bounding across the plains "like a succession of sunbursts against the purple hills" (*WRM* 19).

Most of the brave deeds recounted in *The Way to Rainy Mountain* are the mythical exploits of the twin heroes. In one reference to hunting, the hunter needs magical assistance to know how to kill the "buffalo with horns of steel" (*WRM* 54). Ironically, immediately following this tale is a historical account of a degraded version of hunting buffalo. Rather than the magnificent beast of the previous tale, the hunters chase ''a poor broken beast in which there was no trace left of the wild strain'' (*WRM* 55). Similarly, the personal passage reverses the traditional hunter's tale altogether as the buffalo mother chases Momaday and his father, instead of the other way around.

What we have here is not the nineteenth-century Plains Indian narrative of personal accomplishment, but a contemporary, lyrical narrative, based on pre-contact oral traditions of all sorts, that Momaday modified to educate and inspire contemporary readers. It is, in effect, a series of Momaday's tribal coup tales, but in place of arrows, Momaday uses words. The story of the arrowmaker makes this clear. The arrowmaker, sensing a person outside his tipi, tells his wife to continue their conversation as though everything were normal so as not to reveal to their potential enemy their awareness of him. As he should, the arrowmaker tests his newly made arrow, drawing it in the bow and aiming ''first in this direction and then in that'' (*WRM* 46). The story continues:

> And all the while he was talking, as if to his wife. But this is how he spoke: ''I know that you are there on the outside, for I can feel your eyes upon me. If you are a Kiowa, you will understand what I am saying, and you will speak your name.'' But there was no answer, and the man went on in the same way, pointing the arrow all around. At last his aim fell upon the place where his enemy stood, and he let go of the string. The arrow went straight to the enemy's heart. (*WRM* 46)

This story is about language, says Momaday, ''the repository of [the arrowmaker's] whole knowledge and experience, and it represents the only chance he has for survival'' (Man 172). For the arrowmaker–storyteller, language is not merely decorative, but a tool for self-creation, a weapon for survival. Momaday has shifted the thematic focus from the arrows of the nineteenth-century Kiowa to the language of the twentieth-century author. In the process, he fuses the two in the image of the arrowmaker. Both the toothmarked arrow and the well-crafted word go ''straight to the enemy's heart.'' But arrows did not save the buffalo, or the horses, or Tai-me, or even the Kiowas themselves. When in 1879 they surrendered to the U.S. Cavalry, the hunting and warring ways of their life on the Plains were over. Now, over one hundred years later, Momaday uses language as a means to salvage his personal and tribal story.

Kiowa Pictographs

Momaday's modification of oral personal narrative is accompanied by his transformation of pictographic narrative forms. He does not include pictographs, but like Kiowa tipi painters of old, he employs others (in this case, his father) to help realize his vision in artistic form.[21] "My father was a traditional Kiowa artist," explains Momaday, "he comes directly out of the Kiowa artistic tradition which preceded him" (Woodard 170). And like the pictographic sketchbook artists before him, Al Momaday experiments with subject and materials, both continuing and extending Kiowa artistic conventions. Of the eleven black-and-white illustrations in *The Way to Rainy Mountain,* three are in each of the three major sections, one is in the introduction, and one is in the epilogue. Unlike traditional pictographs, these drawings are not meant to tell the story alone. Rather, they complement the written narrative. According to one scholar, the first six illustrations provide "images of mythic time," and "the latter five . . . could be designated 'historical'" (McAllister 25). Thus the pictures reflect the narrative flow.

As well as linear progression, the illustrations provide an associational circularity. For instance, both the first and last pictures deal with the relationship of the earth and the sky, and the human desire to ascend from one to the other. In the first drawing (Figure 27), the seven sisters, who are now the seven stars of the Big Dipper, hover just above the top of Devils Tower. In the last (Figure 28), seven stars (mirroring the seven sister–stars) fall from a dark cloud at the top right of the page onto a row of five tipis lining the bottom of the page. Just as earlier pictographic coup accounts denoted animal tracks or military movement by a series of marks, the falling stars are linked to the cloud by curved descending lines, indicating their motion and direction. Like the two poems that begin and end *The Way to Rainy Mountain,* these two pictures tell the entire story of the Kiowa. The first drawing depicts the mythical world of the Kiowa—the pre-contact world, which reflected their intimate link to the land, their need to articulate their "wonder and delight" (*WRM* 4) in legends, and their personal relationship to the cosmos. The final picture illustrates the great meteor shower of 1833, "among the earliest entries in the Kiowa calendars," and, according to Momaday, the end of the mythical era and the beginning of "the historical period in the tribal mind" (*WRM* 85). This fundamental transformation of the Kiowa world is summarized in these two contemporary, highly stylized illustrations.

Even though they are not placed precisely at the beginning and end of

FIGURE 27. "Seven Sisters Transformed into the Big Dipper at Devils Tower" by Al Momaday (Kiowa), 1960s. (Courtesy of N. Scott Momaday)

The first illustration in *The Way to Rainy Mountain* suggests the Kiowa myth explaining the origin of Devils Tower (a giant rock formation in northeastern Wyoming) and the Big Dipper. When their brother turns into a bear and begins to chase them, seven sisters climb onto a tree stump to escape his reach. When the bear–brother continues his pursuit, the tree grows miraculously tall, elevating the girls to safety. All the while, the brother pursues his sisters, reaching his huge paws up to snatch them and scoring the growing tree with his great claws. The tree stump, now scratched all around by the bear, becomes Devils Tower, and the seven sisters are transformed into the seven stars of the Big Dipper. As long as the story is remembered, explains N. Scott Momaday, the Kiowa have relatives in the night sky.

FIGURE 28. ''Falling Stars of 1833'' by Al Momaday (Kiowa), 1960s. (Courtesy of N. Scott Momaday)

The final drawing in *The Way to Rainy Mountain* depicts the meteor shower of 1833. Seven stars and countless star fragments fall from a great cloud to the tipis along the bottom of the page. For N. Scott Momaday, the dramatic astronomical event of the falling stars (recorded by peoples throughout North America) suggests the end of the mythical era for the Kiowa and the beginning of the historical period. The seven falling stars hearken back to the first drawing (Figure 27) when the Kiowa had ''kinsmen in the night sky.''

each chapter, the first and last drawings (found in the first and last sections) frame both "The Setting Out" and "The Closing In." The nontraditional left-to-right flow of action in the first illustration and the traditional right-to-left flow of movement in the last drawing emphasize the framing device and a sense of closure. For instance, the cricket, encompassed by a full moon, faces the right side of the page as though it, too, were beginning the journey with the reader. Actually, the cricket illustration is positioned between the introduction and "The Setting Out." Thus it serves as a transition from the introduction, where its tiny presence is "made whole and eternal" by Momaday's angle of vision, to the first chapter. Similarly, it is Momaday's individual vision that attempts to make the story of the Kiowa "whole and eternal" (*WRM* 12). The final image of the first chapter, "The Setting Out," is an elaborate drawing of a water beast (half-dragon/half-amphibian) making an "awful commotion" within the waves. Between its fangs, its arrow-tongue shoots forth from the bow of its mouth. The water monster appears to thrash in all directions, but it is facing left, looking back to the words from which it was imagined.

In "The Closing In," the first picture, located after the first narrative unit, shows four buffalo skulls facing right. Arranged laterally, they seem to move from the top left corner to the bottom right corner of the page, urging the reader forward into the narrative journey, paralleling the Kiowa migration from the Northwest in a southeasterly direction, and reminding the reader of the destruction of the old Kiowa way of life. Certainly, destroying the buffalo was one strategy that helped accomplish that change. The final illustration, the upper torso of a horse with an arrow in its neck, fills the page. The horse faces left, looking back on the chapter and providing a kind of visual closure for the narrative.

The middle illustrations of "The Setting Out" and "The Closing In" are the only two "bilaterally symmetrical" images in the book, and appropriately they are "a thematic pair," notes McAllister. The archaic image of the spider and the modern symbol of "the peyote bird" suggest the historical movement from the early "regard for the natural world" to the later worship in the Native American Church (McAllister 25). Thus, structurally, "The Setting Out" and "The Closing In" are mirror images of each other.

All three illustrations in "The Going On," the middle chapter, face left, suggesting that Momaday is looking backward—in this case, recollecting the golden age of the Kiowa. Like the drawing of the water monster, these three pictures emanate action, a particular trademark of earlier pictographic conventions and of Al Momaday's paintings.[22] The first is the Kiowa storm spirit, "a strange wild animal," depicted here as half-horse/half-water beast, which spits lightning as it roams, "whipping and thrashing" in the moonlit sky (*WRM* 48). Both the geometric zigzag lightning fork and the graceful swirl of the beast's tail fall from the top quarter of the page to the white blankness below. The second illustration is of the buffalo whose steel horns flash in the sun. The viewer's eye moves from the buffalo's rump in the upper right of the page, along its descending curved torso, to its large head, bent to the left as though the animal were about to charge, in the middle of the page. The curves and markings of its body repeat the designs of previous illustrations, especially the lightning and the crescent moon. Above the buffalo's curved back are what look like the flying splinters of trees it has shattered.

The picture of the Kiowa hunter (Figure 29) is the closest thing in *The Way to Rainy Mountain* to the mid-nineteenth-century Plains Indian style of pictographic painting. It depicts strategic position and at least some detail of the hunter's and horse's ornamentation. But, like earlier transitional pictographic artists,[23] Al Momaday has modified the nineteenth-century conventions of tipi and hide painting. He depicts a buffalo being chased by an Indian on a horse. That the chase is at high speed is indicated by the buffalo's flying beard and hair, the horse's streaming mane, and the hunter's flowing hair and feathers. In the traditional Plains Indian pictographic flow of movement, they race from right to left across the page, seeming to emerge from behind a heap of scallops, perhaps representing the mountains from which they came. The hunter has his spear held high in his right hand, ready to thrust it into the buffalo, while his left hand holds his horse's rein lightly. This stylized depiction of physical landscape, the entirely side view, and the realistic rendering of the buffalo, the horse, and the hunter are all modifications of nineteenth-century conventions of hide and tipi painting. Momaday ends this chapter with a contemporary pictograph of the Kiowa who was "transformed into a daring buffalo hunter" (*WRM* 62). This is not Momaday's personal hunting exploit, nor is it an individual Kiowa hunter's animated chase; it is a depiction of a representative Kiowa hunter—a stereotypical emblem of the heroic Kiowa Plains culture.

The dramatic aspects of Momaday's modified forms of personal narrative are not so abundant or so obvious as his experimentation with oral and

FIGURE 29. "A Kiowa Buffalo Hunter" by Al Momaday (Kiowa), 1960s. (Courtesy of N. Scott Momaday)

In the one drawing reminiscent of nineteenth-century Plains Indian conventions of pictographic hide painting, Al Momaday narrates the action from right to left. The hunter races on horseback from the stylized landscape on the right in pursuit of a buffalo. Great speed is suggested by the free-blowing hair of the man, the flowing hair of the buffalo, and the streaming mane of the horse. The legs of both animals are in running positions, enhancing the sense of action as the hunter prepares to plunge his lance into the buffalo. For N. Scott Momaday, such a scene depicts the golden age of the Kiowa people.

pictographic modes. Just as some earlier editors of autobiographies, like Frank Linderman, described the tones of voice, gestures, and other performance aspects of their real-life subjects,[24] Momaday presents a few such details for the recollected and imagined characters of his personal-cultural narrative. He describes Aho's "screwed-up face" and the click of her tongue as she speaks. Another brief dramatic touch, reminiscent of Black Elk's more elaborate incorporation of ritual drama into his autobiography, is Ko-sahn's reenactment of preparations for the Sun Dance Ceremony. Generally, though, Momaday himself is the storyteller–dramatist, and through his structural cues he signals to the reader his changing style and tone. But finally, *The Way to Rainy Mountain* itself dramatizes the mythical, historical, and personal journey of the Kiowa and their consequent transition from an oral to a written tradition. Through the power of the word, Momaday has reclaimed Kiowa myth, recalled Kiowa history, remembered personal experience, and, in the process, reenvisioned himself in terms of each of these. This is, in part, a literary pose and, in part, a personal search for meaning.

As well as resurrecting and modifying pre-contact autobiographical narratives, Momaday continues the tradition of collaborative self-narration. He collaborates with Kiowa tribal elders, with his father, and with Euro-Americans (those, like James Mooney, who collected the ethnographic data on which he relied and those, like Yvor Winters, who influenced his literary taste). Like earlier Indian autobiographers such as Charles Alexander Eastman, he writes as a product of both the Anglo world and a native culture. In the process, he reconfigures a Kiowa identity and modifies the traditional modes of Plains Indian personal narrative, emphasizing the oral.

Finally, we have to ask what is autobiographical about *The Way to Rainy Mountain*. It could be simply an exquisitely written history of the Kiowa tribe, rather than an artfully shaped personal history of a Kiowa individual. Momaday's point, however, is that these are one and the same. He attempts to reclaim the communal sense of self, the land-based sense of identity, and the cosmic-related sense of being of his ancestors. The only way that is possible for him, with his twentieth-century, Stanford-educated literary sensibility, is through an impassioned act of the imagination realized in language. Although he refutes the comparison, Momaday may be likened to a Native American Emerson espousing an Indian oversoul.[25] He wants, like Ko-sahn, to see no distinction between the mythical and the historical, between the individual and the racial experience. But more than that is his decidedly twentieth-century Western obsession to remake himself anew through the power of the word.

The Names: A Memoir

Seven years after the publication of *The Way to Rainy Mountain,* Momaday published a second autobiographical account. In *The Names: A Memoir,* a more straightforward or conventional autobiography following Western forms, Momaday continues to address the themes of his earlier personal narrative. Again, Momaday is concerned with how language, the land, and the past influence one's self in the present. Again, it is through imagination, made substantive in language, that Momaday realizes this. In fact, one scholar sees *The Way to Rainy Mountain* and *The Names* as "two stages of Momaday's self-realization in language" (Schubnell 41). Whereas the first autobiography focuses on Kiowa history and culture, the second concentrates more strictly on Momaday himself. Andrew Wiget describes *The Names* simply as "a series of poetic reflections upon the meaning and emotional tenor of important experiences in the past" during Momaday's process of self-creation (121). Alan R. Velie compares *The Names* with Alex Haley's *Roots* and discusses Momaday's complicated ideas about his Indian identity (13–14, 20). Since Momaday diligently points out his artistic and imaginative awakenings and the influences that led to them, Mick McAllister calls *The Names* "a portrait of the artist as a young Indian" and "an act . . . of personal mythopoesis."[26]

Throughout *The Names,* Momaday reviews the effect of language, land, and ancestors on his sense of himself as a Kiowa and as a writer. He grew up hearing the Kiowa and English voices of his relatives and the Navajo utterances of his neighbors. He states that particularly the voices of his relatives compose "the element of [his] mind's life" (*Names* 8). Having lived in Oklahoma and on the Navajo reservation in New Mexico and Arizona, Momaday insists that these "two landscapes are fixed in [his] mind" (*Names* 59). Later he explains that Jemez was a determining place for him as well: "I existed in that landscape, and then my existence was indivisible with it" (*Names* 142). A variety of languages and landscapes, then, go into creating Momaday's self-conception. Such plurality is reflected in his genetic heritage as well. His Kiowa father, who "moved out of that old world of the Kiowas" (*Names* 36), and his mostly white mother, who moved into the world of the Indians, contribute to Momaday's manifold identity.

As a Kiowa child in the mid-twentieth century, Momaday was bewildered by his Indian heritage. This is clear in the Faulknerian stream-of-consciousness passages in which we see him as a youngster "formulating an idea of [him]self" (*Names* 97). In a vision derived directly from movie-house Westerns, he imagines himself as the heroic cowboy who is going to kill "the ugly Indian" (*Names* 76). His confusion about the precise meaning of Indian identity continues in a series of unpunctuated passages in which he muses:

> Oh I feel so dumb I can't answer all those questions I don't know how to be a Kiowa Indian my grandmother lives in a house it's like your house Miss Marshall or Billy Don's house only it doesn't have lights and light switches and the toilet is outside and you have to carry wood in from the woodpile and water from the well but that isn't what makes it Indian its my grandma the way she is the way she looks her hair in braids the clothes somehow yes the way she talks . . . wait I know why it's an Indian house because there are pictures of Indians on the walls photographs of people with long braids and buckskin clothes . . . and moccasins and necklaces and beadwork yes that's it and there is Indian stuff all around blankets and shawls bows and arrows everyone there acts like an Indian . . . and everyone talks Kiowa and the old people wear Indian clothes . . . and there is laughing Indians laugh a lot and . . . everyone sings . . . and it goes on through the night that's Indian my dad sets out poles on the river and we eat catfish that's Indian and grandma goes to Rainy Mountain Baptist Church that's Indian and my granddad Mammedaty is buried at Rainy Mountain and some of the stones there have peyote pictures on them and you can hear bobwhites there and see terrapins and scissortails and that's Indian too. (*Names* 101–102)

Momaday has a difficult time figuring out "how to be a Kiowa Indian." Finally, he decides that having "Indian stuff" around is what makes someone Indian. Scholars have noted the intended irony of this childlike definition that claims that Euro-American influences (like the Baptist church) and general regional practices (like catfish fishing) are somehow distinctly Indian. Velie says that since Momaday is the first of Alfred Momaday's family to not grow up among the Kiowa, his "ideas of his identity as an Indian are therefore complex and ambiguous" (20). Kenneth Lincoln agrees with Velie, but goes even further to make the important point that "this confusion, this challenge, is an Indian identity in America . . ." (105). *The Names,* then, is Momaday's attempt to weave into a pattern of meaning the disparate threads (the languages, landscapes, and people) of his mixed heritage. To do so, he reclaims traditional Native American modes of personal narrative, modifying them to suit his purpose and blending them with Euro-American autobiography.

Structural Circularity: Momaday's Return Journey

Before looking at how Momaday alters these traditional Native American forms, it is important to consider the overall structure of this memoir. *The Names* is divided into four main parts. These parts are preceded by a title page, an acknowledgment page, a genealogical chart, an untitled pre-prologue, and a prologue, and are followed by an epilogue. Part 1, divided into eight shorter sections, deals with family and tribal history. Part 2, the shortest chapter, containing only two sections, focuses on Momaday's memories of his early life. These recollections of childhood continue in Part 3, composed of four sections. Also having four sections, Part 4 deals with the ceremonial life at Jemez Pueblo and the end of Momaday's childhood.

Just as he did in *The Way to Rainy Mountain,* Momaday begins with the Kiowa origin myth. In the two-paragraph prologue, he recalls how the Kiowa emerged from a hollow log. The prologue ends with one paragraph of Momaday's commentary on this emergence myth. The final sentence of the prologue is: "They could at last say to themselves, 'We are, and our name is Kwuda'" (*Names* 1). Moving from the third-person plural (they) to the first-person plural (we) links Momaday to the "coming out" people and all of them to their name, Kwuda. Names, of course, are important throughout; here, a tribal name recalls the origins of his people.

The epilogue, in contrast, is Momaday's imaginative journey back to his source, told in the first-person singular. Along the way, Momaday calls to life the ghosts of his Kiowa past. He rides Guadal-tseyu (Little Red), the pony whose bones were in his step-grandfather Pohd-lohk's barn, and meets the elders who call him by his Indian name. He writes: "And to each one, face to face, weeping, I spoke his name: Mammedaty, Aho, Pohd-lohk, Keahdinekeah, Kau-au-ointy" (*Names* 166). Ironically, since speaking the names of the dead is taboo among the Kiowa (because the deceased may respond to their names and appear), Momaday has to violate an old Kiowa custom to resurrect the images of his ancestors. As well as his relatives, Ko-sahn was present. And Momaday imagines: "In the evenings, we told stories, the old people and I" (*Names* 166). Through Momaday's stories of their lives, these departed ones have come to life. In his essay "The Man Made of Words," Momaday tells of his surprise when Ko-sahn appeared to him one night. He denies her reality until she reminds him: "You have imagined me well, and so I am. . . . You see, I have existence, whole being, in your imagination" (*Man* 164). Momaday, then, wills these Kiowa elders into existence by imagining them powerfully.

After a time of shared storytelling with these elders, Momaday continues his journey, riding north and west, stopping at Tsoai (Devils Tower), and arriving, finally, at his destination—the original mountain home of the Kiowas: "And then there were meadows full of wildflowers, and a mist roiled upon them, the slow, rolling spill of the mountain clouds. And in one of these, in a pool of low light, I touched the fallen tree, the hollow log there in the thin crust of the ice" (*Names* 167). In the epilogue, then, Momaday makes the return journey of the one he made in *The Way to Rainy Mountain*. Rather than traveling from the source to the destination, he journeys from the end to the beginning. The narrative movement of the work is from the mythical past to the Kiowa–personal historical past to the imaginary mythical past reimagined in the present. This process parallels the very nature of autobiographical activity in which one filters past experience through the present moment. At the same time, the focus shifts from tribal to family to individual back to family and tribal.

Within this overall structure, Momaday has smaller, less conspicuous structural patterns. Stories within stories are one such model. Clearly, Momaday is telling his personal/family/tribal story. Within these autobiographical narratives are the stories his parents and relatives tell him. Momaday comments on these stories as he tells them. For instance, Pohd-lohk recounts the loss of a great horse, taken by an escaping Pawnee boy. For Pohd-lohk, Momaday says, "it was the story of the horse," but it "might have been a different story among the Pawnees, the story of the boy" (*Names* 50). When talking of his mother, he says her arrival among the Kiowa "is a whole story, hers to tell; yet some part of it is mine as well. And there is a larger story; I think of where I am in it" (*Names* 8). This "larger story," of course, is history. For Momaday, it is essential that each of us knows and tells our part of the story, our chapter of the "larger story" that unites us. Some might conclude that Momaday appropriates the stories of his relatives. In fact, all autobiographers, to some extent, tyrannize the telling of others' stories. Perhaps, though, Momaday provides a dynamic model of what Frank Kermode has described as the nature of narrative: "a dialogue between story and interpretation." Momaday, then, is participating in the "progressive interpretation" of personal and tribal stories.[27]

Just as narratives evoke narratives, Momaday's Indian name is a touchstone for a nexus of narratives. Momaday refers to "stories within stories" when he describes his ritual naming at Tsoai. These stories nestle within stories, like Chinese boxes: the myth of Tsoai, the story of Pohd-lohk, and the story of Momaday (a.k.a. Tsoai-talee), each story emerging from one and shaping the next.

At times, Momaday uses typographical devices, another structural component, to cue the reader to a special passage. Most notably, he italicizes certain evocative descriptions of land and place and the three Kiowa myths he includes. Likewise, his pages have generous white space between paragraphs, emphasizing transitions and silences. These are not the kind of prose paragraphs that flow logically from one to the other. Rather, they may be linked by association, image, or tone, or they may be juxtaposed for emphasis or surprise. Often, poems, conversations, and snatches of popular songs and verses are included, especially in Parts 1 and 2, and the first two sections of Part 3. In Part 3, section 3, Momaday relies almost entirely on a stream-of-consciousness style to capture the preconscious or subconscious mental meanderings of his boyhood in Hobbs, New Mexico. Such abundance and diversity of structural and stylistic devices attest to Momaday's mastery of the twentieth-century Western literary tradition. Schubnell, in fact, mentions that Momaday consciously patterned *The Names* after Isak Dinesen's *Out of Africa*. Certainly, that is not Momaday's only influence. Schubnell and others note the "literary echoes" of James Joyce, William Faulkner, Walt Whitman, Albert Camus, and Marcel Proust as well (Schubnell 168–174).

Adaptations of Traditional Kiowa Autobiographical Forms

Names
Besides Western literary influences, Momaday has Kiowa, Navajo, and Jemez narrative traditions on which to draw in shaping his life story. Just as he did in *The Way to Rainy Mountain,* Momaday modifies these

forms to fit his contemporary sensibility. By incorporating family names and stories, tribal myths, and multiple voices, Momaday resurrects in writing a sense of the importance of these for Plains Indians and all native people. In a 1981 interview, Momaday had this to say about names:

> I believe that a man is his name. The name and the existence are indivisible. One has to live up to his name. I think names are terribly important. Somewhere in the Indian mentality there is that idea that when someone is given a name—and, by the way, it transcends Indian cultures certainly—when a man is given a name, existence is given to him, too. And what could be worse than not having a name. (Schubnell 49–50)

Unpopular as Momaday's notion of names may be with postmodern scholars who find no connection between the word and the thing itself, Momaday insists that, for him (and this is true for many traditional Native American people as well), one's name and one's existence are "indivisible." (See Chapter 2 for a fuller discussion of Plains Indian naming practices.) Similarly, Momaday's belief in "the Indian mentality" is controversial among some academics, since it appears to conflate cultural and racial characteristics and to encourage, particularly for nonnatives, reductive notions of Native American identity. Momaday seems to equate "Indian mentality," however, with traditional Indian ways, linking the resulting perspective(s) to what he refers to as "racial memory" and what Charles Woodard calls the "ancestral voice." "I think sometimes that my voice is the reincarnation of a voice from my ancestral past," says Momaday, that sometimes "this voice of mine is proceeding from a great distance in the past" (Woodard 112). Momaday clarifies this further when he explains that he can "take credit for setting down those Kiowa stories in English," but not for inventing them (Woodard 57). In this way, he positions himself not only as a literary creator, but as a cultural conduit, much like John Neihardt does in his retelling of Black Elk's story. He does not, then, encourage reductive notions of Indian identity and its literary expression, but emphasizes the union of traditional continuity and contemporary innovation, of a relational self and an individual identity.

The title, the acknowledgment ("In devotion to those whose names I bear and to those who bear my names"), and the genealogical chart (with the name of each relative handwritten by Momaday) all testify to the significance of names for Momaday. In fact, Momaday explains that "the great principle of selection in the book is the principle of naming," "a very complicated and sacred business" (Woodard 88). The first words of the pre-prologue announce:

> My name is Tsoai-talee. I am, therefore, Tsoai-talee; therefore I am.
>
> The storyteller Pohd-lohk gave me the name Tsoai-talee. He believed that a man's life proceeds from his name, in the way that a river proceeds from its source. (*Names* n.p.)

In essence, the first sentence translates: I have a name, therefore I am that name, therefore I am. For Momaday and, he would have us believe, for his people, a name precedes one's existence, not vice versa. It is worth noting that Pohd-lohk is a storyteller, one who shapes language into meaning and delight. In naming Momaday (Tsoai-talee), he creates him, just as in naming his relatives, Momaday fashions them for the reader. Besides that, the name Tsoai-talee embodies a story, is itself a story—the story of the seven sisters who were transformed into the Big Dipper. Thus the name, like the story, links Momaday and his people to the past and to the heavens. The prologue also begins with a name: the first Kiowa, the contemporary Kiowa, and Momaday refer to themselves as Kwuda—the "coming out" people.

Just as names have been crucial in the prefatory materials, names are important in the first chapter. In fact, the first words are: "The names . . ." (*Names* 3). Momaday begins the paragraph with a list of generic names: "animals," "birds," "objects," "forms," and "sounds." He ends the paragraph with the names of his distant Kiowa relatives: "Pohd-lohk, Keahdinekeah, Aho" (*Names* 3). The very next paragraph continues Momaday's recitation of the names of the dead, this time the Euro-American relatives on his mother's side: "Galyen, Scott, McMillan . . ." (*Names* 3). This centuries-old coalition of names leads inevitably to his own. The Kiowa names—Kau-au-ointy, Keahdinekeah, and Mammedaty—move alongside the Euro-American names—I. J. Galyen, Nancy Scott, and Theodore Scott—before they mingle in his parents (who have both Indian and white names): Huan-toa (Alfred) and Natachee (Mayme). Just as Mammedaty, Momaday's paternal grandfather, "persists in his name," so do all his ancestors who have "invested the shadow of [their] presence in . . . [their] names" (*Names* 26). Like a Kiowa Adam, Momaday delights in creating catalogues of names—of things, events, stories, and people. He begins and ends his autobiography with the names of his ancestors, those whose names he claims as part of his identity.

In section 3 of Part 1, Momaday brings these names to life by describing their histories. Although he discusses other relatives, this section is devoted primarily to Theodore Scott and Anne Ellis, Momaday's maternal grandparents, and to his mother, Natachee, "the namesake of that dark mystery" (*Names* 20)—her Cherokee great-grandmother, Natachee Galyen. For Momaday, her name itself was reason enough for his mother to begin "to see herself as an Indian" (*Names* 25).

Section 4 opens with the name Mammedaty, Momaday's paternal grandfather. Momaday writes:

> Mammedaty was my grandfather, whom I never knew. Yet he came to be imagined posthumously in the going on of the blood, having invested the shadow of his presence in an object or a word, in his name above all. He enters into my dreams; he persists in his name. (*Names* 26)

For Momaday, then, Mammedaty "persists in his name." From the name Mammedaty, the linguistic trace of the grandfather he never knew, Momaday imagines the man himself. As well as his grandfather, Momaday introduces his grandmother, Aho, and his great-great-grandmother, Kau-au-ointy. Similarly, section 5 deals with Momaday's father, Huan-toa, who was renamed Alfred Morris after a white friend of the family (a traditional Plains Indian activity of progressive naming, but now an indication of changing times). In sections 6 and 7, Momaday describes his parents' courtship and marriage, and his birth. He gives special attention to his name on the Standard Certificate of Birth: Navarro Scotte Mammedaty. Next, he mentions the "first notable event" in his life: his family's journey to Devils Tower, from which his Kiowa name derives. He ends this brief section by stating his intention to "imagine a day in the life of a man, Pohd-lohk, who gave [him] a name" (*Names* 42). These seven sections, then, name and describe Momaday's relatives.

The long section 8 is devoted to Pohd-lohk, the name-giver. Pohd-lohk means "old wolf" in Kiowa, and Momaday tells a story about "a young man" who "heard in a high wind the whimper of young wolves," and "had known at once, instinctively, where and what they were, and he went to them quietly, directly, so that there should be almost no fear. . . ." The young man sang softly to the wolves as they "lay huddled among the rocks . . ." (*Names* 46). The next paragraph consists of three italicized words: "*Pohd-lohk, old wolf*" (*Names* 46). Momaday insists here that the relation between a self and a name is mysterious and powerful. Pohd-lohk knows "instinctively, where and what" the wolves were, and he responds to them. With such a personal understanding of the magic of names, Pohd-lohk is an especially powerful bestower of names.

In this section also, Momaday imagines Pohd-lohk reading his winter count (a tribal calendar history). Pohd-lohk recites the names of some of the most transitional events in Kiowa history: *Da-pegya-de Sai* (winter of the falling stars, 1833), *Ta'dalkop Sai* (smallpox summer, 1839–1840), the winter the Pawnee captive escaped with Guadal-tseyu (1851–1852), and *A'dalk'atoi K'ado* (Nez Percé Sun Dance summer, 1883) (*Names* 48–52). Such a recitation is like an informal naming ceremony, confirming the existence and meaning of Kiowa history by rendering it in language.

Next, in the arbor, "a place of strong magic," Pohd-lohk gives the boy a name:

> Pohd-lohk spoke, as if telling a story, of the coming-out people, of their long journey. He spoke of how it was that everything began, of Tsoai, and of the stars falling or holding fast in strange patterns on the sky. And in this, at last, Pohd-lohk affirmed the whole life of the child in a name, saying: Now you are, Tsoai-talee. (*Names* 56–57)

The origin of the Kiowa, their history, and their relation to the universe are all essential aspects of being that converge in the child's name. His name, then, embodies these mythical and historical mysteries. The punctuation of the last line is crucial. It is not "Now you are Tsoai-talee," a simple announcement. Rather, the comma makes all the difference in meaning: "Now you are, Tsoai-talee," is a proclamation of existence itself. In fact, as Momaday would have it, through him (his name), the stories and lives of his people live on.

Throughout the work, Momaday delights in naming, especially places and people. He emphasizes this in a less personal way by cataloguing people at the Jemez Pueblo in Part 4, section 2. He provides brief written sketches of Lupe Lucero, Francisco Tosa, Sefora Tosa, Quincy Tahoma, and an unnamed man who was reputed to be "*muy loco,*" perhaps the result of his namelessness (*Names* 148–151).

Finally, as mentioned earlier, in the epilogue Momaday imagines meeting his ancestors in the arbor. Significantly, they call him Tsoai-talee, and he speaks their names: "Mammedaty, Aho, Pohd-lohk, Keahdinekeah, Kau-au-ointy" (*Names* 166). After he encounters his name-givers, he visits Tsoai, the place for which he was named, and thus prepared, he returns to the hollow log in the mountain meadow of the Kiowa homeland. Thus Momaday ends *The Names* as he began it, with the names of those whose names are part of him.

In keeping with nineteenth-century Plains Indian naming traditions, Momaday himself has several names. Momaday emphasizes his "first Indian name," Tsoai-talee, but he also has a "second Indian name," Tsotohah (Red Bluff), which he downplays (*Names* 170). Since Tsoto-hah does not lend itself to as many mythical, historical, or geographical resonances as Tsoai-talee, Momaday mentions it only twice and relegates it to his Glossary of Indian Terms, an alternative identity lurking among the untold stories beyond this text.[28] In an interview with Charles Woodard, Momaday mentions yet another of his Indian names, Wanbli Wanjila (Eagle Alone), a name conferred on him by a Lakota elder (Woodard 90).

As Garrick Mallery reported in the *Tenth Annual Report of the Bureau of Ethnology, 1888–89,* traditionally, Plains Indian names changed with the deeds or visions of the individual.[29] Momaday does not dwell on this dynamic aspect of Indian naming. However, he shows how Kiowa names have changed historically (his earlier relatives have only Kiowa names, while his more recent relatives have both Indian and Anglo names). He illustrates also how an intimate connection to a landscape and an entire history of a people may be crucial ingredients of a name. He does not reveal the sense of possibility of earning ever new names (and therefore ever new identities) throughout his life. Rather, Momaday treats names, especially his first Indian name, as preservers of tribal identity.

Tribal and Family Stories
As well as names, Momaday incorporates tribal myths and family anecdotes into his autobiographical account. Both of these come from an oral rather than a written tradition. By using them, Momaday emphasizes the orality as well as the communality of the stories that shaped his self-identity. Surprisingly, he includes only three tribal myths: the Kiowa origin myth, the Tsoai myth, and a Saynday (the Kiowa trickster) tale. We have discussed earlier how the first two stories are vital to Moma-day's identity. The trickster tale is important also. On a night when the

people are gathered together in the arbor, an old man tells Tsoai-talee the story of how the man in the moon came to be. Saynday set out to hunt buffalo with the other men. Each evening, instead of fresh buffalo meat, the inept Saynday brought tomatoes home to his disappointed wife. After four such failures at hunting buffalo, Saynday's wife, now quite sick of tomatoes, "began to beat him with a broom." Pursued by his angry spouse, Saynday ran and hid in the moon, where he remains today "because he is afraid of his wife" (*Names* 97). The gathered assembly (presumably the women as well as the men) laughs together at this familiar story, and Momaday writes: "I am created in the old man's story, in his delight" (*Names* 97). Tribal myths and tales, then, provide a group identity, knitting the members of the tribe together through their telling and retelling.

Family stories have the power to create identity as well. "Notions of the past and future are essentially notions of the present," explains Momaday. "In the same way an idea of one's ancestry and posterity is really an idea of the self" (*Names* 97). It is hard to tell if Momaday creates "an idea of the self" and writes his autobiography to conform to that notion or if he invents "an idea of [his] ancestry and posterity" and shapes his autobiography around that. Perhaps these influences work simultaneously, each defining and refining the other. At any rate, Momaday reconstructs numerous family anecdotes—for instance, the stories of his "wild in spirit" great-uncle Granville Scott, who "pulled a gun on a preacher" (*Names* 14–15), or his mother as a young, high-spirited, spoiled "sheriff's daughter" using the mayor's barn for target practice (*Names* 22). Sometimes, as he relates such stories, he takes literary license and imagines the thoughts and words of an ancestor he has never even met. Pohd-lohk's visit to Keahdinekeah comes to mind, complete with Keahdinekeah's private thoughts: "Of this she thought, and she said to herself: 'Yes, old man, I see' . . ." (*Names* 55–56). Such liberty in imaginatively re-creating not only his own past thoughts and feelings but the even older and more distant inner lives of his ancestors results in what Albert E. Stone has called "factual fictions,"[30] or what others might call gross appropriations. Ursula Le Guin explains the mysterious transformations of making the stories of others our own by recounting the story of a German anthropologist who tells a Plains Indian story in English to a young girl in California (an apt model for what has happened to many native traditions): ". . . by remembering it he had made the story his; and insofar as I have remembered it, it is mine; and now, if you like, it's yours. In the tale, in the telling, we are all one blood."[31] By telling the stories of his relatives, which are also his own stories now, Momaday affirms that he and his distant relations are "all one blood."

Orality, Photography, and Ceremony
Just as he did in *The Way to Rainy Mountain,* Momaday emphasizes orality by including oral formulas and multiple voices. He begins the only clearly fictional short story in the autobiography with "Dypaloh" and ends it with "Qtsedaba," traditional Jemez story-opening and -closing conventions (*Names* 137, 142). The same story has a second beginning, the more traditional Western opening: "Once there was . . ." (*Names* 137). Momaday varies the storytellers, allowing different speakers to tell their own or others' stories (even if Momaday has composed the tales for them). He also includes simple conversation and dialect. For instance, a Southerner named Belcher greets Momaday and his mother on their visit to Nancy Scott's grave in Kentucky: "Reckon it's gon' rine. M'nime's Belcher. Y'all got folk hyere" (*Names* 11). In another instance, he envisions the child Momaday's imaginary football announcer: "Ladies and gentlemen this is incredible it looked like a run all the way but Bertelli hid the ball and at the last moment flipped a pass to Momaday . . ." (*Names* 111). Such devices and voices enhance the orality and enrich the verbal texture of the autobiography.

As well as incorporating and modifying oral aspects of personal narrative, Momaday includes three of his own sketches (two of un-photographed relatives in his genealogical chart, and one of Devils Tower) and thirty photographs. Twenty-six of these photographs are of Momaday's relatives, and four are of places (Rainy Mountain, the arbor, a southern cemetery, and Boke's store). Reminiscent of Zo-Tom's, Howling Wolf's, and White Bull's written commentary on their picto-graphic drawings and of the enduring Euro-American tradition of family photograph albums, Momaday writes identifications and comments below each photograph. A family photo album (personal history such as Momaday incorporates into *The Names*) and winter counts (tribal history) perform similar functions.[32] Each records an important event or person; each serves as a mnemonic device to assist the family/tribal historian to remember the past; and each needs an interpreter–storyteller to bring it to life.

Like Native American autobiographers before him, Momaday suggests the performance of his personal narrative by adding dialogue, reenacting childhood fantasies, and reconstructing Jemez Pueblo ceremonies. As discussed earlier, he incorporates dialogue (from a multitude of sources) so the reader hears many varied voices. Similarly, he reenacts some of his childhood games (recalling fantasies of fighting in World War II, escaping from a prisoner-of-war camp, and starring in a football game). Note that these fantasies are all imaginary enactments of "mainstream" American activities that, ironically, recall nineteenth-century Plains Indian coup tales. Perhaps they derive more from gender than from culture in this case. Both cultures encourage males to perform brave deeds and to share stories of their glorious accomplishments.

Finally, like Black Elk, Momaday incorporates Native American ceremonies into his autobiography. In Part 4, he describes the ceremonial year at Jemez Pueblo, bringing to life the feasts, dances, and games of the people. Like Black Elk, he places his spiritual vision at the center of his life and at the heart of his personal narrative. Unlike Black Elk, Momaday's vision is an individual secular inspiration, not a communal religious one. Furthermore, Momaday's personal vision leads to the overriding action of *The Names*—his imagination-induced return journey to the hollow log of Kiowa origin.

Leslie Marmon Silko

In 1948, Leslie Marmon Silko, of Laguna-Mexican-Anglo descent, was born in Old Laguna, New Mexico. There she grew up hearing family and community stories. Growing up mixed-blood in a Keres community that values conformity and continuity gives her a unique perspective—part participant, part observer. In fact, Silko's family history helps to clarify her dual vision, her marginal position. In the late nineteenth century, the Euro-American Marmon brothers married Laguna women and were influential in the process of acculturation. Their outsider position is exemplified by the placement of the Marmon Company and home, which are situated beyond the main pueblo on the margins of the community. Like N. Scott Momaday, who grew up multiculturally also, Silko brings to her writing Native American as well as Euro-American influences. While she spent her early school years at an Indian school, in the fifth grade she was sent to a Catholic school in Albuquerque. By age twelve, she had acquired a literary taste for Milton and Shakespeare and for such American authors as Edgar Allan Poe, William Faulkner, Flannery

O'Connor, and John Steinbeck.[33] In 1969, she earned her B.A. degree in English at the University of New Mexico. Since then, she has traveled, lectured, written, and taught, at Navajo Community College and, most recently, at the University of Arizona.

Like Momaday and other contemporary Native American writers, Leslie Marmon Silko emphasizes how one's land and community, processed by memory and imagination and shaped into language, create one's personal identity. For Silko, community, with its attendant sense of place (geographical, cultural, and social), and personal identity are irrevocably linked. "The community is tremendously important," explains Silko, "That's where a person's identity has to come from, not from racial blood quantum levels." Such an emphasis on community is natural coming from one who is concerned primarily with relationships. "That's all there really is," she explains.[34]

Although acknowledging and affirming communal identity may be a Native American, in this case Laguna, orientation, it is also a profoundly female perspective. Like many Euro-American female autobiographers, Silko does not set up her personal experience and point of view as representative of her people, place, or time. Rather, she insists that hers is not "a Laguna point of view." "It's my point of view," she says, "coming from a certain kind of background and place" (Fisher 21). Silko, then, insists on her individuality as well as her place within a larger familial and cultural network.

Storyteller

Silko's novel *Ceremony* (1977) has received abundant critical attention, while her multiform autobiography, *Storyteller* (1981), has been virtually ignored. Perhaps this is because many of the stories and poems in *Storyteller* are reprinted from other sources; perhaps it is because the work is not readily classifiable. A collection of poetry, prose, and photographs, *Storyteller* includes brief expository essays on Laguna tradition, autobiographical essays, and letters as well as eight short stories and numerous poems and poetic narratives. It is important to clarify that Silko did not conceive of *Storyteller* as autobiography, even though the collection is autobiographical. Ambrose Lucero calls *Storyteller* "a strangely volatile combination of simple autobiography and seemingly simple stories" in which Silko "adds her portion to the conglomerate wisdom of a people working together for an identity." In a more comprehensive reading of this "multi-generic work," Bernard A. Hirsch delineates three main narrative sections, each with a thematic focus: the "Survival Section" (pp. 1–53), the "Yellow Woman Section" (pp. 54–99), and a final section about "learning to see the land rightly."[35]

Although scholars like Lucero and Hirsch agree that *Storyteller* is grounded in oral tradition, what Paula Gunn Allen refers to as "the creative source of [Native American] collective and individual selves,"[36] most dismiss the possibility of *Storyteller* as autobiography because of its communal emphasis. A recent exception is Arnold Krupat, who examines *Storyteller* as a "polyphonic" autobiography "in which the author defines herself . . . in relation to the voices of other storytellers" (*Voice,* 163). Generally, scholars have insisted that Silko "subordinates the individual to the communal and cultural" (Hirsch 2–3), "largely leaving herself out of the book" (Seyersted 35). Such conclusions restrict autobiography to autonomous first-person narratives. The point, though, is that for Silko (as for many indigenous people and many women), identity is created and maintained through relationships and the stories that bear witness to them. The Indian "I," in Bakhtinian fashion, is inherently polyvocal. Paula Gunn Allen notes that Native American, particularly Keres, traditional literature has "the tendency to distribute value evenly among various elements," reflecting the "egalitarian," as opposed to the Western hierarchical, organization of society and literature. "In this structural framework," she claims, "no single element is foregrounded" (240–241). With such a framework, particularly notable in *Storyteller,* it is no wonder that a Western reader, prepared for autonomy, conflict, resolution, and linear narrative, does not find a recognizable autobiographical pattern.

Orality and Autobiographical Narrative

In *Storyteller,* Silko tells her mythical, community, and personal narratives, continuing the Laguna tradition of spinning personal identity from communal stories. Just as Grandmother Spider (Thought Woman) sings creation into being, the storyteller spins words into stories like an autobiographer creating a present pattern from remembered forms. Throughout the work, Silko is concerned with re-creating the spoken word on the page. Her father's aunt, whom she calls Aunt Susie, was of "the last generation here at Laguna, / that passed down an entire culture / by word of mouth / an entire history / an entire vision of the world / which depended upon memory / and retelling by subsequent generations."[37] Due to "the European intrusion" that, among other treacheries, resulted in native children being stolen away from "the tellers," maintenance of this oral tradition was "irrevocably altered" (Silko 6). Nonetheless, Aunt Susie, as does Silko, continues the oral tradition. "What she is leaving with us— / the stories and remembered accounts," writes Silko, "is primarily what she was able to tell / and what we are able to remember" (6). Telling and remembering, storyteller and audience, are crucial to such cultural continuity. Furthermore, Silko acknowledges the responsibility of each individual to sustain and enrich the ongoing yet everchanging tradition of storytelling:

> As with any generation
> the oral tradition depends upon each person
> listening and remembering a portion
> and it is together—
> all of us remembering what we have heard together—
> that creates the whole story
> the long story of the people. (6–7)

"The long story of the people" includes individual life stories as well as community narratives and tribal myths. No one story is more important than another; no one narrative is insignificant. Each story, like each individual, is made whole through connection to shared remembering and telling.

Unlike some who claim to speak as representative Indians, Silko is careful to claim only a single voice in the multitude of Laguna voices. "I remember only a small part," she says. "But this is *what I remember,*" and, she goes on to say, "This is *the way I remember . . .*" (7, emphases mine). The "what" and the "way," the content (and context) and the process, are equally important. In this way, Silko acknowledges the personal quirks and lapses of memory (a crucial issue among autobiography theorists); the individual gifts of each storyteller; the pluralistic voices of her autobiographical tradition, both oral and written, Indian and Anglo; and the possibility of manifold identities. In the process of her remembering and retelling, she does not appropriate the traditional stories, although she embellishes and reinterprets them.

After explaining the significance and importance of the ongoing oral tradition, Silko provides a vivid example of it. Silko's autobiographical persona retells a story, told earlier by her Aunt Susie, "about the little girl who ran away" (Silko 7). Before she tells the story, though, Silko comments on Aunt Susie, a "self-made scholar" and lover of stories, who uses her own distinctive phrases and words to make the stories memorable. Rather than claiming to tell the "authentic" version of this story, to reconstruct her aunt's story exactly (an impossible task), Silko notes: "This is *the way I remember /* she told this one story . . ." (7, emphasis mine). Silko refutes the outdated but persistent Euro-American misconception about the existence of "one true Indian version" of a story (or an oral tradition) unsullied by interpretation and the consequent notion of the supposed stasis of oral transmission. In addition, far from leaving herself out of the book, as many scholars have insisted, she places herself—her memory, imagination, and storytelling voice—as the central but invisible focus.

Throughout the narrative of the little girl, Silko uses italics to provide ethnographic explanation and occasional emphases. Instead of a footnote or preface, italicization functions as an intimate aside to the reader–listener, explaining Laguna traditions and history. For instance, when the little girl–protagonist asks her mother for some "yashtoah to eat" (Silko 8), Silko–storyteller explains in italics:

> *"Yashtoah" is the hardened crust on corn meal mush*
> *that curls up.*
>
> *The very name "yashtoah" means*
> *it's sort of curled-up, you know, dried,*
> *just as mush dries on top.* (Silko 8)

This is, indeed, a type of cultural translation for a non-Laguna reading audience. Similarly, when the little girl jumps into the lake and drowns just as her mother is about to reach her, the narrator pauses to comment: *"Of course the mother was very sad"* (Silko 14). Like some Euro-American editors of Native American autobiographies (such as Frank Linderman, who commented profusely on the storytelling styles of Plenty-Coups and Pretty-Shield and on their Crow culture), Silko uses italics throughout to explain Laguna words and actions, to note emphases, and to highlight performance cues.

After this story has been told, Silko comments again on her aunt's performance, particularly her voice inflections. The mother's words to her daughter were always spoken "with great tenderness," explains Silko, "as if she herself were the mother / addressing her little child"

(15). Similarly, there was "something mournful / in her voice" when Aunt Susie spoke the old man's warning. But as soon as "the little girl's clothes turned into butterflies / then her voice would change and I could hear the excitement and wonder / and the story wasn't sad any longer" (Silko 15). Here Silko emphasizes not only her aunt's storytelling voice, but her own responses to it ("I could hear," she says), uniting the remembered speaker and listener in the present experience of the auto-biographer and again of the reader.

Later, Silko describes the context for another story, this one told by her Aunt Alice. When Silko was seven years old, she felt sad to be left behind when her parents went on a deer-hunting trip to Mount Taylor. Aunt Alice tells Leslie and her two sisters a cheering-up and diversion story about "a young Laguna girl / who was a fine hunter" (Silko 82). The young girl turns out to be Kochininako (Yellow Woman) and, according to Paula Gunn Allen, "the Spirit of Woman" (227). With the help of the Twin Brothers, Kochininako overcomes the giant Estrucuyu. The story not only distracts the young sisters from their disappointment, but inspires them with the grand possibilities of female achievement.

Silko again highlights orality and the dialogic nature of stories when she explains that the Laguna *"always begin their stories / with 'humma-hah': / that means 'long ago,'"* while the listeners respond: *"aaaa-eh"* (38). Together teller and listener(s) narrate the story. Silko develops these ideas further when she reports that her neighbor Nora remembers one of Silko's published poems, "Laguna Coyote," differently. "The way my grandpa used to tell it / is longer," Nora says (Silko 110). "Yes," Silko replies, "that's the trouble with writing. . . . You can't go on and on the way we do / when we tell stories around here / People who aren't used to it get tired" (110). Hirsch notes astutely that this "reminds us of the flexibility and inclusiveness of the oral tradition" (2), but Silko does not merely acknowledge variant versions of the story. She re-creates Nora's reminiscences of the context and scope of her grand-father's coyote tales. Nora does not retell the story; rather, she retells the telling: the audience's anticipation and laughter and her grandfather's hesitation until he was given "something really good to eat" (Silko 110). As Nora explains: "you're supposed to feed the storyteller good things" (Silko 110). The telling, then—its preparation, context, and result—is as crucial as, inseparable from, the narrative itself.

In addition to her aunt's stories, Silko's short story "Storyteller" provides an apt commentary on the nature of autobiography, particularly for Native Americans who wish to tell, perhaps for the first time, their version of Euro-American domination. As the grandmother insists in the story: "It will take a long time, but the story must be told. There must not be any lies" (Silko 26). The young woman in the story tells the story as *she* knows it to be, accepting the consequences of her insistence that she lured the lecherous Gussack (white man) to his icy death intentionally. Likewise, in her numerous renderings of traditional Keres narratives in contemporary contexts, Silko insists that "the story must be told"—not the "official" fiction printed in the U.S. history books or espoused by government officials, but the story as indigenous people have lived it.

Just as Momaday interweaves three narrative strands in *The Way to Rainy Mountain,* Silko blends mythical, community, and personal stories into her autobiographical work. The structure of *Storyteller,* however, is not as obvious, some might say formulaic or crafted, as *The Way to Rainy Mountain,* which routinely interchanges the three narrative modes. For Silko, the old stories not only are still being told, by relatives and community members, but are still being enacted. Her poem "Storytelling" begins by affirming this fact:

> You should understand
> the way it was
> back then,
> because it is the same
> even now. (94)

The short story "Yellow Woman" is the best delineation of Silko's belief in how the oral tradition relates to contemporary life, how the old stories are simply reenacted in our current lives, how today's storytellers and writers are simply renegotiating age-old narratives. The unnamed narrator, a modern-day Yellow Woman, awakens next to a man who, like the Kat'sina in some versions of the Yellow Woman abduction stories, takes her away.[38] Silko's version is somewhat ambiguous because the woman goes willingly, albeit with doubts. After spending a couple of days in the mountains with the mysterious stranger, the woman returns to her husband and children with a story, curiously reminiscent of a Yellow Woman tale, to explain her absence. Like old Grandma explains in the novel *Ceremony,* "It seems like I already heard these stories before . . . only thing is, the names sound different."[39]

Community or village stories, what some critics have referred to as "gossip," provide examples of how certain stories are repeated, but with new characters. "His wife had caught them together before," begins one such story about an extramarital affair in the community. "Then there was the night/old man George was going/down the hill to the toilet" when he "heard strange sounds" from an old barn and found a respectable community member naked with a woman (Silko 92). The daily community happenings, the occasional trysts, and the ever-present humor provide abundant raw material for neighborhood stories. For Silko, just as for Momaday, the mythical, community, and personal narratives of past and present are inseparable or at least irrevocably linked to one another.

The Photographic "I"

As well as the spoken word, the visual image plays a significant part in *Storyteller*. Silko explains that the photographs "are themselves part of the stories" (n.p.). The photographs are included, she notes, "because they are part of many of the stories/and because many of the stories can be traced in the photographs" (1). She suggests a fundamental connection between an image and a narrative. Hirsch claims that the photographs create a "circular design" in *Storyteller*. Certainly, the photographs, taken from the 1890s to the 1970s, vividly link the past to the present. More than that, they link people, particularly Silko, to place and provide insights into the photographer's frame and Silko's prismatic autobiographical point of view.

Of twenty-six photographs, twelve are of relatives, seven are of the land, five are of community members (if we include the picture of Navajos visiting the Laguna Fiesta), and two are of Silko alone (although she appears in four). Seventeen of the photographs were taken by Silko's father, Lee Marmon.[40] Like the text, then, the photographs emphasize relationships—with one's relatives, landscape, and community. As Hirsch points out, Silko begins the book with a photograph of her great-grandparents and her grandfather and ends with one of her great-grandfather, uncles, and father. The first appears to be a studio portrait, while the last is set in the New Mexico outdoors where the family members are framed by a mesa on one side and a car on the other—an apt representation of their connection to both an ancient and a modern culture, to a natural and a technological world. Throughout, she intersperses pictures of her relatives (e.g., Great Grandfather Stagner, Great Grandma Am'ooh, Grandpa Hank, Aunt Susie, Uncle Polly, and her sisters), but it is her father whose presence permeates the book as the primary gaze behind the camera. In one photograph, in fact, he is both the agent and the object of picture-taking, both behind and in front of the camera.[41]

Just as Silko retells, in her own fashion, family, community, and tribal stories, she rearranges her father's photographic perspective into her own meaningful pattern. First we have Silko's point of view as she shows us this selective equivalent to a family photograph album; then her photographer father's as he frames the people and the land; then Denny Carr's as he photographs Silko, appropriately situated in the center of the Tucson mountains, in the only contemporary photograph of Silko included. Overall, the photographs do not constitute a serial self-portrait or linear narrative as Euro-Americans conceive of it. However, such photographic images highlight Silko's continual emphasis on relationships, on connections to one's community and geography. Perhaps it is true that we concoct our notions of ourselves, in part, through the multifarious perspectives of those who observe us. Just as she does with the storyteller's voices, then, Silko shares various photographic points of view. Her vision, though, shapes and unites all of these as she weaves such multiple voices and visions into her own personal narrative.

Silko's captions for the photographs are sometimes as revealing as the photographs themselves. For instance, in at least one photograph caption, the landscape is described very much like a person: "With Pa'toe'ch Mesa visible at the extreme left of the photograph are Uncle Kenneth, Grandpa Hank's brother, my great-grandpa Robert G. Marmon, Charlie Pierce who married Aunt Bess, Grandpa Hank's sister, and Uncle Walter, Grandpa Hank's brother" (Silko 274). Preceding the catalogue of relatives is Pa'toe'ch Mesa. Although they are but a dim outline in the photograph, the mesas and the surrounding expanses define the people. Maybe that is why in the only photograph of the present-day Silko, she erases herself from the caption. Instead of announcing herself in a straightforward manner, such as "Here I am sitting in the Cottonwood Wash," she writes: "In the Cottonwood Wash below Wasson Peak in Tucson Mountains, Arizona" (274). The "I" is absent; the land is foregrounded. A similar self-erasure/evasiveness occurs in the caption for the photograph of Aunt Susie with Silko as a child. In place of an identifying tag (e.g., "This is me"), she shares a memory: "When I was a little girl Aunt Susie spent a good deal of time at the Marmon Ranch . . ." (269). The reader–listener–viewer is left to wonder if this is, indeed, Silko in the picture. While Silko seems to erase herself as an autonomous autobiographer, her voice and image, refracted from the prism of her relations, permeate *Storyteller*. Instead of the Euro-American autobiographical habit of announcing and exalting a separate self, this Laguna Pueblo woman presents a prismatic self, a self that stands with, rather than apart from, her community.

"Getaway" Stories

Escape stories are an essential part of the well-prepared storyteller's repertoire. Tales of escape from natural disasters, tribal disputes, and Euro-American colonization (literally and literarily) are necessary freedom trails to those who follow.[42] The storyteller, according to Silko, "keeps the stories" (247), especially the escape tales. "With these stories of ours," explains the raconteur in "The Storyteller's Escape," "we can escape almost anything / with these stories we will survive" (Silko 247). By knowing all the stories, "even stories told before she was born," the speaker keeps alive the tribal memory of "the dear ones who do not come back" (Silko 247). More important, having one's story ensures survival. The storyteller, pondering her death and her inability to narrate the story of it, hopes her survivors will tell her story. She has her own version of her end, however, and she asks: without her narrative gift, "how could they remember her" (Silko 252). By remembering and retelling the stories, the dead are honored and personal and tribal history endures.

In some ways, the man-become-bear narrative poem, "Story from Bear Country," is an escape story that illustrates the importance of memory and community. The "you" of the poem is seduced into the "canyon and hills" (Silko 206) by the bear people, whose "beauty will overcome . . . memory" (Silko 205), even the memory of one's self. The narrative voice of the poem, speaking on behalf of the community, says to the transformed man: "We can send bear priests / loping after you" (Silko 205). With their "beautiful songs" (Silko 206), they will try to call you back, to pull you back into the story of the tribe. The bear priests, with songs, stories, and the concentrated love of the community, talk the bear-man home. During their ritual, they create a trail of words leading the bear-man home to his people, back to himself. This "getaway story" (Silko 253) illustrates the necessity of collective memory, tribal story, personal narrative, and community effort to bring one back to one's self, to one's people and place (if not in actuality, then in imagination). *Storyteller* itself is a collection of "getaway stories," an anthology of narratives that assist survival in an Anglo-dominated world and that ensure personal and tribal continuity.

Memory, of course, is crucial to the continuance of the oral tradition and to the practice of autobiography. But, notes Silko, "sometimes what we call 'memory' and what we call 'imagination' are not so easily distinguished" (227). The relationship between imagination and memory is as elusive in an oral tradition as it is in a written one.[43] Silko describes how her Aunt Susie and Aunt Alice told her stories they had heard before, "but with changes in details or descriptions." "The story was the important thing," she explains, "and little changes here and there were really part of the story" (227). Throughout the centuries, the oral stories have been passed down, changing continually in the process. Silko's *Storyteller* is "part of the continuing which storytelling must be" (Silko 227). Finally, what remains, she says, are the stories our ancestors were "able to tell / and what we are able to remember" (6).

Conclusion

Like Charles Eastman and Black Elk, Native American autobiographers from the late nineteenth and early twentieth centuries, Momaday and Silko incorporate traditional oral (and sometimes artistic and dramatic) modes of personal narrative into their work. Like them, they modify these forms for a new audience and a new purpose. In *The Way to Rainy Mountain, The Names,* and *Storyteller,* Momaday and Silko write for a complex and varied audience—both native and nonnative. Through imagination, given substance in language, Momaday and Silko attempt to restore, reclaim, and revivify—at least on the page—their personal and tribal heritage. In the process, they expand the Western notion of autobiography to include nonwritten personal narrative (e.g., recorded oral tales and illustrations) and non-Western ideas of self (e.g., a personal-tribal, land-based sensibility). In short, Momaday and Silko continue indigenous traditions of self-narration and incorporate Native American voices into the Euro-American literary tradition, old voices newly calibrated that can begin to address the ethnic plurality of the late twentieth century.

Of the two autobiographers, Silko makes fewer claims to speak for Indian people. Momaday's attempt to universalize Kiowa experience for a diverse audience may be problematic for some readers. This seems to be the case for scholars like Jack Forbes, who insists that *"Native American literature must consist in works produced by persons of Native identity and/or culture for primary dissemination to other persons of Native identity and/or culture"* (emphasis Forbes's).[44] According to this definition, Momaday would not be a Native American author at all, since his work is not for "primary dissemination to other persons of Native identity and/or culture" (Forbes 19). Using such a strict definition of Native American literature excludes not only Momaday, but Silko and such well-known author–autobiographers as Black Hawk, Black Elk, Maria Chona, and Helen Sekaquaptewa, as well as others whose works have been published and read by non-Indians. More important, it denies the possibility of addressing a multiethnic audience while retaining an ethnic identity. Momaday, however, acknowledges no such ethnic or literary limits.

A consideration of Momaday and Silko is a fitting conclusion to a discussion of Native American autobiography because these two authors reflect the influences of a long, often discontinuous, tradition of Native American self-narration. They reclaim pre-contact Native American notions of a communal self that is linked to the tribe, the land, and the cosmos. At the same time, they combine this notion with Western ideas of individuality, revealing the potential conflict as well as the possible reconciliation between the two. In addition, Momaday and Silko continue the collaborative nature of Native American personal narrative. Just as early Plains Indian tribal members joined together to hear a warrior's brave deeds, to paint an individual's pictographic coup tale, or to enact someone's vision, Momaday collaborates with Kiowa elders, his father, and Euro-American scholars to tell, draw, and enact his personal story. Similarly, Silko re-creates the voices of family and community as they narrate select personal and tribal stories. Finally, each brings together the orality and artistry of pre-contact personal narrative and the multi-culturalism of late-nineteenth- and early-twentieth-century autobiography, and modifies them according to a contemporary literary consciousness. Like Zo-Tom, Howling Wolf, and White Bull, Momaday modifies the conventions of nineteenth-century Plains Indian hide and tipi painting in his father's drawings; like Plenty-Coups, Pretty-Shield, and Black Elk, Momaday and Silko incorporate native myths, songs, and ceremonies into their personal accounts, providing performance cues as well; and like Charles Eastman, they adopt a collaborative process, writing from a bicultural (e.g., Eastman's Sioux and Anglo) or multicultural (e.g., Momaday's Kiowa, Navajo, Pueblo, and Anglo) perspective.

Momaday and Silko seek consciously to locate and resurrect a tribal past, to re-create it imaginatively in the present, and to preserve it for the future through the potent power of the word. In so doing, they extend the autobiographical directions of both Black Elk and Charles Eastman. In the tradition of Black Elk, Momaday emphasizes tribal identity, the importance of personal vision, and the spoken word. For Momaday, however, these are conscious personal and artistic choices rather than an unconscious outpouring of his cultural identity. Like Eastman, both Momaday and Silko wrestle with the uncertainties of negotiating in both Native American and Euro-American worlds and with the difficulties of capturing/constructing an Indian identity in writing. Just as Eastman was three-quarters Santee Sioux, Momaday and Silko are mixed-blood Indians. As a consequence of their multicultural backgrounds and their lives in the Southwest, they reflect the influences of indigenous and Euro-American literary traditions in their work. Momaday's autobiographies, in particular, echo many of the traditional Plains Indian autobiographical forms and their modifications in turn-of-the-century life histories. That he did not seek consciously to discover indigenous autobiographies and to pattern his own after them is evident, as Momaday explains to Brumble (Brumble 170). But if, as Momaday informs Woodard, "literature may have proceeded from cave painting," and if painting, drawing, and writing are all forms of "incising" personal "perceptions of the world" (Woodard 163), Momaday's writing may derive, in part, from earlier conventions of Kiowa pictography. Finally, in their personal-cultural memoirs, Momaday and Silko confirm and celebrate their Native American heritage, their Euro-American education, and the literary creations born of them.

Certainly much has changed since Columbus stumbled into this hemisphere five centuries ago. But some things, like stories—of one's land, one's community, one's family, and one's self—endure. Traditional pre-contact modes of personal narrative, such as serial names, coup tales, pictographic robes and tipis, and storytelling performances, modified over the centuries, continue today in new spoken, crafted, performed, and written forms. Such multiple modes of pre-contact self-narration form the basis of a dynamic and enduring Native American tradition of personal narrative. Native American autobiography did not begin when nineteenth-century ethnographers, historians, and literary enthusiasts sought Indian life histories. Rather, the tradition began with pre-contact forms of personal narrative. It was extended in modified form, in the bicultural collaborative life histories of the nineteenth and early twentieth centuries. And it culminated in contemporary written autobiographies that adapt native traditions of self-narration as well as Euro-American modes of autobiography. This movement, from tribal speakers to life historians to autobiographers, reflects the transformation from oral to written cultures. Brumble notes that the movement from orality to literacy, which took two thousand years to develop in the West, often occurred in a "single lifetime" for native people (6). At the same time, contemporary Native American autobiographies reveal how collaboration has changed from intracultural to bicultural to multicultural cooperation. But this is not a simple matter of one tradition replacing another. Rather, contemporary Indian autobiographers, like Momaday and Silko, seek to incorporate Native American oral and artistic narrative modes into Euro-American written autobiography, thus marrying two traditions of personal narrative.[45] As Brumble has noted, Momaday "has taken an important step toward transforming this miscellaneous set of anthropological, historical, and literary documents [turn-of-the-century Indian autobiographies] into a living literary tradition" (3). Even more important, Momaday has revivified *pre-contact* native traditions of personal narrative, reshaping them into a creative configuration of a Kiowa identity. Just as important, though, is Silko's contribution to expanding the Euro-American notion of personal identity, of expressing the performance aspect of personal/tribal stories, and of insisting on the relationship between self and community, self and land, and self and story. Finally, then, the development of Native American autobiography parallels the historical transitions of Native American cultures from the tribal tales of ritual to the life stories of history to the imaginative autobiographies of art.

Notes

Introduction

1. Albert E. Stone, "Introduction: American Autobiographies as Individual Stories and Cultural Narratives," *The American Autobiography: A Collection of Critical Essays,* ed. Albert E. Stone (Englewood Cliffs, N.J.: Prentice-Hall, 1981) 1; Georges Gusdorf, "The Conditions and Limits of Autobiography," trans. James Olney, *Autobiography: Essays Theoretical and Critical,* ed. James Olney (1957; Princeton, N.J.: Princeton UP, 1980) 29.

2. Arnold Krupat, *For Those Who Come After: A Study of Native American Autobiography* (Berkeley: U of California P, 1985) xiii.

3. Arnold Krupat, *The Voice in the Margin: Native American Literature and the Canon* (Berkeley: U of California P, 1989).

4. From here on, I will use the shortened term *pre-contact* for the longer, more awkward phrase "pre-European contact."

5. Gretchen Bataille and Kathleen Mullen Sands, *American Indian Women: Telling Their Lives* (Lincoln: U of Nebraska P, 1984) 1.

6. In the introduction to *I Tell You Now: Autobiographical Essays by Native American Writers,* ed. Brian Swann and Arnold Krupat (Lincoln: U of Nebraska P, 1987), Krupat reiterates this idea: "The form of writing generally known to the West as autobiography had no equivalent among the oral cultures of the indigenous inhabitants of the Americas" (ix).

7. Karl Kroeber, "An Introduction to the Art of Traditional American Indian Narration," *Traditional Literatures of the American Indian: Texts and Interpretations,* ed. Karl Kroeber (Lincoln: U of Nebraska P, 1981) 9.

8. Lynne Woods O'Brien, *Plains Indian Autobiographies* (Boise, Ida.: Boise State College, 1973) 5.

9. H. David Brumble, III, *American Indian Autobiography* (Berkeley: U of California P, 1988).

10. Françoise Lionnet uses the term *autoethnography* in *Autobiographical Voices: Race, Gender, Self-Portraiture,* Reading Women Writing Series (Ithaca, N.Y.: Cornell UP, 1989).

11. H. David Brumble, III, introduction, *An Annotated Bibliography of American Indian and Eskimo Autobiographies* (Lincoln: U of Nebraska P, 1981), and *American Indian Autobiography.*

12. In the forthcoming *Dictionary of Native American Literature,* ed. Andrew Wiget, Arnold Krupat objects to the term "as-told-to" because it is "anachronistic," "ethnocentric," "patronizing," "inaccurate," and "simplistic."

13. Such works are similar to the nineteenth-century slave narratives produced collaboratively by a Euro-American abolitionist and an African-American freed or escaped slave.

Chapter 1

1. For Arnold Krupat's objections to the term "as-told-to," see the forthcoming *Dictionary of Native American Literature,* ed. Andrew Wiget.

2. William Bloodworth, "Varieties of American Indian Autobiography," *MELUS* 5.3 (1978) 69–70; Kathleen Mullen Sands, "American Indian Autobiography," *Studies in American Indian Literature: Critical Essays and Course Designs,* ed. Paula Gunn Allen (New York: Modern Language Assoc., 1983) 57; H. David Brumble, III, *American Indian Autobiography* (Berkeley: U of California P, 1988) 11, hereafter cited in the chapter as Brumble; Arnold Krupat, *For Those Who Come After: A Study of Native American Autobiography* (Berkeley: U of California P, 1985) 31, 33. See also H. David Brumble, III, introduction, *An Annotated Bibliography of American Indian and Eskimo Autobiographies* (Lincoln: U of Nebraska P, 1981); Arnold Krupat, *The Voice in the Margin: Native American Literature and the Canon* (Berkeley: U of California P, 1989), hereafter cited in the chapter as Krupat, *Voice.*

3. It is important to note that although collaborative autobiographies constituted the dominant form of Native American autobiography at the turn of the century, they are still being generated today.

4. William F. Smith, Jr., "American Indian Autobiographies," *American Indian Quarterly* 2.3 (1975) 237; Lynne Woods O'Brien, *Plains Indian Autobiographies* (Boise, Ida.: Boise State College, 1973) 5.

5. Elizabeth Bruss, *Autobiographical Acts: The Changing Situation of a Literary Genre* (Baltimore: Johns Hopkins UP, 1976).

6. Michael Dorris, "Native American Literature in an Ethnohistorical Context," *College English* 41.2 (1979) 147; Harold E. Driver, *Indians of North America,* 2nd ed. (Chicago: U of Chicago P, 1969) 25.

7. Karl J. Weintraub, *The Value of the Individual: Self and Circumstance in Autobiography* (Chicago: U of Chicago P, 1978) xvii, hereafter cited in the chapter as Weintraub, *Value.*

8. Howard Gardner, *Frames of Mind: The Theory of Multiple Intelligences* (New York: Basic Books, 1983) 271–272. See Susan Stanford Friedman, "Women's Autobiographical Selves: Theory and Practice," *The Private Self:*

Theory and Practice of Women's Autobiographical Writings, ed. Shari Benstock (Chapel Hill: U of North Carolina P, 1988) 34–62, hereafter cited in the chapter as Friedman.

9. Peggy V. Beck and Anna L. Walters, *The Sacred: Ways of Knowledge, Sources of Life* (Tsaile, Ariz.: Navajo Community College P, 1977) 11.

10. Paula Gunn Allen, "Iyani: It Goes This Way," *The Remembered Earth: An Anthology of Contemporary Native American Literature,* ed. Geary Hobson (Albuquerque: U of New Mexico P, 1979) 191.

11. Pipestone Indian Shrine Association, *Genuine Indian Made Handcrafts* (Pipestone, Minn.: Pipestone Indian Shrine Assoc., 1965) n.p.

12. Black Elk, *The Sacred Pipe: Black Elk's Account of the Seven Rites of the Oglala Sioux,* ed. Joseph Epes Brown (1953; New York: Penguin, 1971) 6. For more information on Sioux ceremonial pipes, see also Black Elk, *Black Elk Speaks: Being the Life Story of a Holy Man of the Oglala Sioux,* ed. John G. Neihardt (1932; Lincoln: U of Nebraska P, 1979); John (Fire) Lame Deer and Richard Erdoes, *Lame Deer: Seeker of Visions* (New York: Simon and Schuster, 1972).

13. See Maria Chona, *Papago Woman,* ed. Ruth M. Underhill (1936; New York: Holt, Rinehart and Winston, 1979) 57–61, for Maria Chona's description of her female puberty purification ceremony.

14. Margot Astrov, "The Concept of Motion as the Psychological Leitmotif of Navaho Life and Literature," *Journal of American Folklore* 63.247 (1950) 45. Astrov uses *Navaho,* a variant spelling of *Navajo.*

15. Gary Witherspoon, *Language and Art in the Navajo Universe* (Ann Arbor: U of Michigan P, 1977) 48, hereafter cited in the chapter as Witherspoon.

16. This "concept of motion" is not shared by all tribes. Astrov has pointed out that the Pueblo, for instance, were not nomadic, as were the Navajos. They lived in permanent houses and villages and relied on farming for subsistence. Pueblo individuals did, however, acknowledge certain rites of passage in their physical, social, and spiritual development and, like most tribes, saw life as cyclical and flowing rather than linear and static. This is not to say that Euro-Americans have a "static" idea of self. Certainly, there is a belief in a shifting, growing identity. Roy Pascal (as well as other theorists of autobiography) has suggested that with Romanticism, and its attendant elevation of the self, autobiography "truly" begins. At this stage, autobiographical exploration leads to "the discovery that man is not a state of being but a process of development." Roy Pascal, *Design and Truth in Autobiography* (Cambridge, Mass.: Harvard UP, 1960) 52. The basic linguistic distinction between Navajo and English primary verbs is nonetheless revealing.

17. In *Savagism and Civilization: A Study of the Indian and the American Mind* (1965; Baltimore: Johns Hopkins UP, 1967), Roy Harvey Pearce describes savagism as "an American double-mindedness" about Indians that reduced native people to "the noble savage" or "the barbarous savage."

18. M. M. Bakhtin, *The Dialogic Imagination,* trans. Caryl Emerson and Michael Holquist, ed. Michael Holquist (Austin: U of Texas P, 1981), hereafter cited in the chapter as Bakhtin.

19. Albert E. Stone, "Introduction: American Autobiographies as Individual Stories and Cultural Narratives," *The American Autobiography: A Collection of Critical Essays,* ed. Albert E. Stone (Englewood Cliffs, N.J.: Prentice-Hall, 1981) 1–27.

20. Northrop Frye, "Literature, History, and Language," Midwest Modern Language Association, *Bulletin* (1979) 2.

21. Lawrence Evers, prod., "Songs of My Hunter Heart: Laguna Songs and Poems," in videotape series *Words and Place: Native Literature from the American Southwest,* with Harold Littlebird (New York: Russell, 1978).

22. R. D. Theisz revealed a similar desire for a more accurate term when he suggested we replace *autobiography* with *bi-autobiography* in order to note the roles of editor and narrator. His focus, of course, is on the composite autobiographies of the nineteenth and twentieth centuries. R. D. Theisz, "The Critical Collaboration: Introductions as a Gateway to the Study of Native American Bi-Autobiography," *American Indian Culture and Research Journal* 5.1 (1981) 66–67.

23. Georges Gusdorf, untitled lecture on autobiography as cultural expression, Session III, International Symposium on Autobiography and Autobiography Studies, Baton Rouge, La., 22 March 1985.

24. N. Scott Momaday, "The Man Made of Words," *The Remembered Earth: An Anthology of Contemporary Native American Literature,* ed. Geary Hobson (Albuquerque: U of New Mexico P, 1979) 171.

25. Karl J. Weintraub, "Autobiography and Historical Consciousness," *Critical Inquiry* 1.4 (1975) 835.

26. See also James Olney, *Tell Me Africa: An Approach to African Literature* (Princeton, N.J.: Princeton UP, 1973), for a discussion of the tribal self found in African autobiography.

27. Rather than believe that a "lack of individuality" means *no* sense of self, I prefer to think of a collective identity as another form of self. In addition, Brumble points out a couple of important differences between ancient classical autobiographical modes and early Indian self-expressions. First, the Indian versions of autobiography are "products of pre-literate cultures" that predate the literate Greeks and Romans. Second, in memoirs, "a white collaborator usually decided for his Indian informant what was memorable" (Brumble 3).

28. Henry Glassie, *Passing the Time in Ballymenone* (Philadelphia: U of Pennsylvania P, 1982) xiii, hereafter cited in the chapter as Glassie.

29. Paula Gunn Allen, *The Sacred Hoop: Recovering the Feminine in American Indian Traditions* (Boston: Beacon P, 1986) 2; Terry Tafoya, untitled lecture, California State U, Chico, spring 1987.

30. Domna C. Stanton, "Autogynography: Is the Subject Different?" *The*

Female Autograph: Theory and Practice of Autobiography from the Tenth to the Twentieth Century, ed. Domna Stanton et al. (Chicago: U of Chicago P, 1984) 5–22.

31. Felicity Nussbaum, "Toward Conceptualizing Diary," *Studies in Autobiography,* ed. James Olney (New York: Oxford UP, 1988) 137.

32. Elaine Showalter, "Piecing and Writing," *The Poetics of Gender,* ed. Nancy K. Miller (New York: Columbia UP, 1986) 224, 227. I thank Susan Morehouse for introducing me to this article.

33. Germaine Brée. "Women's Autobiography," Session II, International Symposium on Autobiography and Autobiography Studies, Baton Rouge, La., 21 March 1985. For a version of this talk, see Germaine Brée, "Autogynography," *Southern Review* 22.2 (1986) 223. To conclude, however, that gender or race is alone responsible for one's identity and its expression is simplistic. Perhaps we should look to class (as well as ethnicity and gender) for the similarities between some early Native Americans and women autobiographers. Also, both often functioned within a network of social and family relationships, and spoke rather than wrote about their lives.

Chapter 2

1. William Boelhower, *Through a Glass Darkly: Ethnic Semiosis in American Literature* (New York: Oxford UP, 1987) 48, hereafter cited in the chapter as Boelhower.

2. Howard R. Lamar, foreword, *The Indian Frontier of the American West, 1846–1890,* by Robert M. Utley, Histories of the American Frontier Series (Albuquerque: U of New Mexico P, 1984) xv.

3. Richard Slotkin, *Regeneration Through Violence: The Mythology of the American Frontier, 1600–1860* (Middletown, Conn.: Wesleyan UP, 1973); Roy Harvey Pearce, *Savagism and Civilization: A Study of the Indian and the American Mind* (1965; Baltimore: Johns Hopkins UP, 1967); Boelhower.

4. Edward H. Spicer, *A Short History of the Indians of the United States* (New York: Van Nostrand, 1969) 84.

5. Harold E. Driver, *Indians of North America,* 2nd ed. (Chicago: U of Chicago P, 1969) 323, hereafter cited in the chapter as Driver.

6. Alvin M. Josephy, Jr., *The Indian Heritage of America* (New York: Bantam Books, 1968) 114.

7. James W. Schultz, *Why Gone Those Times? Blackfoot Tales,* ed. Eugene Lee Silliman (Norman: U of Oklahoma P, 1974) 116, hereafter cited in the chapter as Schultz.

8. H. David Brumble, III, *American Indian Autobiography* (Berkeley: U of California P, 1988) 83.

9. Such an emphasis on personal heroics is not unique to Plains Indian males. There are Euro-American versions of tales of heroic achievement as well.

Thomas Bangs Thorpe's Indian-harassing character, Mike Fink, comes close to recounting coups when he brags of his prowess in the fight: "Well, I walk tall into varmin and Indian, it's a way I've got, and it comes as natural as grinning to a hyena. I'm a regular tornado, tough as a hickory white, long winded as nor'wester. I can strike a blow like a falling tree, and every lick makes a gap in the crowd that lets in an acre of sunshine." This, of course, is Euro-American Western literary tall-tale braggadocio, not Native American factual coup narrative. See Frederick W. Turner, III, ed., *The Portable North American Indian Reader* (New York: Viking P, 1973), for a small sample of these narratives.

10. Helen H. Blish, ed., *A Pictographic History of the Oglala Sioux* (Lincoln: U of Nebraska P, 1967) 145, hereafter cited in the chapter as Blish.

11. George Catlin, *Letters and Notes on the Manners, Customs, and Conditions of the North American Indians* (1844; New York: Dover, 1973) vol. 1, 145, 147–148, hereafter cited in the chapter as Catlin. This robe was not the only part of Mah-to-toh-pa's outfit that was decorated with pictographs of his achievements. For Catlin's description of Mah-to-toh-pa's mountain-sheep shirt, leggings, and other clothing, see 146–147.

12. Hayward Gallery, *Sacred Circles: Two Thousand Years of North American Indian Art* (London: Arts Council of Great Britain, 1976) 166.

13. John C. Ewers, *Murals in the Round: Painted Tipis of the Kiowa and Kiowa-Apache Indians* (Washington, D.C.: Smithsonian Institution P, 1978) 8, hereafter cited in the chapter as Ewers.

14. James Mooney, "Kiowa Heraldry Notebook. Descriptions of Kiowa Tipis and Shields" (Washington, D.C.: Smithsonian Institution, National Anthropological Archives, 1891–1904) Manuscript 2531, cited in Ewers.

15. Arnold Krupat, *For Those Who Come After: A Study of Native American Autobiography* (Berkeley: U of California P, 1985); Thomas Couser, *"Black Elk Speaks* with Forked Tongue," *Studies in Autobiography,* ed. James Olney (New York: Oxford UP, 1988) 73–88.

16. North and south sides of a tipi are determined in relation to the doorway, which "always faced east—toward the sun" (Ewers 6).

17. Frederick J. Dockstader, *Indian Art in America* (Greenwich, Conn.: New York Graphic Society, n.d.) 46.

18. See also Dockstader's account of Plains Indian personal adornment: "Much of the artistry of these people was expended upon their person. . . . The attention given to the Crow coiffure; the face painting, adornment and make-up of the Cheyenne, and the carriage and bearing of a handsome Dakota man all contributed to this concept of self" (46).

19. William Wildschut and John C. Ewers, *Crow Indian Beadwork: A Descriptive and Historical Study* (New York: Museum of the American Indian–Heye Foundation, 1959) 47.

20. In *Walk in Beauty: The Navajo and Their Blankets* (Boston: New York

Graphic Society, 1977), Anthony Berlant and Mary Hunt Kahlenberg state that Navajo shoulder blankets, woven by women, were seen as markers of individuality, a "means of personal expression" (146), "a diagram of the spiritual presence of an individual" (148). I no longer believe that these designs may be interpreted as autobiographical. Paul G. Zolbrod has noted, however, that "the storytelling art" and traditional Navajo sandpaintings and weavings are "closely linked." By isolating Navajo weavings from "the poetic context which elucidates them," we obscure the full range of their meaning. Paul G. Zolbrod, "When Artifacts Speak, What Can They Tell Us?" *Recovering the Word: Essays on Native American Literature,* ed. Brian Swann and Arnold Krupat (Berkeley: U of California P, 1987) 13–40.

21. Valerie Shirer Mathes, "A New Look at the Role of Women in Indian Society," *American Indian Quarterly* 2.3 (1975) 131–139; Gretchen M. Bataille and Kathleen Mullen Sands, *American Indian Women: Telling Their Lives* (Lincoln: U of Nebraska P, 1984) 18–19, in particular; Paula Gunn Allen, *The Sacred Hoop: Recovering the Feminine in American Indian Traditions* (Boston: Beacon P, 1986).

22. Anthropologist–linguist Dell Hymes and anthropologist Dennis Tedlock seek to capture on the page the rich context of oral performance. Hymes includes gesture, tone of voice, pauses, and audience response, whereas Tedlock notes rhetorical organization. Dell Hymes, *"In Vain I Tried to Tell You": Essays in Native American Ethnopoetics* (Philadelphia: U of Pennsylvania P, 1981); Dennis Tedlock, *Finding the Center: Narrative Poetry of the Zuni Indians* (Lincoln: U of Nebraska P, 1978), and *The Spoken Word and the Work of Interpretation* (Philadelphia: U of Pennsylvania P, 1983).

23. Philippe Lejeune, "The Autobiographical Contract," *French Literary Theory Today: A Reader,* ed. Tzvetan Todorov (New York: Cambridge UP, 1982) 210.

24. For a discussion of "the semantic duplicity of the proper name," see Donna Perreault, "On Women's Stategies Against Their Im/Proper Names: A Psychoanalytic Meditation," unpublished essay, 1988.

25. Marianne Mithun, "Principles of Naming in Mohawk," *Naming Systems,* 1980 Proceedings of the American Ethnological Society, ed. Elisabeth Tooker (Washington, D.C.: American Ethnological Society, 1984) 40.

26. For a discussion of twentieth-century Kiowa autobiographer N. Scott Momaday's insistence on the importance of names, see Chapter 6.

27. Elizabeth Bruss, *The Autobiographical Act: The Changing Situation of a Genre* (Baltimore: Johns Hopkins UP, 1976).

28. Roy Pascal, *Design and Truth in Autobiography* (Cambridge, Mass.: Harvard UP, 1960) 148, 178. See also Georges Gusdorf, "The Conditions and Limits of Autobiography," trans. James Olney, *Autobiography: Essays Theo-*

retical and Critical, ed. James Olney (1957; Princeton, N.J.: Princeton UP, 1980) 28–48.

29. M. M. Bakhtin, *The Dialogic Imagination,* trans. Caryl Emerson and Michael Holquist, ed. Michael Holquist (Austin: U of Texas P, 1981).

30. Pretty-Shield, *Pretty-Shield: Medicine Woman of the Crows,* ed. Frank B. Linderman (1932; Lincoln: U of Nebraska P, 1972) 19.

31. Garrick Mallery, ''Picture-Writing of the American Indians,'' *Tenth Annual Report of the Bureau of Ethnology to the Secretary of the Smithsonian Institution, 1888–'89,* ed. J. Powell, director (1893; New York: Dover, 1972) vol. 2, 445–459, hereafter cited in the chapter as Mallery.

32. Charles Alexander Eastman, *The Soul of the Indian: An Interpretation* (1911; Lincoln: U of Nebraska P, 1980) 43, hereafter cited in the chapter as Eastman, *Soul.*

33. Charles Alexander Eastman, *Indian Boyhood* (1902; Greenwich, Conn.: Fawcett, 1972) 55, hereafter cited in the chapter as Eastman, *Boyhood.*

34. Charles Alexander Eastman, *From the Deep Woods to Civilization: Chapters in the Autobiography of an Indian* (1916; Lincoln: U of Nebraska P, 1977) 22.

35. Alfred W. Bowers, *Mandan Social and Ceremonial Organization* (Chicago: U of Chicago P, 1960) 60.

36. Plenty-Coups, *Plenty-Coups: Chief of the Crows,* ed. Frank B. Linderman (1930; Lincoln: U of Nebraska P, 1972) 27.

37. John Sturrock, ''The New Model Autobiographer,'' *New Literary History* 9.1 (1977) 61. For further information on Indian naming, see Driver 38–90.

38. Karen Daniels Petersen, *Plains Indian Art from Fort Marion* (Norman: U of Oklahoma P, 1971) 53, hereafter cited in the chapter as Petersen.

39. E. Adamson Hoebel and Karen Daniels Petersen, eds., *A Cheyenne Sketchbook,* by Cohoe (Norman: U of Oklahoma P, 1964) 6, hereafter cited in the chapter as Hoebel and Petersen.

40. Leigh Gilmore, personal correspondence, September 1990.

41. N. Scott Momaday, *The Names: A Memoir* (New York: Harper & Row, 1976) n.p.

42. Felicity Nussbaum, ''Toward Conceptualizing Diary,'' *Studies in Autobiography,* ed. James Olney (New York: Oxford UP, 1988) 137, hereafter cited in the chapter as Nussbaum.

Chapter 3

1. Arnold Krupat, *For Those Who Come After: A Study of Native American Autobiography* (Berkeley: U of California P, 1985) 31, hereafter cited in the chapter as Krupat.

2. Helen H. Blish, ed., *A Pictographic History of the Oglala Sioux* (Lincoln:

U of Nebraska P, 1967) 21, hereafter cited in the chapter as Blish. See also Lynne Woods O'Brien, *Plains Indian Autobiographies* (Boise, Ida.: Boise State College, 1973).

3. Karen Daniels Petersen, *Plains Indian Art from Fort Marion* (Norman: U of Oklahoma P, 1971) 27, hereafter cited in the chapter as Petersen.

4. Kathleen Mullen Sands, "American Indian Autobiography," *Studies in American Indian Literature: Critical Essays and Course Designs,* ed. Paula Gunn Allen (New York: Modern Language Assoc., 1983) 57.

5. H. David Brumble, III, *American Indian Autobiography* (Berkeley: U of California P, 1988) 11.

6. Dorothy Dunn, *American Indian Painting of the Southwest and Plains Areas* (Albuquerque: U of New Mexico P, 1968) 136, hereafter cited in the chapter as Dunn, *American Indian Painting.*

7. While Plains Indian men depicted lifelike figures on a variety of materials, women generally were limited to painting geometric designs on parfleches and some articles of clothing.

8. As well as the hide and tipi paintings mentioned below, Plains Indian men narrated their stories in their personal adornment. In *Indian Art in America* (Greenwich, Conn.: New York Graphic Society, n.d.), Frederick J. Dockstader notes how Plains Indian face painting, hair designs, and clothing expressed a "concept of self" (46).

9. John C. Ewers, introduction, *Howling Wolf: A Cheyenne Warrior's Graphic Interpretation of His People,* ed. Karen Daniel Petersen (Palo Alto, Calif.: American West, 1968) 7–8, hereafter cited in the chapter as Ewers, Intro.

10. George Catlin, *Letters and Notes on the Manners, Customs, and Conditions of the North American Indians* (1844; New York: Dover, 1973) vol. 1, 145, 147–148.

11. John C. Ewers, *Murals in the Round: Painted Tipis of the Kiowa and Kiowa-Apache Indians* (Washington, D.C.: Smithsonian Institution P, 1978) 8, hereafter cited in the chapter as Ewers, *Murals.*

12. For a more in-depth discussion of Mah-to-toh-pa's pictographic buffalo hide robe and Kiowa and Kiowa–Apache pictographic tipis, see Chapter 2.

13. Dorothy Dunn, introduction, *1877: Plains Indian Sketch Books of Zo-Tom and Howling Wolf,* ed. Dorothy Dunn (Flagstaff, Ariz.: Northland P, 1969) 7, hereafter cited in the chapter as Dunn, Intro.

14. The Howling Wolf and Zo-Tom sketchbooks I describe were recently donated to the Southwest Museum in Los Angeles by Leonora Curtin's daughter. Another Howling Wolf sketchbook is owned by Anna Bourke Richardson's family and is housed in the Joslyn Art Museum in Omaha, Nebraska. According to Petersen, the Field Museum in Chicago, the Massachusetts Historical Society in Boston, and Yale University in New Haven, Connecticut, have other Howling Wolf drawings, while Hampton University in Hampton, Virginia, the National

Museum of the American Indian in Washington, D.C., and Yale University have Zo-Tom drawings.

15. Throughout this section, "Plate" will refer to the original sketchbook, and "Figure" will refer to the illustration accompanying this text.

16. An examination of the original sketchbook confirmed that Zo-Tom, not the editor, wrote his signature.

17. Paul Radin, introduction, *The Autobiography of a Winnebago Indian*, by Sam Blowsnake, ed. Paul Radin (1920; New York: Dover, 1963) 2.

18. A similar artistic autobiography is that painted in watercolor by Running-Antelope, a chief of the Hunkpapa Dakotas, for Dr. W. J. Hoffman in 1873. This "continuous record of events" includes "the most important events in the life of Running-Antelope as a warrior" between 1853 and 1863. Each of the eleven watercolors is a detailed coup narrative with Running-Antelope's name depicted pictographically in each. Along with the drawings, Running-Antelope provided an oral interpretation. See Garrick Mallery, *Tenth Annual Report of the Bureau of Ethnology to the Secretary of the Smithsonian Institution, 1888–'89*, ed. J. Powell, director (1893; New York: Dover, 1972) vol. 2, 571–575.

19. James H. Howard, ed., *The Warrior Who Killed Custer: The Personal Narrative of Chief Joseph White Bull* (Lincoln: U of Nebraska P, 1968) vii, hereafter cited in the chapter as Howard.

20. These page numbers refer to White Bull's original ledger book housed in the Special Collections Department of the Chester Fritz Library, University of North Dakota, Grand Forks, not to Howard's edition.

21. Plenty-Coups, *Plenty-Coups: Chief of the Crows*, ed. Frank B. Linderman (1930; Lincoln: U of Nebraska P, 1962) 311. In addition, H. David Brumble notes that "the reluctance of early Indian 'informants' to open up 'their souls in the inwardness of true autobiography' is widely remarked upon." H. David Brumble III, introduction, *An Annotated Bibliography of American Indian and Eskimo Autobiographies* (Lincoln: U of Nebraska P, 1981) 3.

22. It is interesting to note that another artistic form of personal expression, blanket weaving, went through a similar change, but with different results. In *Walk in Beauty: The Navajo and Their Blankets* (Boston: New York Graphic Society, 1977), Anthony Berlant and Mary Hunt Kahlenberg trace the design changes of Navajo blankets from prehistoric times to the twentieth century (3). In the late nineteenth century, most of these changes were due to the demands and desires of the market (the wealthy Euro-American purchasers from the East Coast), which insisted on borders, subtle colors, "suitably 'barbaric' designs," and wool rugs rather than cotton blankets (142–145). Some Navajo women, "weaving for trade rather than for the tribe" (141), gave up one means of traditional self-expression in return for economic improvement.

23. According to Petersen, the Fort Marion sketchbooks "may prove to be the Rosetta Stone of Plains Indian pictorial representation" (x).

24. Quoted in Mari Sandoz, introduction, *A Pictographic History of the*

Oglala Sioux, ed. Helen H. Blish (Lincoln: U of Nebraska P, 1967) xx.

25. In a letter, Petersen notes: "Some of the Fort Marion drawings show courting scenes, but I know of no books devoted to this subject." For examples of other pictographic courting scenes, see Amos Bad Heart Bull's pictographs in *Pictographic History of the Oglala Sioux,* ed. Blish; Howling Wolf's drawings in *Howling Wolf,* ed. Petersen; Peter J. Powell, *People of the Sacred Mountain: A History of the Northern Cheyenne Chiefs and Warrior Societies, 1830–1879,* 2 vols. (New York: Harper & Row, 1981).

26. Robert M. Utley, *The Indian Frontier of the American West, 1846–1890,* Histories of the American Frontier Series (Albuquerque: U of New Mexico P, 1984) 184.

27. I have been told that a painted buffalo-hide robe commissioned by a Jesuit priest who lived among the native people in the Plains region during the eighteenth century has recently resurfaced. In addition to pictures of the region's fauna and flora, the artists embellished the buffalo hide with the floral borders popular in Europe at the time. As a cross-cultural counterpart to the Cheyenne diarist, then, the eighteenth-century artists used Native American materials but Euro-American artistic conventions.

28. See, for instance, Walter Ong, *Orality and Literacy: The Technologizing of the Word* (New York: Methuen, 1982) 85–93.

29. Felicity Nussbaum, "Toward Conceptualizing Diary," *Studies in Autobiography,* ed. James Olney (New York: Oxford UP, 1988) 137.

Chapter 4

1. Arnold Krupat, *For Those Who Come After: A Study of Native American Autobiography* (Berkeley: U of California P, 1985) xi. See also H. David Brumble, III, *American Indian Autobiography* (Berkeley: U of California P, 1988), hereafter cited in the chapter as Brumble.

2. Paul John Eakin, *Fictions in Autobiography: Studies in the Art of Self-Invention* (Princeton, N.J.: Princeton UP, 1985), hereafter cited in the chapter as Eakin.

3. M. M. Bakhtin, *The Dialogic Imagination,* trans. Caryl Emerson and Michael Holquist, ed. Michael Holquist (Austin: U of Texas P, 1981) 293–294. Rather than debate "whether the self is a transcendental category preceding language in the order of being, or else a construct of language brought into being by it," Eakin prefers to "conceptualize the relation between the self and language as a mutually constituting interdependency" (8).

4. Such considerations are also relevant to slave narratives, in which former slaves from an oral tradition worked with white editors to tell their lives in writing. For further discussion of the literary parallels between Native American transitional autobiographies and African-American slave narratives, see

Gretchen M. Bataille and Kathleen Mullen Sands, *American Indian Women: Telling Their Lives* (Lincoln: U of Nebraska P, 1984) 6–8; H. David Brumble, III, introduction, *An Annotated Bibliography of American Indian and Eskimo Auto-biographies* (Lincoln: U of Nebraska P, 1981) 9, hereafter cited in the chapter as Brumble, Intro. For an introduction to the oral and communal characteristics of slave narratives, see Elizabeth Schultz, "To Be Black and Blue: The Blues Genre in Black American Autobiography," *The American Autobiography: A Collection of Critical Essays,* ed. Albert E. Stone (Englewood Cliffs, N.J.: Prentice-Hall, 1981) 109–132; Stephen Butterfield, *Black Autobiography in America* (Amherst: U of Massachusetts P, 1974).

5. Robert F. Murphy, "Social Change and Acculturation," *Transactions of the New York Academy of Sciences,* 2nd ser., 26.7 (1964) 845–854. This bicultural model is complicated significantly when more than two cultures are involved. For instance, the nineteenth-century Okah Tubbee was both African American and Native American, but tried to live in a dominantly Euro-American society. A freed slave who claimed that his father was Indian, Tubbee married a Delaware woman and traveled around speaking and performing as an Indian (trying "publicly to dissociate himself from both slave and free black," xiii). Daniel F. Littlefield, Jr., ed., *The Life of Okah Tubbee* (1848 with several editions thereafter; Lincoln: U of Nebraska P, 1988).

6. A. M. Drummond and Richard Moody, "Indian Treaties: The First American Dramas," *Quarterly Journal of Speech* 39.1 (1953) 15.

7. L. L. Langness, *The Life History in Anthropological Science* (New York: Holt, Rinehart and Winston, 1965) 3–19. See also Clyde Kluckhohn, "The Personal Document in Anthropological Science," *The Use of Personal Documents in History, Anthropology, and Sociology,* ed. Louis Gottschalk, Clyde Kluckhohn, and Robert Angell, Social Science Research Council Bulletin, no. 53 (New York: Social Science Research Council, 1945) 78–173.

8. James Clifford, *The Predicament of Culture: Twentieth-Century Eth-nography, Literature, and Art* (Cambridge, Mass: Harvard UP, 1988) 12.

9. Pretty-Shield, *Pretty-Shield: Medicine Woman of the Crows,* ed. Frank B. Linderman (1932; Lincoln: U of Nebraska P, 1972) 11 (originally published in 1932 as *Red Mother*), hereafter cited in the chapter as Pretty-Shield. The internal citation "Pretty-Shield" refers to the text of the life history even when Linderman is speaking.

10. H. G. Merriam, Appendix A, *Montana Adventure: The Recollections of Frank B. Linderman,* by Frank B. Linderman (Lincoln: U of Nebraska P, 1968) 205, hereafter cited in the chapter as Merriam. Note how such a set of names emphasizes how community determines identity.

11. Frank B. Linderman, *Montana Adventure: The Recollections of Frank B. Linderman,* ed. H. G. Merriam (Lincoln: U of Nebraska P, 1968) 181, hereafter cited in the chapter as Linderman, *Montana.*

12. Frank B. Linderman, foreword, *Plenty-Coups: Chief of the Crows,* by Plenty-Coups, ed. Frank B. Linderman (1930; Lincoln: U of Nebraska P, 1957) vii.

13. Plenty-Coups, *Plenty-Coups: Chief of the Crows,* ed. Frank B. Linderman (1930; Lincoln: U of Nebraska P, 1957) 4 (originally published in 1930 as *American: The Life Story of a Great Indian, Plenty-Coups, Chief of the Crows*), hereafter cited in the chapter as Plenty-Coups. The internal citation "Plenty-Coups" refers to the text of the life history even when Linderman is speaking.

14. Frank B. Linderman, author's note, Plenty-Coups 311.

15. Frank B. Linderman, foreword, Pretty-Shield 9, hereafter cited in the chapter as Linderman, Foreword *Pretty-Shield.*

16. Other examples include Pretty-Shield grabbing a broom and pretending to be a contestant in "the hoop-and-arrow game," using Linderman for the hoop no less, and Pretty-Shield demonstrating the childbirth position.

17. See Dell Hymes, *"In Vain I Tried to Tell You": Essays in Native American Ethnopoetics* (Philadelphia: U of Pennsylvania P, 1981); Dennis Tedlock, *Finding the Center: Narrative Poetry of the Zuni Indians* (Lincoln: U of Nebraska P, 1978), and *The Spoken Word and the Work of Interpretation* (Philadelphia: U of Pennsylvania P, 1983). See also Anthony Mattina, "North American Indian Mythography: Editing Texts for the Printed Page," *Recovering the Word: Essays on Native American Literature,* ed. Brian Swann and Arnold Krupat (Berkeley: U of California P, 1987) 129–148.

18. Merriam points out that in a letter to his publisher, Linderman explained that Pretty-Shield "made a mistake in saying that Sitting-heifer was dancing the sun-dance when Plenty-Coups shot her and I am anxious to make a correction" (206).

19. Arnold Krupat doubts this claim because the debate about whether the 1926 edition of *Crashing Thunder* is science or art overlooks "the nature of narrative," which is always "a textualization of the 'facts' and never the 'facts' themselves. . . ." As Indian autobiography, based on "the principle of bicultural composite authorship," *Crashing Thunder* reveals aspects of Radin's mind and culture as well as Crashing Thunder's (i.e., Sam Blowsnake's). Arnold Krupat, foreword and appendix, *Crashing Thunder: The Autobiography of an American Indian,* ed. Paul Radin (Lincoln: U of Nebraska P, 1983), hereafter cited in the chapter as Krupat, Foreword.

20. Paul Radin, ed., *The Autobiography of a Winnebago Indian,* by Sam Blowsnake (1920; New York: Dover 1963) 1, hereafter cited in the chapter as Radin.

21. Nancy Oestreich Lurie, Appendix B, *Mountain Wolf Woman: Sister of Crashing Thunder,* by Mountain Wolf Woman, ed. Nancy Oestreich Lurie (Ann Arbor: U of Michigan P, 1961) 92, hereafter cited in the chapter as Lurie, Appendix B.

22. For a detailed discussion of the expansion of Sam Blowsnake's 1920 autobiography, *The Autobiography of a Winnebago Indian,* into its more literary 1926 form, *Crashing Thunder: The Autobiography of an American Indian,* see Krupat, Foreword.

23. See Indian autobiographers William Apes, *A Son of the Forest: The Experience of William Apes, a Native of the Forest. Comprising a Notice of the Pequot Tribe of Indians. Written by Himself* (New York: Published by the author, 1829), and George Copway (Kah-ge-ga-gah-bowh), *The Life, History, and Travels of Kah-ge-ga-gah-bowh* (Albany, N.Y.: Weed and Parson, 1847). See also Daniel B. Shea, Jr., *Spiritual Autobiography in Early America* (Princeton, N.J.: Princeton UP, 1968).

24. For more information on the peyote religion, see J. S. Slotkin, *The Peyote Religion* (Glencoe, Ill: Free P, 1956); Alice Marriott and Carol K. Rachlin, *Peyote* (New York: New Amer. Lib., 1971).

25. Nancy Oestreich Lurie, preface, *Mountain Wolf Woman: Sister of Crashing Thunder,* by Mountain Wolf Woman, ed. Nancy Oestreich Lurie (Ann Arbor: U of Michigan P, 1961) xiv, hereafter cited in the chapter as Lurie, Preface.

26. Mountain Wolf Woman, Appendix A, ed. Nancy Oestreich Lurie, *Mountain Wolf Woman,* by Mountain Wolf Woman, ed. Nancy Oestreich Lurie (Ann Arbor: U of Michigan P, 1961).

27. For examples of Mountain Wolf Woman's anecdotes, see Mountain Wolf Woman, *Mountain Wolf Woman,* ed. Nancy Oestreich Lurie (Ann Arbor: U of Michigan P, 1961) 9, 13, 27–28, hereafter cited in the chapter as MWW.

28. Ruth Underhill, foreword, *Mountain Wolf Woman,* by Mountain Wolf Woman, ed. Nancy Oestreich Lurie (Ann Arbor: U of Michigan P, 1961) ix.

29. Claire Farrer, personal correspondence and conversation, July 1989. Farrer shared her July 1977 field notes as well. The names have been changed to protect the anonymity of the consultants.

30. For a discussion of stereotypes of American Indians, see Roy Harvey Pearce, *Savagism and Civilization: A Study of the Indian and the American Mind* (1965; Baltimore: Johns Hopkins UP, 1967); Frederick W. Turner, III, introduction, *The Portable North American Indian Reader,* ed. Frederick W. Turner, III (New York: Viking P, 1973).

31. Jeff Todd Titon, "The Life Story," *Journal of American Folklore* 93.369 (1980) 276.

Chapter 5

1. H. David Brumble, III, *American Indian Autobiography* (Berkeley: U of California P, 1988) 11. See also Arnold Krupat, *For Those Who Come After: A Study of Native American Autobiography* (Berkeley: U of California P, 1985), hereafter cited in the chapter as Krupat; Kathleen Mullen Sands, "American

Indian Autobiography," *Studies in American Indian Literature: Critical Essays and Course Designs,* ed. Paula Gunn Allen (New York: Modern Language Assoc., 1983) 55–65; Gretchen M. Bataille and Kathleen Mullen Sands, *American Indian Women: Telling Their Lives* (Lincoln: U of Nebraska P, 1984); Paula Gunn Allen, ed. *Studies in American Indian Literature,* hereafter cited in the chapter as Allen, *Studies.*

2. Roberta Rubenstein, *Boundaries of the Self: Gender, Culture, Fiction* (Urbana: U of Illinois P, 1987) 8.

3. Vine Deloria, Jr., introduction, *Black Elk Speaks: Being the Life Story of a Holy Man of the Oglala Sioux,* by Black Elk, ed. John G Neihardt (1932; Lincoln: U of Nebraska P, 1979) xiii–xiv.

4. Robert F. Sayre, "Vision and Experience in *Black Elk Speaks,*" *College English* 32.5 (1971) 510, 517, hereafter cited in the chapter as Sayre.

5. Sally McCluskey, "*Black Elk Speaks:* and So Does John Neihardt," *Western American Literature* 6.4 (1972) 231, hereafter cited in the chapter as McCluskey.

6. For a detailed discussion of the relationship between Neihardt and Black Elk, see both Sayre and McCluskey as well as Michel Castro, *Interpreting the Indian: Twentieth-Century Poets and the Native American* (Albuquerque: U of New Mexico P, 1983), and Raymond J. DeMallie, introduction, *The Sixth Grandfather: Black Elk's Teachings Given to John G. Neihardt,* ed. Raymond J. DeMallie (Lincoln: U of Nebraska P, 1984), hereafter cited in the chapter as DeMallie, Intro.

7. Carol Holly, "*Black Elk Speaks* and the Making of Indian Autobiography," *Genre* 12.1 (1979) 121; Albert E. Stone, *Autobiographical Occasions and Original Acts: Versions of American Identity from Henry James to Nate Shaw* (Philadelphia: U of Pennsylvania P, 1982) 65.

8. Kenneth Lincoln, *Native American Renaissance* (Berkeley: U of California P, 1983) 9; Calvin Fast Wolf and Mary Sacharoff-Fast Wolf, "'I Have Forsaken These Pagan Ways,'" unpublished paper (1987) 8, 13, hereafter cited in the chapter as Fast Wolf and Sacharoff-Fast Wolf; Krupat 133–134; Thomas Couser, "*Black Elk Speaks* with Forked Tongue," *Studies in Autobiography,* ed. James Olney (New York: Oxford UP, 1988) 79, 84.

9. Black Elk, letter to "Friends," 20 September 1934, Bureau of Catholic Indian Missions, Marquette U, Milwaukee.

10. Raymond J. DeMallie, ed., *The Sixth Grandfather: Black Elk's Teachings Given to John G. Neihardt* (Lincoln: U of Nebraska P, 1984), hereafter cited in the chapter as DeMallie.

11. John G. Neihardt, preface, *Black Elk Speaks: Being the Life Story of a Holy Man of the Oglala Sioux,* by Black Elk, ed. John G. Neihardt (1932; New York: Pocket Books, 1972) xii.

12. Black Elk, *Black Elk Speaks: Being the Life Story of a Holy Man of the*

Oglala Sioux, ed. John G. Neihardt (1932; Lincoln: U of Nebraska P, 1979) 1; hereafter cited in the chapter as Black Elk. Although this 1979 reprint of the 1932 publication of *Black Elk Speaks* does not include Standing Bear's drawings, it does include Neihardt's 1960 preface as well as a new introduction, photographs, and appendixes. The 1961 reprint (also by the University of Nebraska Press) includes Neihardt's 1960 preface and fifteen of Standing Bear's drawings. A new preface written by Neihardt in 1970 and a selection of sixteen of Standing Bear's illustrations are included in the 1972 Pocket Books edition. I will cite the 1979 University of Nebraska reprint for the text of *Black Elk Speaks,* but I will discuss Standing Bear's drawings published in the 1972 Pocket Books edition.

13. John G. Neihardt, *When the Tree Flowered: An Authentic Tale of the Old Sioux World* (1951; New York: Pocket Books, 1973) 1.

14. John G. Neihardt, *Indian Tales and Others* (1907; New York: Macmillan, 1926) 1, 5, hereafter cited in the chapter as Neihardt.

15. Black Elk delineates these categories in his December 21, 1944, interview with Neihardt. See DeMallie 376. For a different explanation of these categories, see Allen, *Studies,* 45–46.

16. Karl Kroeber, "An Introduction to the Art of Traditional American Indian Narration," *Traditional Literatures of the American Indian: Texts and Interpretations,* ed. Karl Kroeber (Lincoln: U of Nebraska P, 1981) 6.

17. Barre Toelken and Tacheeni Scott, "Poetic Retranslation and the 'Pretty Languages' of Yellowman," *Traditional Literatures of the American Indian: Texts and Interpretations,* ed. Karl Kroeber (Lincoln: U of Nebraska P, 1981) 92.

18. Edward H. Spicer, *A Short History of the Indians of the United States* (New York: Van Nostrand, 1969) 88, hereafter cited in the chapter as Spicer.

19. Only one account of an intertribal skirmish is included. When a Crow is caught stealing horses from the Lakota, the Lakota warrior Crow Nose kills him, and many others count coup. By the time Black Elk arrives, "the women had cut [the horse thief] up with axes and scattered him around." Black Elk recalls: "It was horrible." After joining in a kill dance and singing kill songs, Black Elk offers a justification for killing the Crow. The Crows had killed all but one person in the Lakota party that had headed back to the Soldiers' Town (Black Elk 89–90). Such information makes the dead Crow doubly guilty. Although such intertribal troubles provide a colorful backdrop to Black Elk's story, including too many such accounts would deter attention from Neihardt's focus on Indian–white (rather than Indian–Indian) relations and from the emphasis on Black Elk the holy man (rather than the warrior).

20. For more discussion of Black Elk as a "creative theologian," see Clyde Holler, "Black Elk's Relationship to Christianity," *American Indian Quarterly* 8.1 (1984) 37–49; DeMallie, Intro.

21. Blair Whitney, *John G. Neihardt* (Boston: Twayne, 1976) 94.

22. In a seminar address in Northfield, Minnesota, in January 1988, Black

Elk's great-granddaughter Charlotte Black Elk explained the goal of Lakota spiritual seeking. She is also the source for the Lakota words for the four cardinal directions. Fast Wolf and Sacharoff-Fast Wolf note that six is not a sacred number in Lakota tradition, but that holy men have considerable flexibility in articulating their personal visions for the community.

23. See Black Elk, *The Sacred Pipe: Black Elk's Account of the Seven Rites of the Oglala Sioux,* ed. Joseph Epes Brown (1953; New York: Penguin Books, 1971).

24. Helen H. Blish, ed., *A Pictographic History of the Oglala Sioux* (Lincoln: U of Nebraska P, 1967) 145.

25. For a discussion of Plains Indian naming practices, see Chapter 2.

26. Charles Alexander Eastman (Ohiyesa), *From the Deep Woods to Civilization: Chapters in the Autobiography of an Indian* (1916; Lincoln: U of Nebraska P, 1977) 114, hereafter cited in the chapter as Eastman, *Deep Woods.* For a discussion of Eastman's early life-shaping experiences, see Frederick W. Turner, III, introduction, *Indian Boyhood,* by Charles Alexander Eastman (1902; Greenwich, Conn.: Fawcett, 1972) 9–17.

27. For more information on Eastman's life, see Raymond Wilson, *Ohiyesa: Charles Eastman, Santee Sioux* (Urbana: U of Illinois P, 1983); David Reed Miller, "Charles Alexander Eastman, The Winner," *American Indian Intellectuals,* ed. Margot Liberty (Minneapolis: West, 1978) 61–73, hereafter cited in the chapter as Miller, Winner; Marion W. Copeland, *Charles Alexander Eastman (Ohiyesa)* (Boise, Ida.: Boise State College, 1978).

28. Elaine Goodale Eastman, *Sister to the Sioux: The Memoirs of Elaine Goodale Eastman, 1885–91,* ed. Kay Graber (1939; Lincoln: U of Nebraska P, 1978) 173.

29. Among Eastman's works are *Indian Boyhood* (1902), *Old Indian Days* (1907), *The Soul of the Indian* (1911), *The Indian Today* (1915), *From the Deep Woods to Civilization* (1916), and *Indian Heroes and Great Chieftains* (1918).

30. David Reed Miller, "Charles Alexander Eastman: One Man's Journey. . . ." (diss. U of North Dakota, 1975) 336. See also Miller, Winner.

31. Elaine Goodale Eastman, "All the Days of My Life," *South Dakota Historical Review* 2.4 (1937) 179.

32. Charles Alexander Eastman (Ohiyesa), *Indian Boyhood* (1902; Greenwich, Conn.: Fawcett, 1972), hereafter cited in the chapter as Eastman, *Boyhood.*

33. Bo Schöler, "Images and Counter-Images: Ohiyesa, Standing Bear, and American Literature," *American Indian Culture and Research Journal* 5.2 (1981) 48.

34. Eastman softens his account of the dog sacrifice by failing to mention that his dog was to be eaten.

35. Andrew Wiget, *Native American Literature* (Boston: Twayne, 1985) 54.

36. Elaine Goodale Eastman, foreword, *From the Deep Woods to Civiliza-*

tion, by Charles Alexander Eastman (1916; Lincoln: U of Nebraska P, 1977) xvii–xviii.

37. Certainly, Black Elk's sense of "failure" was shaped, in part, by Neihardt's commitment to what Krupat calls the "romantic . . . emplotment" (133).

38. See William Apes, *A Son of the Forest: The Experience of William Apes, a Native of the Forest. Comprising a Notice of the Pequot Tribe of Indians. Written By Himself* (New York: Published by the author, 1829); Sarah Winnemucca Hopkins, *Life Among the Piutes [sic]: Their Wrongs and Claims,* ed. Mrs. Horace Mann (written by Hopkins and edited only slightly by Mann) (1883; Bishop, Calif.: Sierra Media, 1969).

Chapter 6

1. The categories "oral, artistic, and dramatic" are provided by Lynne Woods O'Brien, *Plains Indian Autobiographies* (Boise, Ida.: Boise State College, 1973) 5.

2. For some of the varying definitions of what it means to be Indian, see Jeannette Henry and Rupert Costo, "Who Is an Indian?" *Wassaja: The Indian Historian* 13.2 (June 1980) 15–18; Jack D. Forbes, "Introduction: What Is an Indian?" *The Indian in America's Past,* ed. Jack D. Forbes (Englewood Cliffs, N.J.: Prentice-Hall, 1964) 1–5; Geary Hobson, "Introduction: Remembering the Earth," *The Remembered Earth: An Anthology of Contemporary Native American Literature,* ed. Geary Hobson (Albuquerque: U of New Mexico P, 1979); Kenneth Lincoln, *Native American Renaissance* (Berkeley: U of California P, 1983), hereafter cited in the chapter as Lincoln; Theodore W. Taylor, *The Bureau of Indian Affairs* (Boulder, Colo.: Westview P, 1984); U.S. Dept. of the Interior, Bureau of Indian Affairs, *The American Indians: Answers to 101 Questions* (Washington, D.C.: GPO, June 1974); Murray L. Wax, *Indian Americans: Unity and Diversity* (Englewood Cliffs, N.J.: Prentice-Hall, 1971).

3. Many California Indian tribes are no longer federally recognized. Because they are not legally "Indian" in the eyes of the government, they are not eligible for federal health and education programs designed for native people.

4. The first position is argued by Simon Ortiz, "Towards a National Literature: Cultural Authenticity in Nationalism," *MELUS* 8.2 (1981) 10. The second is articulated by Michael Dorris. "Interview with Louise Erdrich and Michael Dorris." With Hertha D. Wong. *North Dakota Quarterly* 55.1 (1987) 196–218.

5. John (Fire) Lame Deer and Richard Erdoes, *Lame Deer: Seeker of Visions* (New York: Simon and Schuster, 1972); Brian Swann and Arnold Krupat, eds., *I Tell You Now: Autobiographical Essays by Native American Writers* (Lincoln: U of Nebraska P, 1987).

6. For a discussion of Native American autobiography as "bicultural collab-oration," see Arnold Krupat, *For Those Who Come After: A Study of Native American Autobiography* (Berkeley: U of California P, 1985), hereafter cited in the chapter as Krupat; H. David Brumble, III, *American Indian Autobiography* (Berkeley: U of California P, 1988), hereafter cited in the chapter as Brumble; Kathleen Mullen Sands, "American Indian Autobiography," *Studies in American Indian Literature: Critical Essays and Course Designs,* ed. Paula Gunn Allen (New York: Modern Language Assoc., 1983) 55–65, hereafter cited in the chapter as Sands.

7. If Momaday's great-great-grandmother (his mother's great-grandmother) was a full-blood Cherokee, his mother would be one-eighth Cherokee. It is possible she was less. The Cherokee enroll down to one-sixteenth degree of Indian blood.

8. Much of the biographical information on Momaday in this and the following paragraph was obtained from Martha Trimble, *N. Scott Momaday,* Western Writers Series (Boise, Ida.: Boise State College, 1973), and Matthias Schubnell, *N. Scott Momaday: The Cultural and Literary Background* (Norman: U of Oklahoma P, 1985), hereafter cited in the chapter as Schubnell.

9. N. Scott Momaday, "The Man Made of Words," *The Remembered Earth: An Anthology of Contemporary Native American Literature,* ed. Geary Hobson (Albuquerque: U of New Mexico P, 1979) 162, hereafter cited in the chapter as Man.

10. N. Scott Momaday, *The Names: A Memoir* (New York: Harper & Row, 1976) 25, hereafter cited in the chapter as *Names.*

11. N. Scott Momaday, "The American Indian in the Conflict of Tribalism and Modern Society," lecture, Colorado State Univ., Ft. Collins, 31 January 1971 (CoFS), quoted in Schubnell 141.

12. For a more in-depth discussion of this land ethic, see N. Scott Momaday, "Native American Attitudes to the Environment," *Seeing with a Native Eye: Essays on Native American Religion,* ed. Walter Holden Capps (New York: Harper & Row, 1976) 79–85.

13. Robert L. Berner, "N. Scott Momaday: Beyond Rainy Mountain," *American Indian Culture and Research Journal* 3.1 (1979) 57, 67; Kenneth Fields, "More than Language Means: A Review of N. Scott Momaday's *The Way to Rainy Mountain," Southern Review* 6.1 (1970) 200–201, hereafter cited in the chapter as Fields; Thekla Zachrau, "N. Scott Momaday: Towards an Indian Identity," *American Indian Culture and Research Journal* 3.1 (1979) 49; Charles A. Nicholas, *"The Way to Rainy Mountain:* N. Scott Momaday's Hard Journey Back," *South Dakota Review* 13.4 (1975) 156–157, hereafter cited in the chapter as Nicholas; Mick McAllister, "The Topography of Remembrance in *The Way to Rainy Mountain," Denver Quarterly* 12.4 (1978) 20, 31, hereafter cited in the chapter as McAllister; Roger Dickinson-Brown, "The Art and Importance of N.

Scott Momaday,'' *Southern Review* 14.1 (1978) 33; Barbara Strelke, "N. Scott Momaday: Racial Memory and Individual Imagination,'' *Literature of the American Indians: Views and Interpretations,* ed. Abraham Chapman (New York: New Amer. Lib., 1975) 352; Schubnell 29, 38; Arnold Krupat, *The Voice in the Margin: Native American Literature and the Canon* (Berkeley: U of California P, 1989) 177, 181, hereafter cited in the chapter as Krupat, *Voice.* See also Lincoln, 102–116; Jarold Ramsey, *Reading the Fire: Essays in the Traditional Indian Literatures of the Far West* (Lincoln: U of Nebraska P, 1983) 189, hereafter cited in the chapter as Ramsey; Alan R. Velie, *Four American Indian Literary Masters: N. Scott Momaday, James Welch, Leslie Marmon Silko, and Gerald Vizenor* (Norman: U of Oklahoma P, 1982) 24–32; Andrew Wiget, *Native American Literature* (Boston: Twayne 1985) 122, hereafter cited in the chapter as Wiget.

14. N. Scott Momaday, *The Way to Rainy Mountain* (Albuquerque: U of New Mexico P, 1969) 4, hereafter cited in the chapter as *WRM.*

15. According to Schubnell, Momaday claims that "his writing preserves the spirit of Kiowa language, if not the language itself" (144–145).

16. I am indebted to my students at the University of Iowa and at Carleton College for insisting on the significance of the running title.

17. Scholars label these three narrative modes differently. Momaday refers to them as the mythical, historical, and immediate (Man 170); Schubnell calls them the traditional, historical, and personal (145); Fields calls them the legendary, historical, and personal or contemporary (199), while Wiget labels them the mythic, historical-cultural, and personal (122). Lincoln adds a fourth perspective by including the pictures. He refers to these as the tribal, pictorial, historical, and personal (103).

18. Momaday used the same library (and human) resources an anthropologist uses in studying a culture. In this case, he is a member of the group he studies. According to Schubnell, in *The Way to Rainy Mountain* Momaday used the following written sources: James Mooney, *Calendar History of the Kiowa Indians,* Bureau of American Ethnology, 17th Annual Report (1898; Washington, D.C.: Smithsonian Institution P, 1979); Mildred P. Mayhall, *The Kiowas* (Norman: U of Oklahoma P, 1962); Elsie Clews Parsons, *Kiowa Tales* (1929; New York: Kraus Reprint, 1969). Among others, his Western influences include William Shakespeare, Emily Dickinson, Herman Melville, Isak Dinesen, James Joyce, William Faulkner, Marcel Proust, and, of course, Yvor Winters.

19. In an interview with Charles L. Woodard, Momaday makes a similar claim for his art: "My work probably fits into a continuum of American Indian expression which begins with ledger-book drawings and hide paintings and comes up through a traceable line to the present." Charles L. Woodard, ed., *Ancestral Voice: Conversations with N. Scott Momaday* (Lincoln: U of Nebraska P, 1989) 170, hereafter cited in the chapter as Woodard.

20. Helen H. Blish uses the term "bragging biographies" to describe the painted pictographic robes on which Plains Indian warriors depicted their personal battle accomplishments. Helen H. Blish, ed., *A Pictographic History of the Oglala Sioux* (Lincoln: U of Nebraska P, 1967) 145. The remainder of the quotation is from N. Scott Momaday, "The Morality of Indian Hating," *Ramparts* 3.1 (1964) 36.

21. For an example of Kiowa painted tipis, see John C. Ewers, *Murals in the Round: Painted Tipis of the Kiowa and Kiowa-Apache Indians* (Washington, D.C.: Smithsonian Institution P, 1978).

22. For Momaday's discussion of how his father's paintings are "full of motion," see Woodard 171.

23. For instance, see Dorothy Dunn, ed., *1877: Plains Indian Sketch Books of Zo-Tom and Howling Wolf* (Flagstaff, Ariz.: Northland P, 1969).

24. For a discussion of the current theory and practice of applying performance theory to oral traditions, see Richard Bauman, *Verbal Art as Performance* (Rowley, Mass.: Newberry House, 1977); Dell Hymes, *"In Vain I Tried to Tell You": Essays in Native American Ethnopoetics* (Philadelphia: U of Pennsylvania P, 1981); Dennis Tedlock, *Finding the Center: Narrative Poetry of the Zuni Indians* (Lincoln: U of Nebraska P, 1978), and *The Spoken Word and the Work of Interpretation* (Philadelphia: U of Pennsylvania P, 1983). It is important to keep in mind that Momaday is not translating or transcribing individual oral performances, he is re-creating them from books, memory, and imagination.

25. N. Scott Momaday, interview, 12 April 1989.

26. Mick McAllister, *"The Names," Southern Review* 14.2 (1978) 387.

27. Frank Kermode, "Secrets and Narrative Sequence," *On Narrative,* ed. W. J. T. Mitchell (Chicago: U of Chicago P, 1980) 82.

28. One might also note the resemblance of Tsotohah (Red Bluff) to the urban Kiowa preacher Reverend Big Bluff Tosamah in Momaday's novel *House Made of Dawn.*

29. Garrick Mallery, "Picture-Writing of the American Indians," *Tenth Annual Report of the Bureau of Ethnology to the Secretary of the Smithsonian Institution, 1888–'89,* ed. J. Powell, director (1893; New York: Dover, 1972) vol. 2, 445–459.

30. Albert E. Stone, *Autobiographical Occasions and Original Acts: Versions of American Identity from Henry Adams to Nate Shaw* (Philadelphia: U of Pennsylvania P, 1982) 265–324.

31. Ursula K. Le Guin, "It Was a Dark and Stormy Night," *On Narrative,* ed. W. J. T. Mitchell (Chicago: U of Chicago P, 1980) 195.

32. The connection between family photograph albums and winter counts was first suggested by Robert Sayre, class discussion, Native American Literature, U. of Iowa, Iowa City, spring 1982.

33. Per Seyersted, *Leslie Marmon Silko* (Boise, Ida.: Boise State College,

ca.1980) 14–15, hereafter cited in the chapter as Seyersted. Biographical information is based on Seyersted's book and the Silko interview conducted by Lawrence Evers and Denny Carr, "A Conversation with Leslie Marmon Silko," *Sun Tracks* 3.1 (1976) 28–33.

34. Dexter Fisher, "Stories and Their Tellers—An Interview with Leslie Marmon Silko," *The Third Woman: Minority Women Writers of the United States,* ed. Dexter Fisher (Boston: Houghton Mifflin, 1980) 19, 21, hereafter cited in the chapter as Fisher.

35. Ambrose Lucero, "For the People: Leslie Silko's *Storyteller,*" *Minority Voices* 5.1–2 (1981) 1, 10; Bernard A. Hirsch, " 'The Telling Which Continues': Oral Tradition and the Written Word in Leslie Marmon Silko's *Storyteller,*" *American Indian Quarterly* 12.1 (1988) 11, hereafter cited in the chapter as Hirsch.

36. Paula Gunn Allen, *The Sacred Hoop: Recovering the Feminine in American Indian Traditions* (Boston: Beacon P, 1986) 224.

37. Leslie Marmon Silko, *Storyteller* (New York: Seaver Books, 1981) 5–6, hereafter cited in the chapter as Silko.

38. For versions of the Yellow Woman story, see Franz Boas, *Keresan Texts,* 2 vols., American Ethnology Society (1928; New York: AMS, 1974).

39. Leslie Marmon Silko, *Ceremony* (New York: New American Lib., 1977) 273.

40. In addition, three photographs were taken by Silko's grandfather Henry C. Marmon; three by unknown photographers; two by Denny Carr; and one by Virginia L. Hampton.

41. In contrast to the dominance of her father's presence in the book is the obvious and unexplained absence of Silko's mother. The only specific reference to her mother occurs in one photograph caption in which Silko explains: "My mother kept me on the cradle board until I was twelve months old" (270). Once she mentions that "her parents" went deer hunting, and great-grandmothers, grandmothers, sisters, and aunts abound; but concerning her mother, there is only silence.

42. For a discussion of Euro-American readers who wish to restrict Indian writers and their imaginations to suitably "Indian" themes and issues, see Ramsey. See also Duane Niatum, "On Stereotypes," *Parnassus* 7.8 (1978) 160–166; Ward Churchill, "Sam Gill's Mother Earth: Colonialism, Genocide and the Expropriation of Indigenous Spiritual Tradition in Contemporary Academia," *American Indian Culture and Research Journal* 12.3 (1988) 49–67.

43. For a discussion of the problems of memory and imagination in the autobiographical endeavor, see Mary McCarthy, *Memories of a Catholic Girlhood* (New York: Harcourt Brace Jovanovich, 1957), and Darrell Mansell, "Unsettling the Colonel's Hash: 'Fact' in Autobiography," *The American*

Autobiography: A Collection of Critical Essays, ed. Albert E. Stone (Englewood Cliffs, N.J.: Prentice-Hall, 1981) 61–79.

44. Jack Forbes, "Colonialism and Native American Literature: Analysis," *Wicazo Sa Review* 3.2 (1987) 19, hereafter cited in the chapter as Forbes. See also Ramsey and Lincoln. For a further discussion of Native American literature as a "colonized literature," see Elizabeth Cook-Lynn, "American Indian Literature in Servitude," *Indian Historian* 10.1 (1977) 3–6.

45. It is important to note, however, that there are ongoing Native American oral traditions distinct from Western literary models.

Works Cited

Allen, Paula Gunn. "Iyani: It Goes This Way." *The Remembered Earth: An Anthology of Contemporary Native American Literature*. Ed. Geary Hobson. Albuquerque: U of New Mexico P, 1979. 191–193.

———. *The Sacred Hoop: Recovering the Feminine in American Indian Traditions*. Boston: Beacon P, 1986.

———, ed. *Studies in American Indian Literature: Critical Essays and Course Designs*. New York: Modern Language Assoc., 1983.

Apes, William. *A Son of the Forest: The Experience of William Apes, a Native of the Forest. Comprising a Notice of the Pequot Tribe of Indians. Written by Himself*. New York: Published by the author, 1829.

Astrov, Margot. "The Concept of Motion as the Psychological Leitmotif of Navaho Life and Literature." *Journal of American Folklore* 63.247 (1950) 45–56.

Bakhtin, M. M. *The Dialogic Imagination*. Trans. Caryl Emerson and Michael Holquist. Ed. Michael Holquist. Austin: U of Texas P, 1981.

Bataille, Gretchen M., and Kathleen Mullen Sands. *American Indian Women: Telling Their Lives*. Lincoln: U of Nebraska P, 1984.

Bauman, Richard. *Verbal Art as Performance*. Rowley, Mass.: Newberry House, 1977.

Beck, Peggy V., and Anna L. Walters. *The Sacred: Ways of Knowledge, Sources of Life*. Tsaile, Ariz.: Navajo Community College P, 1977.

Berlant, Anthony, and Mary Hunt Kahlenberg. *Walk in Beauty: The Navajo and Their Blankets*. Boston: New York Graphic Society, 1977.

Berner, Robert L. "N. Scott Momaday: Beyond Rainy Mountain." *American Indian Culture and Research Journal* 3.1 (1979) 57–67.

Black Elk. *Black Elk Speaks: Being the Life Story of a Holy Man of the Oglala Sioux*. Ed. John G. Neihardt. 1932. New York: Pocket Books, 1972; Lincoln: U of Nebraska P, 1979.

———. Letter. 20 September 1934. Bureau of Catholic Indian Missions. Marquette U., Milwaukee, Wis.

————. *The Sacred Pipe: Black Elk's Account of the Seven Rites of the Oglala Sioux.* Ed. Joseph Epes Brown. 1953. New York: Penguin, 1971.

Black Elk, Charlotte. Address. Northfield, Minn. January 1988.

Blish, Helen H., ed. *A Pictographic History of the Oglala Sioux.* Lincoln: U of Nebraska P, 1967.

Bloodworth, William. "Varieties of American Indian Autobiography." *MELUS* 5.3 (1978) 67–81.

Blowsnake, Sam. *The Autobiography of a Winnebago Indian.* Ed. Paul Radin. 1920. New York: Dover, 1963.

Boas, Franz. *Keresan Texts.* 2 vols. American Ethnology Society. 1928. New York: AMS, 1974.

Boelhower, William. *Through a Glass Darkly: Ethnic Semiosis in American Literature.* New York: Oxford UP, 1987.

Bowers, Alfred W. *Mandan Social and Ceremonial Organization.* Chicago: U of Chicago P, 1960.

Brée, Germaine. "Autogynography." *Southern Review* 22.2 (1986) 223–230.

Brumble, H. David, III. *American Indian Autobiography.* Berkeley: U of California P, 1988.

————. Introduction. *An Annotated Bibliography of American Indian and Eskimo Autobiographies.* Lincoln: U of Nebraska P, 1981.

————. "Sam Blowsnake's Confessions: Crashing Thunder and the History of American Indian Autobiography." *Canadian Review of American Studies* 16.3 (1985) 271–282.

Bruss, Elizabeth. *Autobiographical Acts: The Changing Situation of a Literary Genre.* Baltimore: Johns Hopkins UP, 1976.

Butterfield, Stephen. *Black Autobiography in America.* Amherst: U of Massachusetts P, 1974.

Castro, Michael. *Interpreting the Indian: Twentieth-Century Poets and the Native American.* Albuquerque: U of New Mexico P, 1983.

Catlin, George. *Letters and Notes of the Manners, Customs, and Conditions of the North American Indians.* 2 vols. 1844. New York: Dover, 1973.

Chona, Maria. *Papago Woman.* Ed. Ruth M. Underhill. 1936. New York: Holt, Rinehart and Winston, 1979.

Churchill, Ward. "Sam Gill's Mother Earth: Colonialism, Genocide, and the Expropriation of Indigenous Spiritual Traditions in Academia." *American Indian Culture and Research Journal* 12.3 (1988) 49–67.

Clifford, James. *The Predicament of Culture: Twentieth-Century Ethnography, Literature, and Art.* Cambridge, Mass.: Harvard UP, 1988.

Cook-Lynn, Elizabeth. "American Indian Literature in Servitude." *Indian Historian* 10.1 (1977) 3–6.

Copeland, Marion W. *Charles Alexander Eastman (Ohiyesa).* Boise, Ida.: Boise State College, 1978.

Copway, George (Kah-ge-ga-gah-bowh). *The Life, History, and Travels of Kah-ge-ga-gah-bowh.* Albany, N.Y.: Weed and Parson, 1847.

Couser, Thomas. *"Black Elk Speaks* with Forked Tongue." *Studies in Auto-biography.* Ed. James Olney. New York: Oxford UP, 1988. 73–88.

Deloria, Vine, Jr. Introduction. *Black Elk Speaks.* By Black Elk. Ed. John G. Neihardt. 1932. Lincoln: U of Nebraska P, 1979.

DeMallie, Raymond J., ed. *The Sixth Grandfather: Black Elk's Teachings Given to John G. Neihardt.* Lincoln: U of Nebraska P, 1984.

Dickinson-Brown, Roger. "The Art and Importance of N. Scott Momaday." *Southern Review* 14.1 (1978) 30–45.

Dockstader, Frederick J. *Indian Art in America.* Greenwich, Conn.: New York Graphic Society, n.d.

Dorris, Michael. "Native American Literature in an Ethnohistorical Context." *College English* 41.2 (1979) 147–162.

Driver, Harold E. *Indians of North America.* 1961. 2nd ed. Chicago: U of Chicago P, 1969.

Drummond, A. M., and Richard Moody. "Indian Treaties: The First American Dramas." *Quarterly Journal of Speech* 39.1 (1953) 15–24.

Dunn, Dorothy. *American Indian Painting of the Southwest and Plains Areas.* Albuquerque: U of New Mexico P, 1968.

——— Introduction. *1877: Plains Indian Sketch Books of Zo-Tom and Howling Wolf.* Ed. Dorothy Dunn. Flagstaff, Ariz.: Northland P, 1969.

Eakin, Paul John. *Fictions in Autobiography: Studies in the Art of Self-Invention.* Princeton, N.J.: Princeton UP, 1985.

———. "Narrative and Chronology as Structures of Reference and the New Model Autobiographer." *Studies in Autobiography.* Ed. James Olney. New York: Oxford UP, 1988. 32–41.

Eastman, Charles Alexander (Ohiyesa). *From the Deep Woods to Civilization: Chapters in the Autobiography of an Indian.* 1916. Lincoln: U of Nebraska P, 1977.

———. *Indian Boyhood.* 1902. Greenwich, Conn.: Fawcett, 1972.

———. *The Soul of the Indian: An Interpretation.* 1911. Lincoln: U of Nebraska P, 1980.

Eastman, Elaine Goodale. "All the Days of My Life." *South Dakota Historical Review* 2.4 (1937) 171–184.

———. Foreword. *From the Deep Woods to Civilization: Chapters in the Autobiography of an Indian.* 1916. Lincoln: U of Nebraska P, 1977.

———. *Sister to the Sioux: The Memoirs of Elaine Goodale Eastman, 1885–91.* Ed. Kay Graber. 1939. Lincoln: U of Nebraska P, 1978.

Erdrich, Louise, and Michael Dorris. "Interview with Louise Erdrich and Michael Dorris." With Hertha D. Wong. *North Dakota Quarterly* 55.1 (1987) 196–218.

Evers, Lawrence, prod. "Songs of My Hunter Heart: Laguna Songs and Poems." *Words and Place: Native Literature from the American Southwest.* With Harold Littlebird. New York: Russell, 1978.

Evers, Lawrence, and Denny Carr. "A Conversation with Leslie Marmon Silko." *Sun Tracks* 3.1 (1976) 28–33.

Ewers, John C. Introduction. *Howling Wolf: A Cheyenne Warrior's Graphic Interpretation of His People.* Ed. Karen Daniels Petersen. Palo Alto, Calif.: American West, 1968.

———. *Murals in the Round: Painted Tipis of the Kiowa and Kiowa-Apache Indians.* Washington, D.C.: Smithsonian Institution P, 1978.

Farrer, Claire. Personal correspondence. July 1989.

Fast Wolf, Calvin, and Mary Sacharoff-Fast Wolf. "'I Have Forsaken These Pagan Ways.'" Unpublished paper. 1987.

Fields, Kenneth. "More than Language Means: A Review of N. Scott Momaday's *The Way to Rainy Mountain.*" *Southern Review* 6.1 (1970) 196–204.

Fisher, Dexter. "Stories and Their Tellers—An Interview with Leslie Marmon Silko." *The Third Woman: Minority Women Writers of the United States.* Ed. Dexter Fisher. Boston: Houghton Mifflin, 1980. 18–23.

Forbes, Jack D. "Colonialism and Native American Literature: Analysis." *Wicazo Sa Review* 3.2 (1987) 17–23.

———. "Introduction: What Is an Indian?" *The Indian in America's Past.* Ed. Jack D. Forbes. Englewood Cliffs, N.J.: Prentice-Hall, 1964. 1–5.

Friedman, Susan Stanford. "Women's Autobiographical Selves: Theory and Practice." *The Private Self: Theory and Practice of Women's Autobiographical Writings.* Ed. Shari Benstock. Chapel Hill: U of North Carolina P, 1988. 34–62.

Frye, Northrop. "Literature, History, and Language." Midwest Modern Language Association, *Bulletin* (1979) 1–7.

Gardner, Howard. *Frames of Mind: The Theory of Multiple Intelligences.* New York: Basic Books, 1983.

Gilmore, Leigh. Personal correspondence. September 1990.

Glassie, Henry. *Passing the Time in Ballymenone.* Philadelphia: U of Pennsylvania P, 1982.

Gusdorf, Georges. "The Conditions and Limits of Autobiography." Trans. James Olney. *Autobiography: Essays Theoretical and Critical.* Ed. James Olney. 1957. Princeton, N.J.: Princeton UP, 1980. 28–48.

———. Untitled lecture on autobiography as cultural expression. Session III. International Symposium on Autobiography and Autobiographical Studies. Baton Rouge, La. 22 March 1985.

Hayward Gallery. *Sacred Circles: Two Thousand Years of North American Indian Art.* London: Arts Council of Great Britain, 1976.

Henry, Jeannette, and Rupert Costo. "Who Is an Indian?" *Wassaja: The Indian Historian* 13.2 (1980) 15–18.

Hirsch, Bernard A. " 'The Telling Which Continues': Oral Tradition and the Written Word in Leslie Marmon Silko's *Storyteller.*" *American Indian Quarterly* 12.1 (1988) 1–26.

Hobson, Geary. "Introduction: Remembering the Earth." *The Remembered Earth: An Anthology of Contemporary Native American Literature.* Ed. Geary Hobson. Albuquerque: U of New Mexico P, 1979. 1–11.

Hoebel, E. Adamson, and Karen Daniels Petersen, eds. *A Cheyenne Sketchbook.* By Cohoe. Norman: U of Oklahoma P, 1964.

Holler, Clyde. "Black Elk's Relationship to Christianity." *American Indian Quarterly* 8.1 (1984) 37–49.

Holly, Carol. *"Black Elk Speaks* and the Making of Indian Autobiography." *Genre* 12.1 (1979) 117–136.

Hopkins, Sarah Winnemucca. *Life Among the Piutes Their Wrongs and Claims.* Ed. Mrs. Horace Mann. 1883. Bishop, Calif.: Sierra Media, 1969.

Howard, James H., ed. *The Warrior Who Killed Custer: The Personal Narrative of Chief Joseph White Bull.* Lincoln: U of Nebraska P, 1968.

Hymes, Dell. *"In Vain I Tried to Tell You." Essays in Native American Ethnopoetics.* Philadelphia: U of Pennsylvania P, 1981.

Josephy, Alvin M., Jr. *The Indian Heritage of America.* New York: Bantam Books, 1968.

Kermode, Frank. "Secrets and Narrative Sequence." *On Narrative.* Ed. W. J. T. Mitchell. Chicago: U of Chicago P, 1980. 79–97.

Kluckhohn, Clyde. "The Personal Document in Anthropological Science." *The Use of Personal Documents in History, Anthropology, and Sociology.* Ed. Louis Gottschalk, Clyde Kluckhohn, and Robert Angell. Social Science Research Council Bulletin, no. 53. New York: Social Science Research Council, 1945. 78–173.

Kroeber, Karl. "An Introduction to the Art of Traditional American Indian Narration." *Traditional Literatures of the American Indian: Texts and Interpretations.* Ed. Karl Kroeber. Lincoln: U of Nebraska P, 1981. 1–24.

Krupat, Arnold. Foreword. *Crashing Thunder: The Autobiography of an American Indian.* Ed. Paul Radin. Lincoln: U of Nebraska P, 1983.

———. *For Those Who Come After: A Study of Native American Autobiography.* Berkeley: U of California P, 1985.

———. *The Voice in the Margin: Native American Literature and the Canon.* Berkeley: U of California P, 1989.

Lamar, Howard R. Foreword. *The Indian Frontier of the American West, 1846–1890.* By Robert M. Utley. Histories of the American Frontier Series. Albuquerque: U of New Mexico P, 1984.

Lame Deer, John (Fire), and Richard Erdoes. *Lame Deer: Seeker of Visions.* New York: Simon and Schuster, 1972.

Langness, L. L. *The Life History in Anthropological Science.* New York: Holt, Rinehart and Winston, 1965.

Le Guin, Ursula K. "It Was a Dark and Stormy Night." *On Narrative.* Ed. W. J. T. Mitchell. Chicago: U of Chicago P, 1980. 187–195.

Lejeune, Phillipe. "The Autobiographical Contract." *French Literary Theory Today: A Reader.* Ed. Tzvetan Todorov. New York: Cambridge UP, 1982. 192–222.

Lincoln, Kenneth. *Native American Renaissance.* Berkeley: U of California P, 1983.

Linderman, Frank B. Author's notes. *Plenty-coups: Chief of the Crows.* By Plenty-Coups. 1930. Lincoln: U of Nebraska P, 1957.

———. Foreword. *Plenty-coups: Chief of the Crows.* By Plenty-Coups. 1930. Lincoln: U of Nebraska P, 1957.

———. Foreword. *Pretty-shield: Medicine Woman of the Crows.* By Pretty-Shield. 1932. Lincoln: U of Nebraska P, 1972.

———. *Montana Adventure: The Recollections of Frank B. Linderman.* Ed. H. G. Merriam. Lincoln: U of Nebraska P, 1968.

Lionnet, Françoise. *Autobiographical Voices: Race, Gender, Self-Portraiture.* Reading Women Writing Series. Ithaca, N.Y.: Cornell UP, 1989.

Littlefield, Daniel F., Jr., ed. *The Life of Okah Tubbee.* 1848. Lincoln: U of Nebraska P, 1988.

Lucero, Ambrose. "For the People: Leslie Silko's *Storyteller.*" *Minority Voices* 5.1–2 (1981) 1–10.

Lurie, Nancy Oestreich. Appendix B. *Mountain Wolf Woman: Sister of Crashing Thunder.* By Mountain Wolf Woman. Ed. Nancy Oestreich Lurie. Ann Arbor: U of Michigan P, 1961.

———. Preface. *Mountain Wolf Woman: Sister of Crashing Thunder.* By Mountain Wolf Woman. Ed. Nancy Oestreich Lurie. Ann Arbor: U of Michigan P, 1961.

McAllister, Mick. *"The Names." Southern Review* 14.2 (1978) 387–389.

———. "The Topography of Remembrance in *The Way to Rainy Mountain.*" *Denver Quarterly* 12.4 (1978) 19–31.

McCarthy, Mary. *Memories of a Catholic Girlhood.* New York: Harcourt Brace Jovanovich, 1957.

McCluskey, Sally. *"Black Elk Speaks:* and So Does John Neihardt." *Western American Literature* 6.4 (1972) 231–242.

Mallery, Garrick. "Picture-Writing of the American Indians." *Tenth Annual Report of the Bureau of Ethnology to the Secretary of the Smithsonian Institution, 1888–'89.* Ed. J. Powell, director. 2 vols. 1892, 1893. New York: Dover, 1972.

Mansell, Darrell. "Unsettling the Colonel's Hash: 'Fact' in Autobiography." *The American Autobiography: A Collection of Critical Essays*. Ed. Albert E. Stone. Englewood Cliffs, N.J.: Prentice-Hall, 1981. 61–79.

Marriott, Alice, and Carol K. Rachlin. *Peyote*. New York: New Amer. Lib., 1971.

Mathes, Valerie Shirer. "A New Look at the Role of Women in Indian Society." *American Indian Quarterly* 2.2 (1975) 131–139.

Mattina, Anthony. "North American Indian Mythography: Editing Texts for the Printed Page." *Recovering the Word: Essays on Native American Literature*. Ed. Brian Swann and Arnold Krupat. Berkeley: U of California P, 1987. 129–148.

Merriam, H. G. Appendix A. *Montana Adventure: The Recollections of Frank B. Linderman*. By Frank B. Linderman. Ed. H. G. Merriam. Lincoln: U of Nebraska P, 1968.

Miller, David Reed. "Charles Alexander Eastman: One Man's Journey . . ." Diss. U of North Dakota. 1975.

———. "Charles Alexander Eastman, The Winner." *American Indian Intellectuals*. Ed. Margot Liberty. Minneapolis: West, 1978. 61–73.

Mithun, Marianne. "Principles of Naming in Mohawk." *Naming Systems*. 1980 Proceedings of the American Ethnological Society. Ed. Elisabeth Tooker. Washington, D.C.: American Ethnological Society, 1984. 40–54.

Momaday, N. Scott. "The Man Made of Words." *The Remembered Earth: An Anthology of Contemporary Native American Literature*. Ed. Geary Hobson. Albuquerque: U of New Mexico P, 1979. 162–173.

———. "The Morality of Indian Hating." *Ramparts* 3.1 (1964) 29–40.

———. *The Names: A Memoir*. New York: Harper & Row, 1976.

———. "Native American Attitudes to the Environment." *Seeing with a Native Eye: Essays on Native American Religion*. Ed. Walter Holden Capps. New York: Harper & Row, 1976. 79–85.

———. *The Way to Rainy Mountain*. Albuquerque: U of New Mexico P, 1969.

Mooney, James. *Calendar History of the Kiowa Indians*. Bureau of American Ethnology, 17th Annual Report. 1898. Washington, D.C.: Smithsonian Institution P, 1979.

———. "Kiowa Heraldry Notebook. Descriptions of Kiowa Tipis and Shields." Washington, D.C.: Smithsonian Institution, National Anthropological Archives, 1891–1904. Manuscript 2531.

Mountain Wolf Woman. *Mountain Wolf Woman: Sister of Crashing Thunder*. Ed. Nancy Oestreich Lurie. Ann Arbor: U of Michigan P, 1961.

Murphy, Robert F. "Social Change and Acculturation." *Transactions of the New York Academy of Sciences*. 2nd ser. 26.7 (1964) 845–854.

Neihardt, John G. *Indian Tales and Others*. 1907. New York: Macmillan, 1926.

——. Preface. *Black Elk Speaks: Being the Life Story of a Holy Man of the Oglala Sioux*. By Black Elk. Ed. John G. Neihardt. 1932. Lincoln: U of Nebraska P, 1979.

——. *When the Tree Flowered: An Authentic Tale of the Old Sioux World*. 1951. New York: Pocket Books, 1973.

Niatum, Duane. "On Stereotypes." *Parnassus* 7.8 (1978) 160–166.

Nicholas, Charles A. *"The Way to Rainy Mountain:* N. Scott Momaday's Hard Journey Back." *South Dakota Review* 13.4 (1975) 149–158.

Nussbaum, Felicity. "Toward Conceptualizing Diary." *Studies in Autobiography*. Ed. James Olney. New York: Oxford UP, 1988. 128–140.

O'Brien, Lynne Woods. *Plains Indian Autobiographies*. Boise, Ida.: Boise State College, 1973.

Olney, James. *Tell Me Africa: An Approach to African Literature*. Princeton, N.J.: Princeton UP, 1973.

Ong, Walter. *Orality and Literacy: The Technologizing of the Word*. New York: Methuen, 1982.

Ortiz, Simon. "Towards a National Literature: Cultural Authenticity in Nationalism." *MELUS* 8.2 (1981) 7–12.

Pascal, Roy. *Design and Truth in Autobiography*. Cambridge, Mass.: Harvard UP, 1960.

Pearce, Roy Harvey. *Savagism and Civilization: A Study of the Indian and the American Mind*. 1965. Baltimore: Johns Hopkins UP, 1967.

Perreault, Donna. "On Women's Strategies Against Their Im/Proper Names: A Psychoanalytic Meditation." Unpublished essay. 1988.

Petersen, Karen Daniels. *Howling Wolf: A Cheyenne Warrior's Graphic Interpretation of His People*. Palo Alto, Calif.: Amer. West, 1968.

——. *Plains Indian Art from Fort Marion*. Norman: U of Oklahoma P, 1971.

Pipestone Indian Shrine Association. *Genuine Indian Made Handcrafts*. Pipestone, Minn.: Pipestone Indian Shrine Assoc., 1965.

Plenty-Coups. *Plenty-coups: Chief of the Crows*. Ed. Frank B. Linderman. 1930. Lincoln: U of Nebraska P, 1957.

Powell, Peter J. *People of the Sacred Mountain: A History of the Northern Cheyenne Chiefs and Warrior Societies, 1830–1879*. 2 vols. New York: Harper & Row, 1981.

——. *Sweet Medicine: The Continuing Role of the Sacred Arrows, the Sun Dance, and the Sacred Buffalo Hat in Northern Cheyenne History*. 2 vols. Norman: U of Oklahoma P, 1969.

Pretty-Shield. *Pretty-shield: Medicine Woman of the Crows*. Ed. Frank B. Linderman. 1932. Lincoln: U of Nebraska P, 1972.

Radin, Paul. Introduction. *The Autobiography of a Winnebago Indian*. By Sam Blowsnake. Ed. Paul Radin. 1920. New York: Dover, 1963.

Ramsey, Jarold. *Reading the Fire: Essays in the Traditional Indian Literatures of the Far West.* Lincoln: U of Nebraska P, 1983.

Rubenstein, Roberta. *Boundaries of the Self: Gender, Culture, Fiction.* Urbana: U of Illinois P, 1987.

Sandoz, Mari. Introduction. *A Pictographic History of the Oglala Sioux.* Ed. Helen H. Blish. Lincoln: U of Nebraska P, 1967.

Sands, Kathleen Mullen. "American Indian Autobiography." *Studies in American Indian Literature: Critical Essays and Course Designs.* Ed. Paula Gunn Allen. New York: Modern Language Assoc., 1983. 55–65.

Sayre, Robert F. Class discussion. Native American Literature. U of Iowa, Iowa City. Spring 1982.

———. "The Proper Study: Autobiographies in American Studies." *The American Autobiography: A Collection of Critical Essays.* Ed. Albert E. Stone. Englewood Cliffs, N.J.: Prentice-Hall, 1981.

———. "Vision and Experience in *Black Elk Speaks.*" *College English* 32.5 (1971) 509–535.

Schöler, Bo. "Images and Counter-Images: Ohiyesa, Standing Bear, and American Literature." *American Indian Culture and Research Journal* 5.2 (1981) 37–62.

Schubnell, Matthias. *N. Scott Momaday: The Cultural and Literary Background.* Norman: U of Oklahoma P, 1985.

Schultz, Elizabeth. "To Be Black and Blue: The Blues Genre in Black American Autobiography." *The American Autobiography: A Collection of Critical Essays.* Ed. Albert E. Stone. Englewood Cliffs, N.J.: Prentice-Hall, 1981. 109–132.

Schultz, James W. *Why Gone Those Times? Blackfoot Tales.* Ed. Eugene Lee Silliman. Norman: U of Oklahoma P, 1974.

Seyersted, Per. *Leslie Marmon Silko.* Boise, Ida.: Boise State College, ca. 1980.

Shea, Daniel B., Jr. *Spiritual Autobiography in Early America.* Princeton, N.J.: Princeton UP, 1968.

Showalter, Elaine. "Piecing and Writing." *The Poetics of Gender.* Ed. Nancy K. Miller. New York: Columbia UP, 1986. 222–247.

Silko, Leslie Marmon. *Ceremony.* New York: New Amer. Lib., 1977.

———. *Storyteller.* New York: Seaver Books, 1981.

Slotkin, J. S. *The Peyote Religion.* Glencoe, Ill.: Free P, 1956.

Slotkin, Richard. *Regeneration Through Violence: The Mythology of the American Frontier, 1600–1860.* Middletown, Conn.: Wesleyan UP, 1973.

Smith, William F., Jr. "American Indian Autobiographies." *American Indian Quarterly* 2.3 (1975) 237–245.

Spicer, Edward H. *A Short History of the Indians of the United States.* New York: Van Nostrand, 1969.

Stanton, Domna C. "Autogynography: Is the Subject Different?" *The Female*

Autograph: Theory and Practice of Autobiography from the Tenth to the Twentieth Century. Ed. Domna C. Stanton et al. Chicago: U of Chicago P, 1984. 5–22.

Stone, Albert E. *Autobiographical Occasions and Original Acts: Versions of American Identity from Henry James to Nate Shaw.* Philadelphia: U of Pennsylvania P, 1982.

———. "Introduction: American Autobiographies as Individual Stories and Cultural Narratives." *The American Autobiography: A Collection of Critical Essays.* Ed. Albert E. Stone. Englewood Cliffs, N.J.: Prentice-Hall, 1981. 1–27.

Strelke, Barbara. "N. Scott Momaday: Racial Memory and Individual Imagination." *Literature of the American Indians: Views and Interpretations.* Ed. Abraham Chapman. New York: New Amer. Lib., 1975. 348–357.

Sturrock, John. "The New Model Autobiographer." *New Literary History* 9.1 (1977) 51–63.

Swann, Brian, and Arnold Krupat, eds. *I Tell You Now: Autobiographical Essays by Native American Writers.* Lincoln: U of Nebraska P, 1987.

Tafoya, Terry. Untitled lecture. California State U, Chico, spring 1987.

Taylor, Theodore W. *The Bureau of Indian Affairs.* Boulder, Colo.: Westview P, 1984.

Tedlock, Dennis. *Finding the Center: Narrative Poetry of the Zuni Indians.* Lincoln: U of Nebraska P, 1978.

———. *The Spoken Word and the Work of Interpretation.* Philadelphia: U of Pennsylvania P, 1983.

Theisz, R. D. "The Critical Collaboration: Introductions as a Gateway to the Study of Native American Bi-Autobiography." *American Indian Culture and Research Journal* 5.1 (1981) 65–80.

Titon, Jeff Todd. "The Life Story." *Journal of American Folklore* 93.369 (1980) 276–292.

Toelken, Barre, and Tacheeni Scott. "Poetic Retranslation and the 'Pretty Languages' of Yellowman." *Traditional Literatures of the American Indian: Texts and Interpretations.* Ed. Karl Kroeber. Lincoln: U of Nebraska P, 1981. 65–116.

Trimble, Martha. *N. Scott Momaday.* Western Writers Series. Boise, Ida.: Boise State College, 1973.

Turner, Frederick W., III. Introduction. *Indian Boyhood.* By Charles A. Eastman. 1902. Greenwich, Conn.: Fawcett, 1972.

———. Introduction. *The Portable North American Indian Reader.* Ed. Frederick W. Turner III. New York: Viking P, 1973.

Underhill, Ruth. Foreword. *Mountain Wolf Woman: Sister of Crashing Thunder.* By Mountain Wolf Woman. Ed. Nancy Oestreich Lurie. Ann Arbor: U of Michigan P, 1961.

U.S. Dept. of the Interior, Bureau of Indian Affairs. *The American Indians: Answers to 101 Questions*. Washington, D.C.: GPO, June 1974.

Utley, Robert M. *The Indian Frontier of the American West, 1846–1890*. Histories of the American Frontier Series. Albuquerque: U of New Mexico P, 1984.

Velie, Alan R. *Four American Indian Literary Masters: N. Scott Momaday, James Welch, Leslie Marmon Silko, and Gerald Vizenor*. Norman: U of Oklahoma P, 1982.

Wax, Murray L. *Indian Americans: Unity and Diversity*. Englewood Cliffs, N.J.: Prentice-Hall, 1971.

Weintraub, Karl. "Autobiography and Historical Consciousness." *Critical Inquiry* 1.4 (1975) 821–848.

———. *The Value of the Individual: Self and Circumstance in Autobiography*. Chicago: U of Chicago P, 1978.

Whitney, Blair. *John G. Neihardt*. Boston: Twayne, 1976.

Wiget, Andrew. *Native American Literature*. Boston: Twayne, 1985.

Wildschut, William. "A Crow Pictographic Robe." *Indian Notes* 3.1 (1926) 28–32.

Wildschut, William, and John C. Ewers. *Crow Indian Beadwork: A Descriptive and Historical Study*. New York: Museum of the American Indian–Heye Foundation, 1959.

Wilson, Raymond. *Ohiyesa: Charles Alexander Eastman, Santee Sioux*. Urbana: U of Illinois P, 1983.

Witherspoon, Gary. *Language and Art in the Navajo Universe*. Ann Arbor: U of Michigan P, 1977.

Woodard, Charles L., ed. *Ancestral Voice: Conversations with N. Scott Momaday*. Lincoln: U of Nebraska P, 1989.

Zachrau, Thekla. "N. Scott Momaday: Towards an Indian Identity." *American Indian Culture and Research Journal* 3.1 (1979) 39–56.

Zolbrod, Paul G. "When Artifacts Speak, What Can They Tell Us?" *Recovering the Word: Essays on Native American Literature*. Ed. Brian Swann and Arnold Krupat. Berkeley: U of California P, 1987. 13–40.

Index

Acculturation, 89
Aho, 162–165, 176, 180, 183
Aleek-chea-ahoosh, 43, 93. *See also*
  Plenty-Coups
Allen, Paula Gunn: gynocracy proposed
  by, 22; land and Indian identity
  discussed by, 14; oral tradition
  discussed by, 188; purpose of
  ceremony defined by, 133–134;
  Yellow Woman defined by, 191
Amanuenses of Native American
  autobiographies, 7, 11, 86, 88–89,
  91–95, 104–105, 109, 152. *See also*
  Editors of Native American
  autobiographies; *specific
  autobiographers and editors*
*American: The Life Story of a Great
  Indian, Plenty-Coups, Chief of the
  Crows* (Plenty-Coups), 93
*American Autobiography: A Collection
  of Critical Essays, The* (Stone), 18
American Horse, 40, 147
American Indian Autobiography
  (Brumble), 4
*American Indian Women: Telling Their
  Lives* (Bataille and Sands), 3
American Indians. *See* Native Americans
Apes, William, 108, 152
Arapaho, 58, 96, 128
Asbury, C. H., 99
Astrov, Margaret, 15, 203 n.16
Autobiographical activity, 12, 24, 55
*Autobiography of a Winnebago Indian,
  The* (Blowsnake), 104–109
Auto-ethnography, 6
Autographs. *See* Name-symbols
Auto-gyno-graphy, 22

Bad Soldier, 112
Badger, 41
Bakhtin, Mikhail, 18, 19, 39, 188

Bataille, Gretchen, 3–4, 111; *American
  Indian Women: Telling Their Lives,* 3
Battle of the Little Bighorn, 68, 76;
  Lakota perspectives of, 129–131. *See
  also* Custer Battle
Beadwork, 36, 37
Bear Dance, 143
Bear Going Straight. *See* Making
  Medicine
Bear-Looks-Back, 41
Bear Paw Mountains, 27
Bear Sings, 126, 134
Bear's Heart, James. *See* Bears Heart
Bears Heart (Nockkoist), 52–53; alias of
  (James Bear's Heart), 52–53
Beaver-that-Passes, 101
Beloit College, 140, 147
Berdache, 22
Berlant, Anthony, 206–207 n.20, 210
  n.22
Berner, Robert L., 158
B.I.A. *See* Bureau of Indian Affairs
Big Dipper, 163, 167, 180, Fig. 27
Big Foot, band of, 131, 136, 140
Big Winnebago, 91, 104, 107. *See also*
  Blowsnake, Sam
Bison (Buffalo) Ceremony, 134–135
Black Cap, 33
Black Elk, Benjamin, 122
Black Elk, Charlotte, 121
Black Elk, Nicholas, 9, 41, 46,
  117–118, 151–152, 161, 173, 186,
  196–198, 215–216 n.12, 216 n.19;
  collaborators with, 37, 122–123;
  emphasis on orality by, 124–126;
  expansion of Lakota autobiographical
  traditions by, 138–139; inclusion of
  coup tales by, 126–132; inclusion of
  spiritual narratives by, 132–135;
  influence of Catholicism on, 121,
  129, 132; Lakota narrative forms used

237